MOTOR
RACING
MAVERICKS

Doug Nye

D1325498

B. T. Batsford Ltd, London & Sydney

First published 1974
Copyright © Doug Nye, 1974

ISBN 0 7134 2856 2

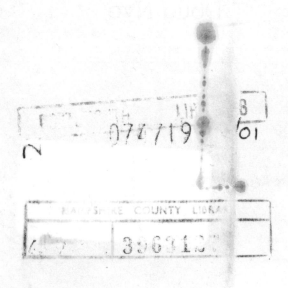

Printed in Great Britain by
Bristol Typesetting Co Ltd Barton Manor St Philips
for the publishers
B. T. Batsford Ltd 4 Fitzhardinge Street London W1H 0AH
and 23 Cross Street, Brookvale NSW 2100, Australia

Contents

Introduction

Roget's *Thesaurus* lists 'Maverick' along with 'Nonconformist', Lone Wolf', 'Revolter' and 'Independent'. . .

All these adjectives describe those men in motor racing history who built and backed unusual and unconventional cars, which tackled the age-old problem of being 'fastest' in an unusual manner, or in a muddled way which doomed them to failure from the outset.

For most of them there was no reward, but while most competition cars are by definition unsuccessful, those described in these pages all had a vital spark of originality or non-conformity. This put them far ahead of their time or set them aside from those who failed simply because they did not try hard enough. These are the glorious or obscure projects which are glorious in their obscurity.

Some never made it as far as the starting or timing line, while others successsfully achieved their objectives but did so by adopting an unusual approach which has earned them their place in this volume.

This is by no means a comprehensive catalogue of motoring 'oddballs'. It is purely a personal choice of subjects which interested me. It is the colourful tale of the men and their cars now recalled as 'Motor Racing Mavericks'.

Doug Nye, Lower Bourne, July 1974

Acknowledgements

The idea for this story occurred to me some three years ago, for some reason just as I was driving by Ealing Broadway underground station . . . It would not have reached fruition but for the encouragement and assistance of Anthony Harding, and from the long list of those who have offered help, information and photographs I must single out Geoffrey Goddard, Denis Jenkinson, Karl Ludvigsen and Cyril Posthumus for special mention. There was nothing too much to ask from them, and their prompt response every time was beyond price. Thanks also to my wife Valerie, for listening patiently while I enthused about Jano's Tipo A and the air-cooled Ruggeri, and to:

Eric Bellamy, Librarian, National Motor Museum, Beaulieu; Arthur Birchall, former Team Lotus Indianapolis chief mechanic; Al Bloemker, Indianapolis Motor Speedway; John Bolster, Technical Editor, *Autosport*;

Michael Bowler, Editor, *Classic Car*; Stefano Bricarelli, Editor, *Motor Italia*; Fritz Busch, proprietor, Schloss Wolfegg Automobil Museum; Archie Butterworth, constructor-driver of the AJBs; Pete Coltrin, ever-helpful man about Modena; Don Davidson, USAC statistician and memory man extraordinary; S.C.H. 'Sammy' Davis, former sports editor, *The Autocar*; Andrew Ferguson, former Team Lotus racing manager; G. N. 'Nick' Georgano, Editor, *The Encyclopaedia of Motor Cars*; Tony Gosnell, owner of the only Sima-Violet running in Britain; Peter Hull, Alfa Romeo authority, Vintage Sports Car Club; Karl Kizer, Indianapolis Speedway Museum; Jim Lee, of *Autocar* and *Motor* archives; Dr Camillo Marchetti, of Alfa Romeo SpA; Dale Porteus, former Team Lotus Indianapolis mechanic; M. Serge Pozzoli, Editor, *L'Album du Fanatique*; Maurice Phillippe, former Team Lotus chief designer; Herr Reichert, Porsche System Engineering; Michael Sedgwick, Director of Research, National Motor Museum; Nigel Wollett, owner of the Aston-Butterworth F2 car; Tim Parnell (son of Reg), BRM Team Manager; Henry 'Smokey' Yunick, Constructor of the Hurst Floor-Shifter Special. Of the photographs on the jacket the Opel Rocket Car and the 1923 GP Benz come from Cyril Posthumus, the Pat Clancy Special and the Tucker Torpedo Special are by courtesy of the Indianapolis Motor Speedway, the Alfa is from Wide World Photos and the Lotus-Ford 64 is by PP Photographs. Grateful acknowledgement is made to the following for the photographs in the book: 1, 2, National Motor Museum; 3–6, 8–11, 13–17, 19, 23, 25–6, 28, 30, 32–4, 42–3, 56, 57; 12, Taso Mathieson; 7, 20, 22, 24, 31, 39, 51, 62, Indianapolis Motor Speedway; 18, Stefano Bricarelli; 21, 40, 52–3, Ludvigsen Archives; 27, 29, 35, 41, 48–9, 54–5, 58–9, 63, Geoffrey Goddard; 36–8, 50, Alfa Romeo; 45, M. L. Rosenthal; 46, *Autocar*; 47, *Motor Sport*; 60, Donington Collection; 61, Guy Griffiths, 64, PP Photographs. The drawing on p. 25 appears courtesy of *Autocar*; those on pp. 56, 117, 142 are taken from Pomeroy's *The Grand Prix Car* (Motor Racing Publications Ltd); that on p. 125 is by courtesy of Alfa Romeo; the drawing on p. 88 is by James F. Drake, Jr, and appeared in Floyd Clymer's *Indianapolis Race History*.

I must also make mention of the diligence and enthusiasm of the staffs of *Autocar*, *Autosport*, *Car & Driver*, *The Light Car*, *Motor*, *Motoring News*, *Motor Sport*, *Road & Track*, *Scientific American* and *Speed* over the years, for these are the men who record motoring history as it happens. Without their efforts a work such as this could never be written.

'The man with the new idea is a crank
until the idea succeeds.'
MARK TWAIN

1

In Quest of Speed –
America, 1902-1907

The hundreds of holidaying New Yorkers had never seen anything quite like it. They pressed close against the paling fences separating them from the world's fastest automobiles, riveted by one particular projectile, gleaming white in the spring sun.

It was unlike any car they had ever seen. It was unlike anything they could dream of beyond a kind of futuristic Jules Verne idea of a high-speed submarine.

Unlike any contemporary motor vehicle, this machine paid no heed to its horse-drawn heritage. Its bodyshell was slim and stream-lined, low-slung between its tall disc wheels. It had a drooping, sharp-pointed nose, from which its smoothly curving lines rose and diverged to smooth themselves round a neatly rotund centre section before sleeking downwards and inwards to a pointed stiletto of a tail.

Perched on top of this flat-bottomed torpedo-like hull was some-thing we would instantly compare to a modern fighter plane's canopy: a sleek opaque bubble with a tiny mica windscreen in its forward face.

This was the much-rumoured Baker 'Torpedo' electric record car, and it was here on Staten Island to produce what had been billed as 'The Very Fastest Kilom. and Mile Ever Made by Mankind or Locomotive . . .'.

Torpedo was a product of the Baker Motor Vehicle Company of East 65th Street, Cleveland, Ohio. It was the brainchild of company founder Walter C. Baker, who was a gifted mechanical engineer born on 27 June 1868, at Hinsdale, New York. He was educated at Cleveland, and in 1893 assisted in building the 'Electrobat' electric runabout which was one of the sensations of the World's Columbian Exhibition in Chicago. In 1894 he had joined the Cleveland Screw Machine Company, an early producer of high-grade ball bearings, and there he learned the possibilities of producing good performance from low power outputs by the use of near frictionless drive-lines made possible by wide use of ball-bearings.

In addition to being a good engineer, Baker was a good business-man, and he founded his own American Ball Bearing Company to supply the growing national motor industry with these increasingly vital components.

In 1897 Baker and his assistant, Fred C. Dorn, experimented with their first electric vehicle. Their workshops, on Jessie Street just off Cleveland's Central Avenue, were a hive of advanced industry for on the ground floor worked Elmer Sperry, struggling to perfect his gyro compass and similar fine equipment. The first Baker electric was very successful, weighing only 550lbs and achieving a claimed 20mph from a three-quarter horsepower motor powered by ten battery cells. It was the first left-hand drive American car.

Fred R. White came along in 1898 to provide backing for Baker's electric motor vehicle company, and its products ('The Aristocrats of Motordom') starred at the Madison Square Garden Motor Show in New York in 1900. Baker made extensive use of ball-bearings in his Electric Runabouts, and their friction-free drivelines contributed to a good range of around thirty miles. They were credited as being the first shaft-driven American cars, and the first with bevel-gear back axles.

Mrs Hamilton Fish, a pillar of East Coast society, bought one of the Motor Show cars, and without taking driving lessons (which she obviously considered beneath her) she took it out for a run. It had a simple fore-and-aft two-way controller; the further you pushed it in either direction, the faster it went.

The story goes that she turned smartly into a side street and promptly ran down a jay-walking pedestrian. He was just picking himself out of the mud when she realised what she had done, yanked the controller backwards to stop and smartly reversed over him again! Before she could return he threw himself onto the verge and yelled ' Fo' God's sake Ma'am, before yo' git through yo' sure is goin' to run me over!' Mrs Hamilton Fish abandoned her Baker Electric in the middle of the street, and never drove again. . . .

Despite her experience, by 1902 the USA claimed 300 factories building mechanical road vehicles, turning out nearly 19,000 units in that year, and total automotive products were valued at 20,000,000 dollars. Baker had combed all the bugs out of his production cars, and now he set his sights on the speed arena to help publicise them.

Electric cars were very popular with the early record breakers. For road use they were generally slow and sluggish, with conservation of current a vital necessity to give reasonable range. With a record car range wasn't important, and in Europe the Comte de Chasseloup-Laubat and Camille Jenatzy had proved the electric car's potential by forcing a heavy current through an uprated motor in the shortest possible time.

These two had shunted the world record back and forth in a duel lasting throughout 1899. They pushed the record mark up from 42.42mph to 65.79mph, but not without their occasional failures, as when the French aristocrat applied too much current to his Jeantaud motor, burned it out and sulphated its batteries.

With these precedents Baker set about his record car design. He chose to carry a two-man crew; one managing the motive power and the other steering and braking. For stability he adopted a long wheel-base and large diameter wheels, and he built low, small and stream-lined to maintain a low centre of gravity and to minimise wind resistance.

The car quickly took shape, based on an angle-iron chassis which tapered inwards at front and rear to match its futuristic body form. A straight, tubular front axle was suspended on a transverse leaf spring, and the driven rear axle was sprung by semi-elliptic leaves mounted on the chassis side rails. Baker considered light and precise steering of vital importance, and adopted a marine system with three steel cables winding round a spiral-grooved three-inch spool mounted on the end of the steering column. Eyelets on the outboard ends of the cables linked with brackets brazed onto a hefty track rod, and there were adjuster springs on either side to maintain tension. This unconventional scheme was to bring Baker many brickbats. . . .

Wire-spoked wheels with fabricated wooden rims were made up, thirty-six inches in diameter, and they carried three-inch cross-section tyres made specially by B. F. Goodrich. They were inflated to 125psi. Wheelbase of the new car was 9ft 9ins and track 4ft 8½ins.

Power came from a nominally 7hp motor made by the Elwell Parker concern of Cleveland. It was actually capable of producing twice that output for short periods, and was mounted between the back axle and the new car's centre in the manner now seen in all modern single-seater racing cars. Small sprockets were attached to either end of the motor's armature shaft, from which one-inch pitch drive chains ran rearwards to twelve-inch diameter final drive sprockets mounted either side of an enclosed differential. Internal spring drives were built into the centre of these large sprockets to cushion the transmission and to minimise the danger of breaking a chain. Two cable-operated external contracting brakes were mounted inboard, between the sprockets and the differential. Operation of the handbrake lever automatically cut off current to the motor.

Current was supplied by *forty* Gould accumulator cells carried in ebonite boxes. Eleven of them were sited in the tail, behind the back axle, four between it and the motor, fifteen arranged around the rearward of the two tandem seats and ten ahead of the foremost seat, between the 'helmsman's' splayed-apart legs.

Two futuristic features were seen in the cockpit area. The crew were provided with full restraint harnesses made from very broad webbing, designed to pass over each shoulder, cross over chest and back bandolier-style, and attach to pick-ups on the hammock seats. Each crewman, the 'electrician' in the rear seat and the 'driver' in the front, was strapped securely into his post. Ahead of the driver was a tiny seven-inch diameter steering wheel with thickly padded rim, some fifty-nine years before similar 'kiddy-car' wheels became widespread in Grand Prix racing. . . .

Great attention was paid to the streamlined bodyshell, which like the steering mechanism owed much to marine experience. Its flowing, compound curves were virtually impossible to reproduce in metal at that time, and so a boat-builder was employed to produce what amounted to an inverted yacht hull.

It was made up carvel-style from quarter-inch (or thinner) pine planking, with hardwood internal ribs to give the shape. When complete the whole thing was sealed and covered with stretched oil cloth, which was then enamelled white and polished. Slots in the sides allowed movement for the axles, and a full-length flat undertray hung beneath the chassis to give a six-inch ground clearance.

A detachable streamlined coaming formed the hatch top, internally padded to protect the crew's heads and with that tiny mica screen providing driver visibility. What little light filtered into the ' cabin ' allowed the electrician to see his voltmeter and tachometer. To his right was a control lever, mounted in a quadrant on the chassis rail, beside a canister of liquid carbonic acid gas for the hooter, which he also controlled.

'To avoid air resistance and the catching up and throwing of pebbles and road drift' as a contemporary report put it, each wheel was covered with stitched-on stretched discs of oil cloth, both inside and out.

Despite this lightweight construction the forty electric cells forced the new car's weight up to 3,100lbs, or over twenty seven hundred-weight, and it cost Baker an estimated $10,000, roughly £2,500 at that time.

Baker himself was to drive the car, with C. E. Denzer as his intrepid electrician, and with its striking body shape the name 'Baker Torpedo' was a natural. Shake-down trials were held on an empty road just outside Cleveland, where Baker claimed to have topped 85mph. This was a staggering figure, for the official Land Speed Record had then only just been raised to 75.06mph in Europe by Leon Serpollet's steam car.

Plans were made for an official tilt at the world record, but it was to be a fateful decision when the publicity-conscious constructor opted for a speed meeting in spectacle-hungry New York, rather than heading south to the new venue at Ormond Beach, Daytona.

Friday, 30 May 1902 was the annual 'Decoration Day' on which America combined remembrance for her half-million Civil War dead with the opening of the outdoor sports season. The Automobile Club of America ran a 100-mile endurance test from New York City out to Bridgeport, Connecticut, and back along the North Sound shoreline that day, but it was a tame event with a 15mph speed limit imposed. The next day, Saturday the 31st, was to be much more exciting, with speed trials on the Staten Island Boulevard and the Baker Torpedo as their star entry.

The ACA had made a strange choice of course. They disregarded the perfectly flat and straight Coney Island Boulevard which they had used before, and chose instead the poorly-surfaced, steeply cambered, curving road on Staten Island. Tram tracks crossed the road at one point, and thick clay had to be laid there to level the hump!

Spectators flocked to the course that spring morning, many knowing the Boulevard well and fully expecting a day of thrills and spills.

In the morning Baker made a practice run with the Torpedo, swaying through the two deceptive bends and bounding over the tramlines in an heroic drive to average 78mph for the flying mile – almost 3mph faster than the official record.

By the afternoon the cosmopolitan crowd had swelled to thousands, overwhelming the few police trying to keep the road clear and hold them back from dangerous sections.

The official runs began, with 'gasoline waggons under 1,000lbs' showing the way, smokey, clattery and slow. Two more gasoline classes were run off, and then came the moment the crowd had been waiting for, the time for the Torpedo's record attempt, and they pressed onto the road to watch its coming.

At the start-line Baker had helped Denzer down into the tiny claustrophobic cockpit, then climbed aboard, drawn and tense, supposedly remarking to a nearby policeman ' Here's where I'm taking a chance. I don't know if I'll get out of this alive. . . .'

With its crew firmly strapped into place and the cockpit hatch clipped down the Torpedo whined into life, began to roll and gathered speed as it whistled off along the high-raised crown of the road towards the start of the measured distance.

Denzer, sitting straight-legged in the rear seat must have had a terrifying ride in the dim light. He was timing the run and as Baker yelled that the kilometre mark had passed he knew their time was down and disappointing; 36.2-seconds, 6.4-seconds behind Serpollet's record. He took a deep breath and gave the Torpedo full power. . . .

It was bounding along over the potholed road, and one of the deceptive bends was fast approaching. Baker wheeled it into the curve, the crowd blurring past outside his mica screen.

Accounts vary as to what happened next. One blames a rear wheel collapse, another a rut, another claims the unusual steering failed. Baker was later able to disprove the latter theory, but the result could not be altered. . . .

Torpedo rushed out of the curve with Baker fighting for control and Denzer just hanging on and hoping. It dived to the right side of the road, swept back onto the high crown and then hit the raised tram tracks. Suddenly the offside rear wheel was seen to collapse, Baker was braking hard and the car careened into a tree stump on the left of the road, bounced off and charged into a knot of spectators.

Two men were brushed aside by the Torpedo's smooth nose, but another was killed by a whirling wheel and another died trapped beneath the heavy chassis. Ten others were injured, including some women, and while rescuers tended them police broke open the

Torpedo's hatch to find her crew. They were shaken but unhurt, apart from a lump on Denzer's head raised by the cops' clubs! The whole split and torn body shell was eventually removed to release them, the first competition motorists to owe their lives to a safety harness.

Denzer's watch reputedly showed a mile time of forty seven seconds, which would have brought the record to America at over 76mph, but the slow kilometre time makes this seem suspect. Whatever the truth, the run had ended in tragedy, and after being jailed overnight the Torpedo's crew were released and the disaster blamed on public over-enthusiasm. Baker claimed that the wheel had collapsed when he locked his brakes in trying to avoid people on the course, but the Torpedo was not to run again, although rebuilt and exhibited at the Crystal Palace Motor Show in London the following year.

Baker turned to track racing, and in 1903 he built 'Torpedo Kid' which was a much smaller 700-pounder with a similar body shape to the record car, an open cockpit and a dozen cells powering a Baker motor. The 'Kid' appeared in the Cleveland races on September 5, in the hands of a driver named Chisholm.

E. W. Gilbert's Waverley electric beat the Baker in a one-mile speed trial, but Torpedo Kid won the 800lb class. It then made another run, lowering the five-mile circuit record for electrics from 8 minutes 40 seconds to only 6 minutes 29.6 seconds. Then, in a final event, Gilbert's Waverley was just overtaking the Kid when a crash was heard, the Kid careered under the guard fence without touching it and ploughed into the crowd, breaking one spectator's hip and badly bruising two more, while a fourth passed out from shock! Chisholm was OK and explained that the Waverley's left rear wheel had clipped the Kid's right front as it pulled ahead.

This second near-tragedy was almost too much for Baker to bear, but in 1904 the rebuilt Kid ran at Ormond Beach, on Florida's east coast at Daytona, and there it broke the American class kilometre record at 37.25 seconds. By this time the electric car's days were numbered in record-breaking, and within twenty years it was obsolete as a road car as well, the Baker company folding in 1916.

The boat-like body shape was a trend-setter, and two years after the Kid's brief Daytona success it was seen again in new high-speed vehicles built by Stanley, the steam car people.

These cars were Louis Ross's 'Teakettle' and Fred Marriott's 'Beetle'. Ross's car was the more Baker-like of the two, with drooping nose and tail, high-sided open cockpit and fared disc coverings to its wire wheels. Teakettle covered the mile in 38 seconds in 1905, and then it was Marriott's turn in the Beetle.

This was the faster of the two cars, with a straight-stemmed vertical sided body with turtle back and low-sided open cockpit. Marriott won the Dewar Cup Mile with it in 1906 at 111.8mph, and then covered five miles at 107.65mph to prove that this Stanley steamer was not just a very short distance sprint machine.

Beetle's engine was virtually standard, with a 20 horsepower boiler of 13 inches diameter whose tubing internals gave about 265 square feet of heating area. The twin-cylinder horizontal engine itself had internal dimensions of $4\frac{1}{2}$x$6\frac{1}{2}$ ins, and this drove to a giant $1:1\frac{3}{4}$ final drive gear ratio which allowed the engine to revolve only 500 times while covering a whole mile in distance! At 800psi boiler pressure, which could be maintained for ten miles, the engine was rated at fifty horsepower, and for a shorter distance double the pressure and nearly three times the power was available.

On the day after his five-mile run, Marriott donned his denim jacket and goggles and stroked Beetle along the Atlantic-swept beach at a staggering 127.56mph for the mile and 121.57mph for the kilometre. The mile time represented an improvement of 18mph on the existing Land Speed Record, standing to Hemery's Darracq in France, but the world governing body in Paris couldn't credit such speed and only recognised the kilometre time as the new world record—come to America for the first time—officially.

In 1907 Marriott returned to Ormond Beach with a new Stanley steamer, originally named 'Wogglebug' but to go into history as the 'Rocket'. Using 1,300psi pressure Marriott hissed away over the hard sand on a run which was not to be completed.

Spectators' watches reflected incredible speeds as *Rocket* sped into a patch of uneven sand, began to pitch furiously, then skidded broadside and hurled itself into a flurry of rolls and somersaults during which it totally disintegrated. By a miracle Marriott was helped from the wreckage little injured, but like Baker before them the Stanley concern retired from the performance business. Just how fast had these unconventional American cars become in the five years since that fatally futuristic appearance at Staten Island?

Observers from the Massachusetts Institute of Technology claimed that Marriott had been travelling at '196-198mph' as the accident began, and this grossly exaggerated estimate was later regarded as

1 The futuristic Baker 'Torpedo' electric record car before its fateful run at Staten Island, 1902.

2 The 'Torpedo's' crew, with Walter C. Baker in the forward seat, and his 'electrician', C. E. Denzer, seated behind him. Denzer is wearing his restraint harness. By his right-hand is the power control.

3 Rigolly's monstrous Gobron-Brillié, with opposed-piston engine, tubular chassis frame, and the distinction of setting the first over-100mph Land Speed Record, in 1904. The Baker shape (above) had been far in advance.

4 Fred Marriott in the Stanley steamer 'Rocket' on Ormond Beach, Daytona in 1906. Before it crashed, 'Rocket' covered the mile at over 127mph, a full 20mph faster than the contemporary Land Speed Record!

5 An advertisement of about 1914 showing Barney Oldfield's famous barnstorming front-drive Christie.

6 André Morel in one of the streamlined Voisins on the airfield at Issy-les-Moulineaux in 1923. The car has sports-racing wings fitted here. It was the first monocoque-chassised Grand Prix car.

gospel by Marriott himself. According to an *Automobile Quarterly* report, F. E. Stanley hand-timed the first quarter-mile at six-seconds, and on this basis the whole mile would have been covered at around 150mph . . . in 1907 . . . in a steam car . . . on a seaside beach. . . .

2

Europe's 100mph Monster –
1903-1904

America had no monopoly on advanced and unconventional—indeed, often eccentric—ideas on the way to build a performance motor car, and this was proved in 1903, less than a year after the Baker Torpedo's fateful debut on Staten Island.

At this time the official World Land Speed Record had stood to a Parisian merchant and amateur driver named Augières for less than five months. His 60hp Mors had thundered through the flying kilometre in twenty nine seconds, a speed of 77.13mph, electrically timed on a new course at Dourdan in France.

Europe's first big speed meeting of the new year was at Nice, early in April, and there a Parisian manufacturer entered the record business with a radical new racing car: the 13½-litre Gobron-Brillié.

This remarkable machine featured the unusual but strong and surprisingly reliable features of the company's road cars. It had a four-cylinder engine of monstrous proportions, with twin opposed pistons operating in each cylinder!

Gobron's unlikely-sounding lump was mounted in a similarly unconventional chassis. In place of the normal hefty channel-section steel members of the day, the company used a light but still reasonably stiff structure formed from jointed steel tubes in a manner which would have done credit to a master plumber.

The engine cylinders had a 140mm bore and a combined stroke—considering both upper and lower pistons—of 220mm, giving a displacement of 13,547cc. A six-throw crankshaft was used, carried in three main bearings, and the upper pairs of pistons hung from a giant bridge piece, connected by studs of enormous length passing down outside the cylinders to connect with their respective big-ends. There were two of these assemblies, with two separate blocks of two cylinders each, on a common crankcase.

Valve operation was desmodromic, with a single camshaft both opening and closing the valves. Earlier Gobrons had used atmospheric inlet valves with no positive mechanical operation, while later ones were to use separate camshafts for inlet and exhaust. In the record car the valves were housed in combustion chambers set to one side of the cylinders, so we could consider the unit a 'side-valve'.

Earlier models had fuel piped direct to the cylinders, but now a constant-level float-type carburettor was being introduced to this remarkably individual marque. Plumbing 'of positively heroic dimensions' carried mixture between the paired cylinder blocks, and was water-jacketed to the engine cooling system.

This monstrous piece of machinery is said to have been four feet long and 3ft 6ins in height. The tubular chassis frame had a wheel-base of 9ft 11ins.

Starting this monster was something of a party piece for its mechanics, who evidently had to attach a giant crowbar to a starter shaft and then crank it a quarter-turn at a time. Features claimed for the design included an increased piston area (ie effective capacity to produce power) at decreased piston speed (ie increased reliability) and freedom from vibration as the whole assembly was self-balancing. Certainly the Gobron-Brillié record car was in a class of its own, for whereas its competitors boiled and bubbled and spluttered and coughed at low speed the well-bred Parisian grumbled docilely around with perfect good manners.

The company had no chance to test it before rushing down to Nice for the speed week, and it was no surprise to find testing troubles when trying to run it fast. Sadly, Count Zborowski was killed in the associated La Turbie hill-climb that week, which threw the organisers into turmoil, and when Gobron's driver Rigolly had to return to Paris hurriedly the car missed its intended one-mile races.

Two more 110hp Gobron-Brilliés were prepared for the Paris–Madrid capital-to-capital race in May, when the three were to be driven by Rigolly, the Belgian Arthur Duray and by Koechlin, but when the race was stopped at Bordeaux after a series of fatal accidents they did no better than 29th, 64th and 75th places respectively. The cars might have been reliable, but they certainly didn't seem very fast.

Then, early in July that year, Rigolly took one car to Dublin's Phoenix Park where he was only narrowly beaten in a flying kilometre event by the two Mors cars of Baron de Forest and Fernand Gabriel. The Baron covered the distance at 84mph, but as the course was slightly downhill this could not be recognised as a new outright record.

Later that month, on the 15th, a new speed event was being run on a level ten-kilometre strip of road between Ostend and the French border; the Nieuport–Snaaskerke road, which had been newly completed with a fresh, smooth and *flat* macadam surface.

Rigolly was still on his way home from his Irish outing, so Arthur Duray climbed into his Gobron and boomed along the featureless Belgian road to cover the standing-start mile in 58.8 seconds and the flying kilometre in 26.8 seconds, a speed of 83.47mph which made him and his car new holders of the official World Land Speed Record.

On November 3 Duray took his successful car out onto the French record road at Dourdan, and this time galloped through the kilometre traps in a rumbustious 26.4 seconds, a speed of 84.73mph.

In America early in 1904 two combinations bettered the complex Gobron's record. Henry Ford's much publicised 'Arrow' managed a chilly 91.37mph on a frozen Lake St Clair on January 12. There has been discussion ever since as to whether this should qualify as an early Water Speed Record! Then, on January 27, William K. Vanderbilt sped along Ormond Beach in a '90' Mercedes at 92.30 mph. Neither record was recognised by myopic European authority.

So Gobron still officially had the fastest motor car in the world, when on March 31 Rigolly returned to the Promenade des Anglais at Nice and brutally smashed his way through the sea air in a bonnetless 13.6 litre variant to set a new official record at 94.78mph. Duray drove a new Gobron with a capacity of over fifteen litres, intended for the Gordon Bennett race—forerunner of the International Grand Prix—which was to be run later in the year. He could not better his team-mate's speed, but joined him in the exclusive 150kph club.

Still the 100mph mark, so meaningful in Britain and America, failed to be surpassed by the big, beautiless Gobrons, and at Ostend two months later Baron Pierre de Caters took his Gordon Bennett road-racing ' 90 ' Mercedes along the Snaaskerke road to chop 0.6 of a second off Rigolly's record and edge close to the magic hundred at 97.25mph. Monsieur Gobron at once challenged the good Baron to a match race, but he smiled that he had '. . . just annoyed Panhard, Mors and Gobron-Brillié a little . . .' and declined the offer.

It was on 17 July 1904 that Rigolly growled out onto the Snaaskerke road in his gigantic 130hp Gobron, and prepared to meet a new opponent in Paul Baras' 100hp 11.3 litre Darracq. They thundered off along the standing-start mile course, and both cars just nipped the 100mph mark in the closing yards of their run. Baras stopped the clocks at 48.6 seconds but over the vital flying kilometre the Gobron's power told and Rigolly howled through 0.4 of a second faster than the Darracq to average a record-breaking 103.56mph.

The unlikely Gobron-Brilliés became the first cars in history to set a record in excess of 100 miles per hour. It took twenty-three years before Major H. O. D. Segrave cracked the 200mph barrier, and thirty-two until Sir Malcolm Campbell almost tripled Rigolly's figures. In 1947 John Cobb moved into the uncharted realms of 400mph, and then the new age of reaction-driven flightless aircraft finally saw Craig Breedlove go through the 600mph barrier on Bonneville Salt Flats on 15 November 1965.

That was more than fifty-one years after the Belgian coastal plains saw Rigolly set his record, yet how spectacular his lofty, bulky, borborygmic Gobron-Brillié must have seemed to those brave enough to watch. . . .

3

America's Luckless Prophets

To which end do we apply the power? This is a question which has been haunting racing and record car designers since the birth of their profession. The first-ever self-propelled land vehicle was Nicholas Cugnot's gigantic steam-powered tricycle gun tractor, built in France in 1769. For simplicity's sake he drove the single front wheel, in a way being faithful to the concept that horses pulled carts, therefore any 'mechanical horse' might as well pull itself along in similar manner.

When Carl Benz introduced what is generally accepted as being the first practical 'horseless carriage' in 1885 he used a rear-mounted engine driving to the rear wheels, and this largely set a fashion for the vehicles to follow. Crude front-drive vehicles still appeared, often with the motor mounted on the front wheel and steering effected by swinging the whole assembly to-and-fro. As road speeds increased so terms like 'feel' and 'handling' began to have meaning, and such unsophisticated systems proved downright dangerous. Rear-wheel steering was found to be very deceptive, and so rear-drive and front-wheel steering became the accepted norms.

In 1902 the Dutch firm of Spyker produced a 60hp four-wheel-drive racer which they demonstrated by driving up the Crystal Palace steps in London, but that remained its most notable feat. Then in America a prophetic project, born for competition, anticipated the BMC Mini saloon car layout of transverse front engine and front-wheel drive by some *fifty-five* years. The cars concerned were not successful, but they were exciting!

John Walter Christie was a gifted engineer who had made a considerable reputation and fortune for himself by producing mech-

anical gun turrets for naval ships and land forts. In 1904 he took out
a front-drive system patent in the name of his Christie Iron Works
Company, of New York city.

His system used a block-cast four-cylinder engine mounted transversely between the front wheels, which were coupled to either end
of the crankshaft via simple cone clutches. These clutches slipped
during sharp cornering to provide a differential effect.

I believe that the first two cars were powered by conventional in-
line engines, the later 60hp model winning a fifty-mile race at the
Ormond-Daytona Speed Carnival. Late in 1905 the Christie 'Double-
Ender' made a petrifying appearance, with 60hp engines mounted at
either end driving all four wheels. It covered a mile in thirty-eight
seconds or at 99mph, but generally didn't perform very well
and Christie dropped the rear engine idea and concentrated purely on
front-wheel drive.

During that year he set-up the Christie Direct Action Motor Car
Company to build, promote and market taxis. He didn't get down to
detailing their design until well into 1907 and concentrated on
production of his fearsome racing cars in the meantime.

In January 1904 W. K. Vanderbilt Jr had presented a cup to the
Automobile Club of America for an international motor race to be
run on Gordon Bennett lines, with teams competing from each of the
major manufacturing countries. He stipulated that the first two events
be run on American soil, and on 23 September 1905 eliminating trials
began on the Long Island road course to choose the American team
for the second Cup Race.

J. Walter Christie entered the Double-Ender there, minus its rear
engine, and gave George Robertson his first major race—he was later
to emerge as one of America's great pioneer racing drivers.

Starting at 5.30am, the eliminating trial cars were despatched at
two-minute intervals. Robertson lasted two indifferent laps and then
his car expired on the third, but the Cup Race Commission still
selected the car for the Vanderbilt Cup race proper, to be held that
October.

October 14 dawned to see German, French and Italian teams facing
the Americans, and despite the first car starting as early as 6am a
huge crowd was already becoming unruly.

Vincenzo Lancia, driving a Fiat, rushed into an immediate lead
and held it for seven laps while Christie, driving his own car, found it
misfiring for most of the race. Lancia was running with a twenty-

minute lead when he stopped for fuel at the Willets Avenue supply depot.

He heard the Christie's thunderously distinctive exhaust note approaching down the tree-lined road, and rushed to get back into the race ahead of it. 'The American car was not easy to pass, as it swung considerably from side to side', he later explained, but unfortunately the front-drive's engine had chimed in on full song and it was booming down the road much faster than ever before. Lancia misjudged its speed, accelerated out in front of it, and poor Christie had no alternative to running full pelt into the Fiat's tail!

Lancia lost the lead in a forty-five minute stop for repairs to his car's back axle, but the Christie was out for good. When the crowd flooded the course to hail Hemery's Darracq as the winner, remaining runners were flagged off and Christie was finally classified eleventh out of thirteen starters.

At about this time Christie met Louis Chevrolet, whose name was to be immortalised by the General Motors' marque, but who at that time worked for Fiat's New York agency. The Swiss-born engineer joined Christie briefly to build a new front-drive racer, and returns to our story later. . . .

In the 1906 American races, Christie was back at the wheel of his own car on Long Island. His 50hp V4-cylinder front-drive racer was upstaged by the peculiar 110hp forced-draught air-cooled twelve cylinder Frayer-Millers, but once again Christie was selected for the Vanderbilt Cup team through no fault of his own . . . the car was unmanageable, gobbling up the straights but attempting to spear straight off at the corners as its driver leaned on the almost solid steering and tried to talk his car into making the turn. In the Cup Race proper Christie had similar problems, but was still running when the crowd again invaded the course, and was classified thirteenth.

This 1906 car was a giant of thirteen litres, and in an Ormond Beach meeting in Florida earlier that year it had covered the mile at a best of 35.2 seconds—demonstrating enormous traction in a straight line—and finished second to Wogglebug in a thirty-mile race.

That Christie was perhaps a visionary of more obstinacy than sense is demonstrated by his entry for the 1907 Grand Prix, at Dieppe in France. His contender was the biggest-engined Grand Prix car ever to be built, with a monstrous V4 of no less than nineteen litres! The car was built in Christie's unpretentious machine shop on the western edge of New York city, beside the Hudson River.

Its basis was a deep channel-section steel frame, quite compact for those days (and for that size of engine) with a wheelbase of 9ft 4ins and a track of 4ft 5ins. At around 1,800lbs it was to be one of the *lightest* cars in Grand Prix racing. Front suspension was by enclosed coil springs and rear suspension by semi-elliptic leaf springs, while hollow-spoke steel wheels replaced the bronze castings used formerly. The Grand Prix wheel had ten spokes instead of twelve, which meant two less retaining bolts to be undone while tyre-changing. Christie's patent wheels had no felloe, so that when a worn tyre was removed with its rim, all that remained was a hub with its radiating spokes. This saved considerable weight when compared to the double rims seen in other 'dismountable' designs.

The gigantic engine featured a three main-bearing crankshaft, and it was mounted as before on the front axle line and canted rearwards so that its forward pair of cylinders were raked back at a gentle angle, and the rearward pair laid back closer to the horizontal. Bore and stroke of each cylinder was no less than $7\frac{1}{4}$ x $7\frac{1}{4}$ ins, and overhead valves were used. To allow more efficient drive and easier steering, drive-shaft length had been increased from five inches to nine inches on either end of the crankshaft with its clutch drives, and the transmission included two forward speeds and reverse. The engine was water-cooled with a bucket pump, and as on earlier Christie cars the radiator was formed from very fine tubes forming a kind of cooling blanket arched over the bodywork between engine and cockpit.

Christie travelled to France in optimistic mood. His car cornered with the alacrity of a well-flung housebrick, but it was light and after all, he had the biggest engine in Grand Prix racing. But his misfortunes started immediately on reporting to the circuit, for he was allocated the race number 'WC1', and then in the race an exhaust valve jammed—so the reports say—and America's hope was out of the race, to be classified thirty-third.

This was the end of the road with no autumn races in America that year due to continual crowd-control problems. Christie took his fearsome front-drives on the dirt-track circuit, setting a record for the dirt-track mile at 69.2mph which salvaged something from the wreck of his front-drive promotional campaigns.

At about this time W. Gould Grokaw and Morris Gest organised a New York company to be called the Front Drive Motor Car Co, capitalised for $250,000, which was intended to operate the forthcoming Christie cabs. The prototype cab featured an in-line four-cylinder engine mounted transversely in the front and with an in-unit transmission driving to the front wheels through universally-jointed half-shafts—exactly mirroring Alec Issigonis' British Mini layout of 1959. Advantages offered were great comfort for the occupants of the cab itself, well-insulated from all the mechanical fuss up front, but its steering would be very heavy for a driver who had to spend all day and every day heaving the thing around the city, and drive-shaft and steering-joint reliability was dubious. Above all the Direct Action Taxi was too unusual and unconventional to appeal to the essentially conservative taxi companies, and in any case the asking price of around $2,600 (£650) was almost prohibitively expensive.

Christie still tried to prove the system's potential with his sporting activities, and in December 1909 he blasted one of his racers along part of the newly brick-paved Indianapolis Motor Speedway to set a flying quarter-mile record of 97.6mph. Come the following year and John Walter Christie abandoned his attempts to convert the disbelievers and began manufacturing fire engines, tractors and tanks. He developed some revolutionary suspension ideas for tanks, building one model during the Great War which was good for 25mph and in 1938 demonstrating a prototype with 430bhp Curtiss aero engine which could operate with or without its tracks in place and which was clocked at 67mph. This almost—but not quite—won him a fat Government contract, yet while ignored in the US his ideas appeared in British and Russian tanks and found their way back across the Atlantic to their birthplace. It was too late to help Christie, who died almost destitute in 1944.

Meanwhile Barney Oldfield had bought the biggest of the seven front-drive Christie racers, and this bluff, cigar-chewing showman barnstormed it round the American dirt tracks for years.

The car was a star attraction, renowned for its unmanageability as it blasted down the straights, Oldfield slinging it tail-out into the turns, backing-off until it pointed in the right direction and then slamming on the power to storm off along the next straight section with the front wheels scrabbling for grip and showering shale and stones into the open-mouthed crowds! The car at one time bore the legend 'Firestone Tyres—My Only Life Insurance', and although much-loved by dirt-track fans the car's appearances did little to impress the public with the safety of front-wheel drive.

Even so, it proved very fast, and in 1913 Oldfield raised the dirt-track mile record to 77.6mph in California; in 1915 he covered a flying mile on the Tacoma Board Speedway at 113.9mph and as late as 1916 set a new Indianapolis lap record at 102.6mph. Another Christie front-drive, the 120hp V4, admirably renamed *Big Bear*, appeared regularly at Daytona beach events in the hands of E. B. Blakely. The Christie's day was a long time passing and front-drive was to be adopted often in dirt, speedway, endurance and Grand Prix racing in years to come.

While Christie had been going along his eccentric path, Louis Chevrolet's name had been immortalised as that of a nerveless racing driver and of a new car marque which was to become the hub of the mighty General Motors group. When GM boss W. C. Durant decided to go into the bread and butter market Chevrolet was no longer interested and walked out.

He set up his own Frontenac company, and while preparing its first products he became involved with an obscure little car which gave a blinding glimpse into the monocoque-chassised, all-independently suspended future of motor racing.

In 1906-7 private interest had built the artificial banked autodrome at Brooklands, near Weybridge in Surrey. The new form of speedway became a terrific success for both racing and development testing, and in America in 1909 a group of Indianapolis businessmen combined to build and open a 2.5-mile rectangular speedway of their own. In 1911 the first annual 500-mile race was run there, and as the Indianapolis '500' this was to develop into the best-known of all American sports events and certainly the richest motor race in the world.

In 1912 the Blood Brothers Machine Company of Allegan, Kalamazoo, Michigan, produced the prototype of a striking new cyclecar. It was designed by Howard Blood, a graduate of Cornell University. In view of his surname, his place of education and the fact that he had a wife named Cornelia, the adoption of the 'Cornelian' name (as that of the semi-precious 'Blood stone' gem) was perhaps predictable.

Prime design parameters for a cyclecar were small size, economy of operation and a brisk performance. Accordingly Blood had concentrated on lightweight construction to produce a good power-to-weight ratio, and he dispensed with the conventional steel channel frame and built himself a combined body-chassis structure in welded and riveted sheet metal.

He suspended all four wheels on transverse leaf springs, with two at the front—above and below hub height—and three at the rear where one at the top and two side-by-side at the bottom held the wheels more-or-less parallel.

Neat hub carriers fitted on the springs' tips, carrying knock-off wire wheels with 3.50x30 pneumatic tyres. There were no dampers in the system, but the springs used were extremely stiff. To give the rear wheels as much independent movement as possible the combined gearbox and back-axle unit was bolted to a bridge-piece fitted inside the body unit, and double universal-jointed half shafts drove to the wheels.

Blood's earliest prototype used simple flexible leather discs as universal joints, but they tore constantly and later models used tempered steel strips which were more robust but still far from ideal. In this form the new Cornelian was pronounced ready for a production launch in mid-1915, but first came a surprising competition debut.

26 September 1914, saw a hundred-mile race run on the Kalamazoo dirt-track. Blood decided to enter a stripped-out prototype Cornelian, very much as a sudden impulse, and he found a driver named 'Cap' Kennedy who was strolling around the track trying to find something to run against all the established stars who were competing.

Nobody can have been more staggered than Kennedy when he came home seventh among modern Peugeot, Delage and Mercedes racing machinery in a stripped out prototype cyclecar!

This result fired Blood's imagination, who foresaw a brilliant success at Indianapolis providing the perfect springboard to launch his production run. He was using Sterling engines at the time, made by part of Durant's burgeoning GM empire, and Sterling's manager was an ex-Chevrolet employee. When approached about the possibilities of a tuned-up Sterling engine for an assault on Indianapolis he suggested Louis Chevrolet as being the perfect man to run the programme. Blood approached Chevrolet, and the great man agreed to assist.

He came to the Allegan works with his brother Arthur, and they took over a production prototype Cornelian and began to develop it for serious racing.

The back-end of the standard touring body was sawn-off and replaced by a tapering racing tail, and the crude universal drive-shaft joints were junked and replaced by properly-made Hooke joints. The engine was stripped down, modified to accept racing carburettors and reworked from its standard 1688cc, 18bhp form, to a full 1883cc. Alloy pistons, enlarged inlet valves and a higher compression ratio were adopted, and power output for this 'racing' four-cylinder grew to some 33bhp at 3,500rpm. In a car weighing only 950lbs this produced a reasonable power-to-weight ratio, and it remained to be seen how much advantage would be gained on the vast expanse of Indianapolis with the good handling offered by full independence and the speed potential of a minuscule frontal area.

Chevrolet wanted someone slim and light to co-drive the car, and chose Joe Boyer. The Cornelian was the first car on the Speedway on opening day, and was the first to qualify as Boyer stroked it round at 81.1mph, about one-and-a-half miles per hour slower than the previous year's winning Delage average for the whole 500-Miles. It was unlikely that the car could achieve a good finish, but it could still do sufficiently well to sell some cyclecars.

Louis Chevrolet took the start in the cream-painted number 10 Cornelian, and he was running nineteenth of forty-two starters in the early stages when the little Sterling engine began to run hot and stuttered onto three cylinders.

He stopped to add water and change a plug, and at the 100 mile mark was running twelfth, looking as one contemporary report put it, like 'a veritable grasshopper'. Then the engine abruptly gasped and died, falling silent on the back straight and leaving a furious Chevrolet to coast to a halt – out of fuel. He managed to top-up the tank and restart, but then made two more stops for water and finally retired after seventy-seven laps when a valve broke, damaging the engine.

It was the end of a brief entry into the 'big time' for the Cornelian, and that September production of the cyclecars ceased almost before it had begun. The Blood Brothers were overwhelmed with orders for universal joints and other components, and the Cornelian project died with only perhaps a hundred built.

The Indy car, if a 33-horsepower 'grasshopper' can be so described, was sold to Roscoe Dunning and he attempted to race it on the dirt where it proved even more out of its depth than at Indy. Its true métier would have been in road racing where its nimble handling would have come into its own, but on a power-course like Indianapolis or an untidy, tail-sliding arena like the dirt-tracks it simply lacked the cubic inches to succeed. Dunning is remembered as the man who introduced Wilbur Shaw, three-times Indy winner and eventually owner of the Speedway, to motor racing, but his little Cornelian soon disappeared and was forgotten and disregarded.

Monocoque chassis structures appeared in Grand Prix racing in 1923, 39 years before Colin Chapman introduced the true age of monocoque racing cars with his stressed-skin Lotus 25 at the 1962 Dutch Grand Prix. Today, all major Formula single-seaters and the vast majority of sports cars feature monocoque chassis construction, but credit for being 'first' must go to Gabriel Voisin – the mercurial French aviation pioneer whose SA des Aéroplanes G. Voisin company was based upon the airfield at Issy-les-Moulineaux, Seine.

Voisin's earliest aviation experiments had been made as early as 1898, when he was eighteen years old. He eventually developed a powered version, which flew for 260 feet on 10 March 1907, and on 13 January 1908 Henri Farman flew the Voisin machine for the first circuit in Europe, a distance of about a mile, at around 54mph.

The French pioneer claimed with some reason that this was a better performance than anything yet achieved by the Wright brothers, whose historic powered flight of December, 1903, had been catapult launched and depended upon considerable wind speed to produce the necessary lift. Voisin contended that '. . . such flights have no practical value', and after opening the world's first aircraft factory as early as 1905 he worked hard to prove his point. In the Great War, Voisin-type flying machines dominated the air, with hardly a Wright to be seen. Gabriel's works built 10,400 aeroplanes at Avenue Gambetta, Issy-les-Moulineaux, and then came the Armistice, and the end of hostilities. . . .

He began manufacturing motor cars during the first years of post-Great War depression, and his enterprising and daring character led him immediately into motor racing. When his works team of stream-lined sleeve-valve engined sports cars came home first, second, third and fifth in the 1922 Touring Car Grand Prix at Strasbourg, he set about building entries for the following year's event. Unfortunately the use of streamlining was regarded with distaste by the French authorities, and with less than six months remaining before the race at Tours they announced a ban on such 'cheating'.

Voisin was furious, withdrew his Touring Car entries and announced that he would attack the Grand Prix de l'ACF instead. The Tours circuit was not quite as fast as Strasbourg, so that the all-enveloping bodies to be adopted by Voisin and Bugatti were unlikely to produce such startling lap speeds. Voisin also knew that he could not challenge Fiat and Sunbeam on level terms with his limited resources in both money and time, but he was willing to have a go.

He announced that his company was entering Grand Prix racing because there was nowhere else to go, and that too much was not to be expected of them. However, in a letter to the ACF he wrote: 'We will field cars able to go fast with engines of low power . . .'. He was going to make the most of his aviation knowledge.

With designer André Lefebvre he devised a strikingly wedge-shaped body form, with a low chisel nose which rose to the broad two-seat cockpit opening, after which a long sweeping tail section curved back towards ground level. The front wheels were exposed, mounted on either end of a massive tubular front axle suspended on semi-elliptic leaf springs, while at the rear the narrow-track back axle pulled its wheels inside Voisin's broad new aerodynamic tail.

To save weight the aviation engineers decided to adopt aircraft-style construction for this body-chassis unit, dispensing with the conventional channel-section side frames and forming a stressed fuselage ribbed in ash with steel fletch-plating bolted on as reinforcement. Aluminium skinning was pinned onto this sub-structure, forming body sides and top and adding a full-length heavy-gauge undertray which gave a very low ground clearance and which was a major load-bearing member. This forerunner of today's racing chassis scaled just 83½lbs!

Unfortunately Voisin's basic racing engine—a 62mm x 109mm, 1992cc 'six' with Knight double sleeve valves—was extremely heavy despite its use of an alloy block, and its power output of 75bhp at 4,000rpm was pitiful in Grand Prix company. It was also a tall engine, which demanded an ugly rectangular housing breaking-up the new car's striking chisel nose-line.

Despite its shortcomings, this innovative design appeared at Tours for the Grand Prix, where four works cars were entered to be driven by Rougier, Duray, Morel and the works engineer, Lefebvre. In practice they were swamped by the powerful red and green cars, and Voisin himself was alarmed when his drivers came in complaining of wandering on the straights and dreadful instability under braking. The cars' narrow track was blamed and was duly widened slightly before the race.

The cars were very slow, with a top speed of about 105mph compared to the 120mph plus produced by Fiat and Sunbeam. Gabriel Voisin hoped that trouble might hit the faster runners, but found to his bitter disappointment that his own cars were unreliable. Only Lefebvre's car survived to the finish, running for 496 miles while his faster and harder-driving team-mates dropped out one by one. The sole surviving Voisin was placed fifth and last, $1\frac{1}{4}$-hours behind H. O. D. Segrave's winning Sunbeam.

Voisin brought out his cars once more, for the European Grand Prix at Monza (see page 30), but the Italian circuit proved even less lucky for him and the whole team retired with mechanical failures.

The pioneer aviator returned to road car production, pursuing a constant quest for quiet refinement which resulted in a line of vast and often virtually unsaleable machines of doubtful aesthetic appeal. The last Voisin cars were produced in 1937, by which time the visionary, eccentric company founder had sold his name to an outside syndicate. The company itself collapsed in 1939, leaving many remarkable designs and prototypes in its wake, including steam cars, monstrous V12s, even a six litre *straight*-twelve engined model!

Post war years saw Voisin running a small drawing office in the Rue des Pâtures, in Paris. His 197cc front-drive two-seater 'Mini-cars' were put into production by Autonacional SA of Barcelona from 1950–58, under the name 'Biscuter', and among more visionary exercises were a 50cc single-seater town car which would slip-in beneath France's vehicle taxation umbrella, a steam tank for the Army, a military amphibian and even a revolutionary 'traffic-city' plan for Paris worked out in conjunction with Le Corbusier.

In his declining years, Voisin wrote two volumes of memoirs, vivid works for a man well into his eighties, recalling his '10,000 aeroplanes' and '1001 motor cars', plus the innumerable women in his life. He seems to have been appalled that the public took more interest in his love life than in his engineering, so turned to philosophising and writing on hunting instead. On Thursday, 27 December 1973, his obituary appeared in the London *Telegraph*. He had died at his home near Tournus at the age of 93 – his futuristic Grand Prix cars passed unmentioned. . . .

During the thirties the monocoque cudgel had been taken up by Greek-born Alec Issigonis in England, with the incredible 'Lightweight Special'. Its monocoque shell was formed from plywood faced on both sides by aluminium sheet, and suspension was by

7 Louis Chevrolet in the 1915, monocoque-chassised, all-independent suspension Cornelian at Indianapolis. It was to be 50 years before Jim Clark's monocoque Lotus 38 won the famous '500'.

8 The Rumpler 'Tropfenwagen' road car – it was *very* peculiar . . .

9, 10 The Benz 'Tropfenwagen' Grand Prix car of 1923, with and without its striking body. The chassis was extensively drilled for lightness, the engine was mid-mounted with the saddle radiator above and swing-axle independent rear suspension was fitted.

11 A signed photograph of test driver Kurt Volkhart in the prototype Opel-Sander rocket car. It had small negative incidence 'wings' on either side to ensure it remained earthbound.

rubber bands. It used a Murray Jamieson-developed Austin engine, and in this form scaled just 587lbs when completed in 1939. Postwar this car ran in many hill-climb events where another unitary-construction single-seater appeared, this being Laurie Bond's tiny 500cc Rudge-powered front-drive Bond Special which was far too powerful for its negligible weight and which skipped and bounded along like a little rubber ball!

In 1965 the Indianapolis '500' was won by Jimmy Clark in a works-entered Lotus-Ford 38—a car developed from the Formula 1 monocoque design of 1962. The wheel had then come full circle—it took fifty years from the Cornelian's introduction of monocoque principles to Indy for a monocoque-chassised car to win the race.

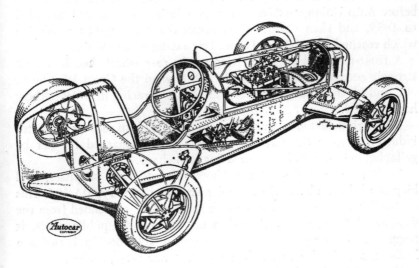

An early monocoque: Alec Issigonis' 1939 'Lightweight Special'
(courtesy of *Autocar*).

C

4

The Engine's in the Back! –
Europe, 1921-1925

Just as there was an early forerunner to the monocoque racing chassis so there were early rear-engined racing cars, introduced long before Auto Union contrived to 'unpopularise' the theory from 1934 to 1939, and then Cooper Cars began the rear-engined revolution which reached its height in Grand Prix racing in 1959–60.

A front-mounted engine driving to the rear wheels had become a strongly-entrenched fact of life by 1914 when the Great War broke out, and on the return of peace and of motor racing in 1919 nothing had changed.

Although defeated in war, Germany was quick to recover its motor industry, despite the twenties being a decade marked for her by galloping inflation and continued financial chaos.

In 1921 the Berlin Motor Show offered some surprises, and biggest of them all was the Rumpler Tropfenwagen Typ OA 104. This outlandish vehicle looked as though it should be suspended from the gas-bag of a Zeppelin rather than set free on the public roads. It suggested the result of a close triangular relationship between a lifeboat, a taxi-cab and a light aircraft. It was *very* peculiar.

Dr Edmund Rumpler himself came from Bohemia, and he produced his first car designs for Nesselsdorfer, Daimler and Adler before the Great War. He had many advanced ideas, including an early engine in unit with its gearbox, and swing-axles allowing independent suspension to the driven wheels, which he patented. Both these features appeared in his Adler period, but then he turned his attention to aviation and designed the Rumpler Taube, a strikingly graceful monoplane scout which saw wide service during the war years.

After the war Germany's aviation was stamped out, and Rumpler returned to motoring to apply his aviation expertise to advanced projects. He established Rumpler Motoren Gesellschaft GmbH in Berlin at the start of 1921, and there the 'Teardrop Car' was built.

Rumpler was aiming to achieve a good aerodynamic shape which would provide the utmost performance and economy from a given power unit, and to provide his passengers with the best possible ride he concentrated them near the middle of the car. With further regard to their comfort he tucked engine noise and fumes well out of their way in the tail, and then provided an extensively-glazed two-door saloon body based on a complex punt-type frame.

The body had a flat-topped deck and sweeping flanks which met in boat-like points at front and rear. Two headlights reposed one above the other on the stem, and rakish horizontal 'wings' projected from either side of the hull to act as splash guards above the road wheels.

Even the chassis frame was teardrop-shaped, and at the front it carried a solid axle beam on two semi-elliptic springs mounted within the frame members, and at the rear two more semi-elliptics angled rearwards to suspend the outboard ends of long swing-axles.

Neither was the engine anything mundane, for Rumpler had a W6-cylinder unit produced on contract by the outside firm of Siemens & Halske. This form—known in Britain as a 'broad arrow'—had three banks of cylinders (in this case with two cylinders in each bank) with the outside pair mounted at a broad vee angle and the centre bank vertical on a common crankcase. This compact, short, water-cooled unit had cylinder dimensions of 74mm x 100mm, giving 2,600cc, and produced 36bhp at 2,000rpm. It had pushrod-operated overhead valves, with a tiny camshaft in each bank, and leaf-springs closed the valves with one for each pair of inlets or exhausts. The con-rods gathered in threes on the two crankpins which were arranged 180 degrees apart. A vertical shaft drove fan and magneto, and a single Pallas carburettor was used with complex inlet manifolding. Transmission was through a three-speed gearbox.

All this unconventionality produced a road car with a top speed of 70mph, but Rumpler fixed the price of this remarkably unsaleable product at the equivalent of £7,500. His company kept going, and he later produced a modified Typ 4A 106 model with a 2,595cc 'four' of conventional design giving over fifty horsepower. This produced a top speed of seventy-five mph and reportedly was a desperate thing to drive at such speeds. In 1926 he turned his design about and went in for front-drive, but then his small concern collapsed and the brief flirtation was over.

In the meantime the famous concern of Benz & Cie in Mannheim was trying to change its staid, conservative image, and with permission from the directors the head of the technical division, Dr Hans Nibel, prepared to build the company's first Grand Prix car since 1908.

Nibel and engineer Max Wagner approached Rumpler and gained permission to incorporate his patents into their new Grand Prix design. Thus was born the first rear-engined, swing-axled, inboard rear-braked car to tackle Grand Prix racing. They even borrowed the Tropfenwagen ('Teardrop Car') tag, and this has since become more synonymous with the Benz than with the original Rumpler designs.

Of course this was not to be the first rear-engined racing car. Almost everything has been done before, and nearly contemporary competition cars with the engine aft of the driver included the Brooklands AV cyclecar of 1920–22 which had its twin-cylinder engines projecting behind the back axle, and the mid-engined Crouch cars of 1921–22 which had the power unit sited within the wheelbase, between the back axle and the driver.

This latter arrangement is that seen in modern Grand Prix design, and this was the way Nibel and Wagner laid out their new car for Benz.

It was intended for the 2-litre Grand Prix formula of 1922–25 and work was soon under way at Mannheim. The chassis frames were built up from channel section steel, carefully curved and shaped and designed to pass under the swing-axles at the rear. Hefty cross members gave the chassis its torsional rigidity, and the whole assembly was then extensively drilled for lightness and probably lost it all again!

A combined three-speed gearbox and final drive was used, with the gearbox fitting neatly between the engine and differential unit. When this idea returned to mid-engined Grand Prix design in the postwar Cisitalia-Porsche and the 1963 ATS it failed to impress, but when the 1970 Porsche 908/3 sports cars adopted it to concentrate their mass within the wheelbase it was hailed as a generally 'good idea'.

This 'transaxle' assembly was bolted to the rear chassis cross-members, and then mated to the engine which was an unsupercharged six-cylinder with shaft-driven double-overhead camshafts, the cylinders arranged in separate steel barrels with welded-on water jackets and carrying four valves per cylinder. Roller bearings were used on a Hirth-type built-up crankshaft for both mains and big-ends, and bore and stroke dimensions were 65mm x 100mm, giving 1,997cc. There were twin Zenith carburettors, and the factory eventually released modest power output figures of 80bhp at 4,500rpm.

Quarter-elliptic leaf springs were used front and rear, disposed similarly to those on Rumpler's original car, with friction-type dampers at the front but none – it would appear – at the rear. The rear drum brakes were mounted inboard on the cheeks of the final-drive unit, with the drums themselves carefully drilled, and they were cable-operated.

The whole car was clad in a nicely-formed teardrop-shaped light metal body with a bulbous nose and tapering slimline tailcone. Detachable louvred panels enclosed the engine, and a broad cockpit accommodated two seats for the driver and his regulation riding mechanic.

To achieve a clean and unbroken nose-line the radiator was formed into a crescent-shaped saddle, which wrapped over the tail just behind the engine cover. A streamlined nacelle formed its header tank, and the whole assembly was beautifully nickel-plated and polished. An oil cooler projected from the right-side of the body just behind the driver's right elbow.

There was no windscreen as such, but the cockpit coaming was curled into a raised lip just ahead of the driver to divert the airstream over his head. The whole car was painted white, with nickelled hub caps and an enormous "BENZ" badge was sign-written onto the nose.

Nibel intended to enter a team of three new cars for the 1922 Italian Grand Prix at Milan's brand-new Monza Autodrome, but labour troubles delayed their construction, and it was not until the following year that the rear-engined Benz made its debut.

Once again the company aimed high, choosing the European Grand Prix at Monza for their re-entry into racing. Drivers were to be Willy Walb, Franz Horner and the Italian Nando Minoia.

The sleek white cars were a sensation in practice, but out on the track they were far overshadowed by the supercharged Fiats which had been introduced in the French Grand Prix at Tours. These were the first supercharged cars to enter Grand Prix racing, but their debut had been a disaster with flying gravel entering the unguarded supercharger intakes and wreaking havoc within. Now, on their home ground, Fiat were better prepared, and drivers Pietro Bordino, Carlo

Salamano and Felice Nazzaro used their 146bhp to the full. Their demonstration of speed and power in practice was interrupted when Bordino somersaulted his car, killing his mechanic and damaging his arm.

Ugo Sivocci, driving the brand-new Alfa Romeo P1, was also killed in this practice period. Other entries preparing for the race included three of the Tours Voisins, two Rolland-Pilains and a semi-official works team from Miller in America. They were using their board speedway-bred cars, driven by Jimmy Murphy, Count Louis Zborowski and the wealthy Argentinian enthusiast, Martin de Alzagar. Murphy had won the 1921 French Grand Prix for Duesenberg in the last virtually all-American GP win until 1967 when Dan Gurney won the Belgian GP in his Eagle.

Against such opposition the one-year-late Benz cars were markedly underpowered, and the race developed with Bordino rushing away into the lead (scarcely betraying the fact that his arm was in a sling, and his mechanic was changing gear!) with his team-mates fanned out behind and Murphy putting up a terrific fight to maintain contact in the Miller.

Bordino wore himself out, and at half-distance he retired exhausted. Since the Fiat relief driver Cagno had taken himself off somewhere, their leading car had to be withdrawn on the spot. This left Salamano to win from Nazzaro with the gallant Murphy third only five minutes behind the winner. Walb had retired his Benz Tropfenwagen with unspecified engine trouble, but Minoia finished fourth, and Horner fifth.

The cars had proved quite tricky to drive, with their rear wheels liable to tuck and skip in corners, and back at Mannheim the engineers developed the design to cure its tail-happiness. The rear brakes were taken outboard—perhaps to protect them from transmission oil leaks?—and in 1924 a modified car appeared with its radiator resited in the nose, presumably to improve weight distribution.

Willy Walb drove it in the Feldberg and Köhnigstuhl hill-climbs and won both handsomely against poorish opposition. Hill-climbing continued into 1925 when Walb won at Stettener and Schriesheim-Weisenthal, while Jewish businessman and amateur driver Adolf Rosenberger won the Herkules climb and the Stuttgart road race outside Solitude in a similar car.

Germany's financial chaos had hit Benz hard, and with money short there were no more Grand Prix entries for their Grand Prix team. They built a sports-racing version of their Tropfenwagen for 1924, with a saddle-radiator GP model carrying high cantilevered mudguards, twin headlights fared into the nose cowling and a rudimentary vee-shaped windscreen.

Walb raced it regularly, winning his class at Baden-Baden in 1924 and at Freiburg in 1925. An obscure Dr Tigler also drove a sports model in 1925, and he won at Wiesbaden and Stolzenfels.

The end came when Benz merged with Mercedes in 1926, for the Mercedes-Benz cars were to be strictly front-engined, rear-wheel-drive models disregarding the compact, weight-saving rear-engine location suggested by Dr Rumpler. His swing axles were a different matter, and they are still with us today.

A fellow Bohemian—Dr Ferdinand Porsche—championed the swing-axled rear-engined cause long after Benz dropped the idea, and used the axles in his Steyr designs of the late twenties. When Steyr were absorbed into Austro-Daimler in 1929, Porsche found his style cramped so resigned and set up his own design office which opened at Kronenstrasse 14, Stuttgart, on 1 December 1930.

He chose as his commercial manager the same Adolf Rosenberger, the driver from Pforzheim, who had raced the Tropfenwagen in 1925 and had later become a Mercedes works driver.

In the early thirties both the Ardie and Adler companies produced minor rear-engined prototype cars, and Porsche also dabbled, with the assistance of Rosenberger and another ex-Benz man—Willy Walb.

When the governing body of motor sport, the AIACR, announced their new 750-kilogram maximum weight formula in October 1932 (for introduction in 1934), Porsche decided to build a racing car.

Within a month the Porsche team of engineers had a scheme roughed out for a Grand Prix car incorporating a mid-mounted engine and swing-axle suspension. The design office set up a new company, catchily-titled the 'Hochleistungsfahrzeugbau GmbH' (High Performance Vehicle Construction Co Ltd) to build the new 'P-Wagen', and it was intended to use the same mid-mounted 4.4 litre V16-cylinder engine in an aerodynamic bodied sports car.

At this same time Joergen Skafte Rasmussen had formed his Auto Union empire from the well-known firms of Horch, Audi, Wanderer and DKW. His directors were very competition-minded and when he gave the go-ahead for the construction of a 750Kg Grand Prix car they approached Porsche and asked if he would design one for them.

Porsche presented them with his experimental 'P-Wagen' design and so the famous mid-engined Auto Union Grand Prix cars came into being, ten years on from the original Rumpler-inspired Benz cars.

When Hitler came to power early in 1933 the Auto Union and Daimler-Benz Grand Prix programmes received state backing, but an unfortunate sign of the times was Rosenberger's resignation from the Porsche office on the eve of Hitler's election. He was a Jew, a far-sighted man, and he knew what was coming.

During the twenties there was another brief but interesting 'rear-engined' development in the German motor industry. It came to the public's notice in April 1928, when the sounds of unusual explosions and brief glimpses of fast-moving smoke-wreathed vehicles were rumoured around the Opel works at Russelsheim.

Fritz von Opel, grandson of company founder Adam Opel, made a public announcement to prevent idle speculation. His company was developing a rocket-powered experimental research vehicle!

Engineers Valier, Sander and Volkhart had fitted a dozen solid-fuel rockets into the extreme tail of an old retired racing chassis. They lit the blue touch paper, then retired to watch the unfortunate driver —usually Volkhart—steer the car until its rockets exhausted themselves. Five of the twelve failed to fire on the first public demonstration at the Opel works, but Von Opel himself was delighted with the impression made on his important guests and planned a full-blown public demonstration of an improved car at Berlin's AVUS test-road-cum-racing circuit.

The Automobil-Verkehrs-und-Ubungstrasse had been planned in 1908 and was built through the Grünewald after the Great War and opened with a race in 1921, when a Benz won. In 1926 the first German Grand Prix had been held there in pouring rain, won by Caracciola in one of the tricky eight-cylinder Monza Mercedes, but his team-mate—our old friend Rosenberger—had crashed into a scoreboard hut and killed a scorer. This tragedy shut down the AVUS for some time, and now Opel's rocket car demonstration was bringing it back to life.

Eugen Sander built a classically bullet-shaped car with solid axles and leaf-spring suspension, while Max Valier—the rocket expert—mounted twenty-four sequentially-fired solid-fuel rockets into its extreme tail, separated from the driver's cockpit by a hefty armour plate.

Prophetic additions on either side of the car's cylindrical hull were fifty-inch long negative-incidence 'wings', looking just like an aircraft's but being designed to promote downthrust at speed and so ensure that the car remained earthborne.

In the fifties Swiss engineer Michel May was to arrive at the Nürburgring with a tall strutted wing mounted on his Porsche to perform the same function, Mercedes used smaller devices on their racing coupés and an Indy car named 'Mad Dog' streaked round the Daytona bankings with wings on either side in exact imitation of the Opel rocket car. By 1966–67 Jim Hall's Chaparral sports cars were carrying enormous strutted aerfoils operating directly on the cars' rear suspension, and in 1968–69 'wings' proliferated and spread into Grand Prix and minor formulae single-seater racing. Today no serious competition car is without some form of aerfoil aid.

Sander's car was lacquered black and sinister, with large 'OPEL RAK 2' lettering on its flanks, its constructor's name written smaller underneath. Fritz von Opel himself was to drive the car, and on May 23 this well-engineered publicity stunt took place.

Nattily-dressed in leather flying jacket and white silk scarf, the bespectacled Von Opel clambered down into the highsided cockpit, resting his begoggled but bare head back against a fared tail-rest.

Once in place, with final instructions from Valier, he fired the first of his rockets and RAK 2 began to roll, gathering speed as thick white smoke and incandescent embers poured out of its tail.

Its sibilant hiss became a shattering roar as Von Opel fired-off all 260lbs of solid-fuel rocketry behind his back, and the black car completed a sensationally spectacular swerving run at over 125mph—some later reports claiming as much as 160mph which seems most unlikely.

The media were breathlessly impressed by this exhibition, and Opel authorised building RAK 3 which was to be a rail vehicle to be tested without passengers. A length of track was chosen near the village of Burgwedel, on the Hanover plains, and despite bursting some of its rockets RAK 3 recorded 180mph and coasted safely to a halt.

Then thirty rockets were loaded on board, each two feet long, five inches in diameter and containing $27\frac{1}{2}$ pounds of powder. Twenty yards down the track the first rockets began to explode and detach from the vehicle, and the uneven thrust remaining then skewed the rail-car off its tracks and sent it rampaging along the cutting to smash through a line of trees and destroy itself.

On August 3-4 RAK 4 was ready to be tested on the same stretch of line, this vehicle weighing 1,750 lbs, with twenty-four rockets mounted in a tray on the rear of the chassis pointing upwards at a sixty-degree angle. After seventy-five yards sheets of flame emerged sideways from the smoke cloud surrounding the rail-car, and almost instantaneously it reared-up and soared and rolled through the air to explode on impact with the ground 300 yards away!

The Opel image was suffering badly, so RAK 5 was junked. Fritz von Opel took to building a rocket-powered plane which was also unsuccessful. Kurt Volkhart built himself a 24-rocket car of his own which he demonstrated successfully at the Nürburgring with a female passenger in 1929, but on 17 May 1930 poor Valier was killed in his laboratory while experimenting with liquid rocket fuels. The day of the rear-engined, reaction-powered high-speed vehicle was not to dawn until well into the sixties.

5

Front-Wheel Drive Revived –
America and Europe, 1918-1927

Nobody in America who had witnessed it could forget the awe-inspiring sight of Barney Oldfield's front-drive Christie erupting out of the dirt-track turns with its front wheels scrabbling for grip, hurling plumes of debris far into the air on each burst of power.

In 1918 an ex-US army sergeant named Ben F. Gregory set up the Front Drive Motor Company in Kansas City, Missouri. During the next four years he built several cars, all using an ingenious form of front-drive far in advance of Christie's Edwardian ideas.

Some Gregory cars were racers and some tourers, but all featured a normal in-line engine mounted behind the front axle line. The front axle itself was a De Dion tube which served purely to tie the front wheels together, and it was arched to give clearance to a gearbox and final drive unit mounted in front of the turned-about engine. The wheels were powered through universally-jointed half shafts, and springing was by transverse leaf.

Gregory's own stark single-seater racing car used first an OX-5 and later an Hispano-Suiza aero engine, and like Oldfield before him he barnstormed it round the nation's dirt tracks with some considerable success.

In 1922 Gregory's company was wound up and Jimmy Murphy won at Indianapolis with a Miller-engined Duesenberg. He wanted a potent speedway car for the coming year, and mechanic Riley Brett is said to have suggested front-wheel drive, recalling Oldfield's lap record successes with the crude Christie. Murphy and Brett went to see Harry Armenius Miller in Los Angeles, and work began on the Miller front-drive which eventually became a classic in racing car design and a potent force in speedway racing.

Meanwhile in England a less well-publicised project was taking shape, working along similar lines. The Alvis Car and Engineering Company of Coventry ran a comprehensive competition programme, using stripped versions of their 1,496cc 12/50 four-cylinder models.

The 12/50s had been introduced in 1923, and during that summer the works driver, Major C. M. (Maurice) Harvey, scored several successes in sprints and hill-climbs with 'Racing Car No 1'. This was a 12/50 with extensive drilling to save weight, dry-sump lubrication and a three-speed gearbox. It weighed 1,700lbs, which was considered very light for its type, and later in the year some rather less sketchy variants built up on experience with 'No 1' gave Alvis their biggest competition success when Harvey won the 200-Miles race at Brooklands, averaging over 93mph.

The company's works manager and chief engineer was another ex-military man, Captain G. T. Smith-Clarke, and under his direction a pair of more specialised 12/50-based racing cars were built-up for 1924 plus a single-seater intended for Brooklands racing and record work. The new cars scaled 1,232lbs., and their engines were rumoured to produce 70bhp at 4,500rpm. They were still no match for their deadly rival, J. A. Joyce's Sprint AC, which was well over 100lbs lighter.

'Beating the AC' became one of Smith-Clarke's minor ambitions, and with designer W. M. Dunn he schemed a sprint car to use a more powerful 1½-litre engine and a much lighter chassis.

The only available engine was the 12/50, and to wring more power from it Smith-Clarke and Dunn decided to adopt the then-novel idea of supercharging.

Initial experiments were made with a cupola-type supercharger, powered by its own electric motor, but then a conventional Roots-type unit was adopted, driven from the engine crankshaft. This drew mixture from a Solex carburettor, and the engine produced close on 100bhp on the test bed.

With the engine well on the way to providing the necessary power, Alvis tackled the problem of making a lightweight car which would also be stable and offer good traction.

This problem was solved at a stroke. Smith-Clarke and Dunn decided to drive the front wheels. Concentrating the works at the driven end of the chassis would automatically save weight by dispensing with a long propeller shaft. It would also put most of the available weight on the driven wheels, and without a shaft to get in the way the driver could be seated very low down and the whole car could be low-slung to promote stability.

Work began on the new Alvis late in 1924, and it was released to the British press the following Spring. It was a sensation.

The chassis was formed completely in duralumin, with eight-inch deep channel section side members and stressed-skin dural boxing around the rear of the cockpit to form a kind of semi-monocoque structure! The bodywork terminated abruptly in a stressed panel forming the backrest for the seats, and the back axle was exposed, offering educational views of its reversed quarter-elliptic springing.

The engine was turned about-face in the chassis, with a single-plate clutch, four-speed gearbox and straight-tooth bevel final drive and differential all housed in the very nose of the car. The front drum brakes were mounted inboard on the cheeks of the final drive unit, and a twin-tube rigid De Dion axle assembly hooked round the drive unit to locate the front wheels. It was suspended on quarter-elliptic leaf springs, and drive to the wheels was via exposed half-shafts with an inboard universal joint buried within the brake drum and an outboard joint integral with the hub.

Wheelbase was 8ft 0in, with a 4ft 6in front track and 4ft 0in rear track. The car stood just on 3ft 0in high, and weighed under 1,120lbs. In initial form it was unsupercharged, but the Roots unit was soon added, driven off what was now the 'back end' of the crankshaft, and mounted by the driver's ankles.

In tests the new Alvis proved itself a vivid performer, with terrific acceleration off the mark or away from a corner. It tracked well through the corners while the driver was content to grit his teeth and keep his foot hard on the power. Under deceleration, in particular under heavy braking, weight transference made the car a real handful for its tail weaved and juddered and threatened to overtake the nose at every opportunity!

Harvey gave the car its competition debut at the Kop public road hill-climb on 28 March 1925, two months before the first front-drive Miller was to make its debut at Indianapolis.

In America Miller had experienced problems developing his compact design of front-drive unit, and draughtsman Leo Goossen did not perfect the watch-like mechanism until well into 1924. Late that season Jimmy Murphy was killed in a 100-mile dirt-track race at Syracuse, NY, and so was cheated of driving 'his' car. In the 1925

Indianapolis '500' it was driven by Bennett Hill and Dave Lewis, who very nearly won but finished a good second.

While the American car was proving itself, Harvey's fwd Alvis went on to have a good season, actually matching and beating Joyce's AC on occasion. A second car was added to the team, with an over-1½-litre engine, but meanwhile Smith-Clarke's ambitions were growing.

The AIACR regulations for a 1½-litre Grand Prix formula were shortly to come into force, and with the front-drive sprint car proving successful Alvis decided to enter Grand Prix racing.

Smith-Clarke and Dunn drew a straight-eight cylinder engine with bore and stroke of 55mm x 78.75mm, giving a swept volume of 1,497cc. They adopted an unusual valve gear, for they were going to use a supercharger which at that time was very akin to black art, and they wished to keep the sparking plugs well divorced from the piston crowns to keep heating problems within known limits. The cooling properties of alcohol fuels and the characteristics of special alloys were little understood, and so horizontal valves were adopted, one on either side of each combustion chamber, actuated by short vertical pushrods from high-mounted side camshafts.

The crankshaft ran in five plain main-bearings, and dural con rods were made in which the body metal doubled as the bearing surface. The block was cast in one piece with the head and upper crankcase half, while the lower half incorporated a dry sump. The rear end of the crankshaft drove a Roots supercharger which encroached on the regulation two-seater cockpit with its unoccupied mechanic's seat, and which drew from a Solex carburettor. Twin magnetos provided the ignition.

Unfortunately this unit cannot have been very powerful, and Alvis were very reticent where its output was concerned. It was probably around 110bhp, which was no match for the contemporary 144bhp Talbots and 170bhp Delages.

The abandonment of lightweight construction tended to compound the engine's poor power output, since the Alvis engineers adopted a conservative steel channel frame with unstressed aluminium-panelled bodywork. Fuel tankage was concentrated forward in the car to maintain a bias towards the driven wheels, and the tail cowling enclosed nothing but empty air.

While attempts were made to complete the cars and to persuade more power from the straight-eight engines, the 1926 season quickly passed by. Alvis were not a wealthy company, and they quickly discovered that a Grand Prix programme was both expensive and time-consuming.

The cars had been intended to run in the British Grand Prix at Brooklands in August, but Alvis's eventual lone entry was scratched after proving itself ill-prepared and unraceworthy in practice.

A great effort was made to have the cars running well for the 200-Mile race in September, and one car was sufficiently advanced for Harvey to run it for the first time at Shelsley Walsh hill-climb early that month. It was wrongly-geared but sounded superb as it bellowed up the hill.

Both cars were ready for the 200-Miles, with the Earl of Cottenham joining Harvey as second driver. Unfortunately the Grand Prix Talbot team was also present, with Segrave, Divo and Moriceau driving, but the Alvis was still able to impress.

Artificial Ess-bends had been formed on the finishing straight by laying down banks of loose sand. The organising Junior Car Club claimed that this new feature enabled the public '. . . to enjoy the unique opportunity of witnessing at close quarters the driving prowess of some of the best-known racing car exponents in this country and abroad. . . .'

Harvey's Alvis was one of the fastest cars through these bends. He would come swaying into the corner under braking, then lock the car over, back-off on the throttle to bring the tail round and then give it full power to show explosive acceleration away from the corner, with the engine howling through the gears very satisfactorily.

In the race he was third away behind the two French-driven Talbots, but they just powered away from him round the long Brooklands bankings. On the 23rd lap he was lying fourth behind Segrave when Longden's back-marker Fiat pulled across his path as he rushed out of the Ess-bend. Harvey dodged the obstruction, but suddenly closing the throttle and throwing on steering lock was fatal, for the Alvis' tail whipped round and the car spun off the road backwards. Its tail clanged onto the railings of the public enclosure, then thudded against a telegraph pole and cut-off the telephone in the timekeeper's box. Harvey was out of the race.

Cottenham inherited fourth place in the sister car, but then saw his oil pressure gauge zero and wisely retired. It was not until the engine was stripped down at Coventry that the gauge was found to be faulty . . . he could have continued.

So ended Alvis's first year 'in Grand Prix racing', and for 1927 a large improvement programme was begun. New engines were made having twin-overhead camshafts operating inclined valves in hemispherical combustion chambers, and the supercharger was repositioned alongside the engine block while the front-drive system was rejigged to place the gearbox ahead of the final-drive unit, projecting beyond the front of the car to put more weight on the front wheels. This allowed fuel tankage to be more evenly distributed, with a twenty-five gallon tail tank being introduced, designed to drain down before a twenty gallon secondary tank fitted into the scuttle. Twin magnetos fired four cylinders each.

Then the first independent front suspension to appear in Grand Prix racing since Christie's in 1907 was adopted. This consisted of four small quarter-elliptic springs mounted transversely on either side, two above and two below each drive shaft. Separate steering drag links appeared on either side and the driver's seat was shuffled across the chassis to provide a central driving position virtually coincidentally with an Italian car we shall meet shortly.

The new engine produced a more respectable 125bhp, and two cars were planned for the new 1927 Grand Prix season. Unfortunately Alvis again lost their battle with time, and it was not until the British Grand Prix at Brooklands on October 1, the last Grand Prix race run to the 1½-litre formula, that the new car appeared.

Harvey took the car out for practice only to return with something variously reported as a defective oil pump or a broken piston. As one could conceivably follow the other, perhaps both reports were true. Damage was sufficiently serious for the car to lose its last chance in Grand Prix racing, and it was withdrawn with Alvis never having started a GP race.

Two cars returned to Brooklands for the 200-Miles, but the Earl of Cottenham had to stand down for family reasons and race-horse jockey George Duller took over as Harvey's team-mate. The two cars had indifferent practice sessions, but then fled away from the field at the start, again displaying immense acceleration.

Harvey was leading Duller until the latter's car misfired by the pits and was instantly swamped by Campbell and Eyston in their Bugattis. On lap seven Duller stopped to change plugs, and Harvey was passed by the Bugattis and by Morel's wildly-driven Amilcar-Six. At quarter-distance Harvey's Alvis was seen creeping into the pits, spluttering and coughing, and one of Britain's now redun-

12 Giulio Foresti rumbles 'Djelmo' down onto Pendine Sands for its ill-fated attempt on the Land Speed Record, 1927.

13, 14 Front-wheel drive: The early-model Alvis which Major Harvey crashed at Brooklands in 1926, and Cappa's incredible 1100cc V12 Itala which was never raced.

15 Monza Autodrome, September 4, 1927. Pietro Bordino in the brand-new Fiat 806 talks with Felice Nazzaro before the start of the Milan Grand Prix.

dant Grand Prix challengers retired with piston failure.

Duller's misfiring sister car soon followed Harvey into retirement with another piston failure when lying second in the 1½-litre class. Again the Alvises were said to be the quickest cars through the corners, but that was achieving far too little, far too late.

The company concentrated on racing sports versions of their front-drive cars later in the twenties, and ten straight-eight models were produced in 1929–1930, finally winning their class in the 1930 Tourist Trophy race with a best placing of fourth overall.

But their Grand Prix programme may be likened to the famous V16 BRM of twenty years later, which also ran out of time and was left high and dry by the receding tide of a Grand Prix formula. The Duller GP car is still in existence in Australia, but it is yet another memorial simply to what might have been.

During this same period another small British effort produced a 1½-litre Grand Prix car. Major Frank Halford – later to become renowned for his aero-engine designs – put together a six-cylinder, twin overhead camshaft engine, with cast-iron head on an aluminium block carrying 'wet' cylinder liners. Bore and stroke dimensions were 63mm x 80mm, giving a displacement of 1,496cc, and with a large Roots supercharger mounted between the dumb-irons of an old Aston Martin chassis and transmission, the Halford Special produced about 96bhp at 5,300rpm and later modifications brought this up to around 120bhp. Major Halford raced the car quite often, notably in the 1926 British Grand Prix when transmission failure put him out after eighty one laps, and after he had held fourth place. George Eyston later drove the car which was eventually converted for road use, but it was interesting as one of the last genuine specials in Grand Prix racing. . . .

Turin's Museo dell-Automobili Carlo Biscaretti di Ruffia positively brims with such specials. Tucked away in one of the museum's well-lit halls is another front-drive car which never saw the formula to which it was built, and which suffered a worse fate than the Alvises for in fact it was never to be raced at all. This is the wooden-chassised, front-wheel drive 1,100cc V12 Itala of 1926.

Fabbrica Automobili Itala SA had been formed in Turin in 1904 by Matteo Ceirano and Guido Bigio. Ceirano was a man who flitted about the Italian industry, starting Ceirano itself in 1901, then founding Itala and later moving on to establish SPA in 1906. Bigio stayed on with Itala until he met his death in a road accident seven years later.

In this time Itala built its reputation on competition, Raggio's 15.3-litre model being the first shaft-driven car to win a major race, in the 1905 Coppa Florio at Brescia. Cagno's stripped touring Itala won the first Targa Florio in Sicily in 1906, and then a similar model was driven by Prince Scipione Borghese to win the incredible Peking – Paris in 1907.

Bigio's death and a disastrous attempt to build Hispano-Suiza V8 aero engines during the Great War left Itala in a sorry state. Their postwar models were scantily updated versions of their prewar offerings, and sales slumped badly.

But in the early twenties Itala attracted an engineer named Giulio Cesare Cappa from Fiat. He set about revitalising the marque, and he had just the track record for the job. He had built a shaft-driven motorcycle in 1905, and as chief engineer of Aquila-Italiana he had produced four-and six-cylinder engines cast *en bloc*, aluminium pistons, ball-race crankshaft bearings, and a form of unit engine-gearbox construction all virtually unheard of in 1906, when they were all released. During the war years he had worked with Fiat designing aero engines, and postwar had aided Guido Fornaca in designing the dominant Grand Prix Fiats of the early twenties.

Fiat pulled out of racing after 1924, by which time Cappa was with Itala and fighting hard to hold their head above water. It was known that a new 1,500cc Grand Prix formula was to be introduced in 1926, and logically this meant a demotion of the junior Voiturette class from 1,500 to 1,100cc. Cappa aimed to build a racing car easily capable of being run in both Voiturette and Grand Prix events, and capable of dominating both. His design was to be one of the most remarkable racing cars of all time.

He took a virtually clean sheet of paper, disregarded all conventions regarding racing design, and outlined a scheme for a car using front engine and front-wheel drive, and super-light construction. He began his design months before he would hear of the first front-drive Miller's success at Indianapolis, and roughly contemporary with Smith-Clarke's Alvis team in Coventry.

Cappa wanted nothing so hefty as a De Dion axle wobbling about on the front of *his* Grand Prix car, and he adopted fully independent front suspension with splined and ball-jointed drive shafts to allow for bump and steering movements of the wheels.

He used transverse leaf-springs as the front wheels' upper locating members, enclosing them in smooth steel farings which hinged on the chassis through moulded rubber shrouds. The outer ends of the springs sat in shaped hard-rubber blocks on the hub carrier. The bottom of the carrier was attached to the chassis through short swinging links, which were similarly fared and hinged. At the rear a similar transverse leaf and short link system was adopted, using the same neatly formed streamlined farings and with the wheels running on dead half-axles.

These neat suspension units attached to a novel chassis frame, for in search of lightness Cappa had gone back to the dawn of motoring, and had adopted an ash frame with steel plate reinforcing bolted through from each side. Sitting in the front of this light assembly was Cappa's *tour de force*, unfortunately to become the car's downfall.

The Autocar of 25 June 1926 put it in a nutshell when it commented: 'It is rarely one encounters a car embodying so many original features as are to be found in the new Italas, which have a piston displacement of 1,100 or 1,500cc—there are two sizes—with twelve cylinders in one casting'. A cross-heading read 'Lilliputian Engine Parts!' and was deadly accurate. Not until the 1,500cc V16 BRM was completed in December, 1949, were smaller parts to be found in a racing design.

Cappa's V12 was reputedly scaled down from a projected 700hp aero engine design and used two banks of six cylinders each, disposed at sixty degrees within a single aluminium alloy casting whose box-like external appearance betrayed nothing of its complex V12 internals.

Inserted steel cylinder liners were used, with detachable cylinder heads formed in 'Silumin' with bronze valve seats. Bore and stroke were 45mm x 55mm, and capacity of the prototype Tipo 11 Voiturette was just 1,049cc.

The valves were operated by a single central camshaft mounted high above the centre of the vee, and gear-driven from the crankshaft. Each of twelve cams on this shaft operated two valves on either side. These tiny components were less than seven-eighths of an inch across the head and weighed three-quarters of an ounce each. Their horizontal mountings necessitated special Borgo pistons with stepped crowns, and they were controlled by hairpin springs.

Ignition was by twin Bosch magnetos, and the one-piece crankshaft ran in seven roller-bearings. As often used in two-stroke engine designs, there were six master connecting rods each carrying a lug to which was attached a shorter connecting rod from the opposite piston.

Careful attention was paid to lubricating this mechanism with a large simple pump pressurising the system, fed by a three and a quarter gallon oil tank. The whole of the valve gear was open to the crankcase for lubrication, with an aluminium cover making the chamber oil-tight.

Even in its supercharging the Itala Tipo 11 was unusual. Here a Roots-type compressor was driven from the rear of the crankshaft, but it neither drew from nor fed to the carburettors!

Instead it fed pressurised air direct through ports let into the cylinder barrels, where a set of special valves were actuated by a second camshaft set deep into the vee. Air driven into the cylinders at the end of the power stroke scavenged the exhaust gases, while air forced in at the end of the induction stroke merged with a basically very rich mixture to produce a highly explosive charge.

Ahead of the engine, which of course drove forwards in the frame, a complex two-part aluminium casting was mounted, containing clutch, gearbox and final-drive units and providing a mounting for the radiator. Steering gear was mounted above the gearbox, controlled by a horizontal column carrying a vertical steering wheel, and the simple drum brakes appearing on all four wheels were borrowed direct from Cappa's road-going Tipo 61 design. This lively road tourer appeared in 1924, featuring an attractive seven-bearing, pushrod light-six engine of 1,991cc, with alloy block and pistons and three-speed gearbox.

The Tipo 11 was completed with a strikingly sleek and smooth bodyshell, built low to take advantage of the missing rearward drive line, and with a neatly veed section which appeared in the radiator and which was mirrored in the bonnet, scuttle and tail. A completely smooth undertray was fitted, and in apparent disregard of the Grand Prix regulations Cappa set his steering and controls dead-centre in the cockpit, with a single central driving seat. Can Smith-Clarke have studied Cappa's design in 1926, before adopting fully independent front suspension and a central driving position for his own front-drive Alvis 'Mark 2' of 1927?

Twin exhaust pipes emerged from either side of the Itala's engine, discharging into jacketed expansion chambers integral with the body sides. A curious feature was that the pipes ended within the car's tail cowl, which was liberally louvred to allow the gases to escape. Wheelbase was a modest 8 feet 2 inches, and overall height was only 33¾ inches.

The Tipo 11 was about 450lbs lighter than its Grand Prix contemporaries, in 1,100cc trim, and Bugatti driver Bartolomeo Constantini was hired to test it at the Monza Autodrome.

He found it good for about 105mph on the straights, but reported that it was skittish through the corners – perhaps because he was unused to front-wheel drive. Generally he thought very highly of the little car, but felt that it would require more power. . . .

Cappa's theory fell down badly in this department, for although his V12 revolved easily up to 8,000rpm Itala seldom published its output, and when claims *were* made they seldom exceeded 50bhp. The contemporary 1,100cc Voiturettes from Amilcar and Salmson were good for 80bhp or more at that time, so the Tipo 11—for all its sophistication—was woefully inadequate.

Perhaps its curious supercharging system was at fault, but in any event Itala fortunes were sinking to an all-time low and they could not afford the expense of a long drawn-out development programme. Their racing car had to go, straight out of the box. It did not, and there was to be no second chance.

The Tipo 11 was never to be joined by the projected Grand Prix Tipo 15, and the Italian Government soon called in the sinister-sounding Societa Finanzaria di Liquidazione, which was a reconstruction agency formed to bolster ailing Italian industry in those difficult days. Itala were left with their revolutionary racing car and no money with which to develop it into a raceworthy proposition. In 1929 the company lost 21,000,000 lire and collapsed, but were reorganised by the government. Another major reorganisation followed in 1931, but it was all to no avail and this famous old marque finally lay down and died in 1934.

Four years later V12 engines and all-independent suspensions, albeit with rear-wheel drive, were unbeatable on the Grand Prix circuits of Europe as the 3-litre cars from Auto Union and Mercedes-Benz ground relatively feeble opposition into the dust.

In Italy the pretty but forlorn little Itala stood by silently and watched, its day long past, silent, and half-forgotten.

6

Blue-Blooded Record Breakers –
Europe, 1923-1931

The Marquis Ivanrey de Soriano and the Prince Djelalledin: two names which are written fairly modestly into the catalogue of French-built record breaking cars which didn't actually succeed in breaking many records.

Soriano was a Spaniard, and he joined forces with a fellow aristocrat, the Marquis de San Carlos de Pedroso, to form a company named SA des Automobiles Soriano-Pedroso, based at Neuilly. It was founded in 1919, and small prototype sporting vehicles were built in Biarritz before the move to the outskirts of Paris.

The small sporting Sorianos used side-valve Ballot engines of 1,131 or 1,590cc, and the smaller unit could be sleeved down or underbored in manufacture to just 1,094cc to gain entry to the 1,100cc racing class. An unusual feature of these light cars was their final drive by side chains. Soriano-Pedrosos were raced, without success, in the 1920 Cyclecar Grand Prix, and were then entered in the 1921 Brooklands 200-Mile race but failed to start.

Both blue-blooded founders of the firm built record cars of their own, Pedroso's being an obscure three litre straight-eight, and Soriano's an advanced and neat little single-seater, built as a contemporary of the mid-engined Benz Tropfenwagen.

It was one of the earliest of Europe's single-seaters, built at a time when most competition cars still retained a second seat for a riding mechanic.

Soriano chose a Ruby engine for the car, a unit built by Godfroy & Levêque of Levallois-Perret. This company was better known for its proprietary engines than for its own cyclecars, and Soriano adopted their Type P Sport four-cylinder side-valve unit, which had a capacity of around 950cc and produced 20bhp at 3,500rpm.

This was mounted in a neat little chassis, with transverse leaf spring suspension, and chain drive was hidden within a striking slab-sided bodywork which in profile offered a near perfect aerofoil section, picturesquely described as a *"section parallelipipédique"* in French. The nose radiator was neatly cowled and the wheels were provided with disc streamlining. The car was quite light, at 320kg (706 lbs), and capable of about 70mph.

This interesting little forebear of Europe's classical single-seat racing cars, which were not to become popular or successful in major road races until the advent of the Alfa Romeo Monoposto in 1932, is still in existence in a French museum.

In passing it is interesting to recall the Chevallier single-seater which was built around a 1,086cc Ruby engine in the thirties. This remarkable little car had an interlinked suspension system which caused all four wheels to bank into corners, motor-cycle style, and its designer/driver, M. Chevallier himself, raced it in the Bol d'Or 24-Hour races of 1933–35 at St Germain, and actually won the 1934 event in a dead-heat with Maillard-Brune's MG!

Also French-built during the twenties was a far more potent car, a contender for the outright World Land Speed Record, and one which rated very much as a ' mystery car ' of its day.

This was ' Djelmo ', built to satisfy the ambition of a Prince Djelalledin who is variously described as a Turkish or Egyptian emigré resident in Paris. Some time in 1923 he decided to sponsor an ambitious record contender, and all that seems certain is that he gained the services of an Italian-born ex-Sunbeam-Talbot-Darracq combine engineer named Edmond Moglia, who began to have parts made for the new car in September 1923.

There is a story that Djelalledin had bought a design from STD, or from one or more of its employees, for £6,000. This design was developed by Louis Coatalen and Vincenzo Bertarione of Sunbeam as a reply to the 10½-litre V12 Delage which René Thomas was shortly to take to a new record of 143mph along the Arpajon road.

Moglia took over a workshop in the northern part of Paris and built the chassis, while its special engine was contracted out to Janvier Sabin & Cie. The work was completed from scratch in an incredible eleven months, and the result was a very impressive single-seater of suitably imposing size.

The engine was a straight eight cylinder, with bore and stroke dimensions of 107mm x 140mm, giving a displacement of 10,071cc. The cylinders were arranged in two blocks of four, with welded-on aluminium water jackets. There were four valves per cylinder, operated by twin overhead camshafts. Nine main-bearings carried a massive crankshaft, and ignition was by a single sparking plug per cylinder. Four carburettors were fitted, made by either Claudel-Hobson or Zenith (the car's career was long enough for both to have been tried at some time). Compression ratio was 6:1 and the unit was quoted as producing 355bhp at 3,000rpm.

Moglia was talking of an eight-carburettor modification, in which each unit would feed direct inlet tracts to each pair of the sixteen inlet valves, but this was evidently never adopted, although 400bhp was confidently predicted in this form. Supercharging was also discussed, but again was never applied.

This imposing engine was bolted direct to the chassis frame, acting as a valuable stiffening member, and a simple two-speed and reverse gearbox was added. The exhaust system was a monumental piece of plumbing, feeding its gases away through the middle of the car's undertray. There was extensive use of aluminium alloy, including an elaborate casting which encased the front dumb irons, springs and radiator mounting. Front leaf springs passed right through a forged front axle, and the narrow rear axle was entirely enclosed, with its semi-elliptic leaf springs underslung, beneath the chassis rails.

A neat body-shell was fitted, with a kind of mitre-shaped radiator cowl, and its panelling fitted very closely around the massive engine. This was one problem with the proposed supercharging idea, for there was no spare room beneath the bonnet to carry a supercharger, and it would have to be mounted in the commodious tail section, driven from the propeller shaft.

This was a centrally-seated record car in the grand manner, with a wheelbase of 10ft 2ins, a front track at 4ft 8ins and a very confined rear track of 3ft 1½ins, with the wheels snuggled cosily against the body sides.

The name 'Djelmo' was arrived at by combining those of its constructors, and Prince Djelalledin contracted Giulio Foresti, a driver of sleeve-valve Schmids and Bugattis at that time, to attack the world record in it.

Foresti and Djelalledin tested Djelmo at Arpajon and on the bleak, featureless Miramas Autodrome outside Marseilles, but there was little sign of the outfit actually attacking any records with it.

Back in Paris, Moglia was juggling with a design of his own for a more powerful record breaker, using two of the ten-litre engines at either end of a simple chassis frame driving to all four wheels. Unfortunately Djelmo was proving slow and temperamental, and the Prince's ambitious plan to ship it to America to run on the new Muroc Salt Flats venue or on Daytona beach had to be shelved.

Meanwhile the record had been raised, first by René Thomas to over 140mph and then in 1926 by Parry Thomas's Liberty aero-engined car Babs to 171.02mph. This run had been made on the smooth sands of Pendine, on the Atlantic coast of Wales, and in August 1927 Djelmo was shipped across the Channel, bound for the Carmarthen coast. By this time the record had been forced even further away, for in March Malcolm Campbell had clocked 203.792 mph on Daytona beach!

So, with the record already way beyond Djelmo's reach, the Prince's crew arrived in Wales to see just what their car would do. On Saturday 26 November 1927 persistent engine problems were considered cured, and Foresti rumbled Djelmo down the stone slip-way onto Pendine Sands and set out on a final run to check the car's capabilities. He covered the mile in 20.6 seconds, a speed of around 175mph. On the return run Djelmo flicked into a violent tail-skid but Foresti managed to wrestle on corrective lock in time to maintain control and brought her safely to a halt.

This speed was considered sufficient for the French crew to book the official RAC time-keepers for the following Monday, the 28th.

For the last time Djelmo lumbered down onto the firm sands with the cigarette-smoking Foresti bare-headed in the cockpit. Once the car was warmed up he turned about and drove rapidly out of sight of the timekeepers, and then turned and began his official run, pounding along the damp and uneven beach with a thin spray of sand and mist churning into a high rooster-tail in his wake.

Djelmo was flying along the beach at a good 150mph when she hit a treacherously soft patch of sand, staggered momentarily, and veered off course. This time Foresti couldn't control her, and as the car skidded broadside so her Dunlop tyres dug into the yielding sand, gripped, and flipped her sideways. The car went rolling and pounding along the beach, hurling her driver clear to land in a dazed and shaken heap while it ended its gyrations right-side up, battered and bent, with her wire wheels smashed and her belly resting disconsolately in a pool of corrosive sea water.

It was the end of her career. Djelalledin had her taken back to Paris where she lay in the back yard of the Bugatti agents until at least 1940. Not long afterwards the rotting remains were cleared away and sold to some gypsies, who cut them up and sold the metal for its scrap value. Perhaps that's all Djelmo was ever worth, for she was virtually obsolete even as Moglia began to build her.

Moglia himself had a way with the nobility, and 1929 found him in Spain working with Enrique de Pescara whose brother, the Marquis Raoul de Pescara, had founded the Fabrica Nacional de Automoviles in Barcelona. Their products were to be enthusiastically patronised by King Alfonso XIII himself, and Moglia had a big share in designing the twin-overhead cam 180bhp competition models which featured many elektron parts, weighed only 1,344lbs, and which brought Juan Zanelli and Esteban Tort the 1931 European Mountain Championship. The cars were known as Nacional Pescaras, and with their light weight and visible reserves of power it was hardly surprising that British enthusiasts who saw Zanelli drive one at Shelsley Walsh should instantly christen it, 'The National Cascara'. I doubt if Moglia ever recovered. . . .

The early thirties also saw a little-known but extremely potent record-breaking special appear in England. The Austin and MG companies were locked in battle in the 750cc class, every racing and record success they could achieve being extensively advertised. The class became virtually a factory preserve in this time, and one which any amateur must have felt well-advised to leave alone.

Lord Ridley—a very capable engineer—felt otherwise, and in September 1930 he began to design a 750cc high-performance engine. He had been toying with a horizontal unit using many proprietary parts, but finally decided to use a conventional in-line four-cylinder layout with three main-bearing crankshaft, gear-driven twin overhead camshafts, wet sump lubrication, and a Powerplus supercharger. Bore and stroke were 66mm x 54.5mm, providing a 746cc displacement, and Ridley and his assistant, G. U. L. Sartoris, developed twin-valve per cylinder pent-roof cylinder heads, one cast in iron and a later component in bronze.

In May 1931 Lord Ridley's engine was tested, using 13lbs boost on 50–50 petrol and benzole fuel. It produced 54bhp at 6,500rpm.

and in record trim with the iron head, boost was raised to 14½lbs and 72bhp at 7,500rpm was achieved from RD1 alcohol fuel mixture.

His lordship now installed the engine in a 7ft wheelbase channel chassis, with suspension by four pairs of quarter-elliptic leaf-springs, the rears being reversed in Bugatti-style. Transmission was via a Parry Thomas multi-plate clutch and five-speed gearbox, and with an offset cockpit the car was clad in a low-slung flat body very reminiscent of Parry Thomas's famous Flat-Iron cars.

On 12 August 1931 Lord Ridley trespassed into Austin and MG preserves, and took the Class H mile record at Brooklands at 104.56 for the mile and 105.42mph for the kilometre. This was a brilliant achievement against the professional manufacturers' teams, and Lord Ridley watched confidently as his figures were bettered, knowing that with the bronze head and other modifications he had plenty more performance up his sleeve.

In its final record-breaking form the Ridley Special was given 19lbs supercharger boost and gave 87bhp at 7,500rpm. Lord Ridley now planned to wrest the record back from his giant competition on Brooklands' last open day before its annual winter shut-down. In this way he could at least retain the record well into the new year.

At Brooklands the strikingly low-slung car with its bulging cockpit surround was howling round the long bankings at over 112mph when Lord Ridley lost control. Whether he was dazzled by the autumn sun or too-soft springing allowed the undertray to strike the track was never properly established, but both car and driver were badly knocked about as they careered off the course.

Lord Ridley eventually recovered, but only the engine and gearbox could be salvaged from his incredibly potent Special. He detuned the engine to produce a reliable 62bhp at 7,200rpm, and mounted it in a modified 1,100cc Amilcar Six chassis to form a road-going sports car. Work proceeded very slowly, and the car was still awaiting a body when war broke out in 1939. Today the chassis carrying this ambitious, successful but obscure little engine is housed in Britain's National Motor Museum at Beaulieu, Hampshire.

7

Brief Encounter, Last of the Grand Prix Fiats –
Italy, 1927

Monza Autodrome, 4 September 1927; a cold, grey and dark place to be. The day had dawned to lowering skies and an incessant drizzle fell from grey clouds to drip from the dying autumn leaves of Milan's Royal Park.

Despite the weather a huge crowd was assembling at the Autodrome to watch the Italian Grand Prix, hoping to see a battle of the giants between the French Delages, trying to defend an unbeaten record, and the brand-new Fiat which was headline news that morning. The more knowledgeable among them knew that Delage had sent just one car to defend their record in this the most important race of the year, and they also had the disappointment of knowing that the new Fiat would only be running in the Milan Grand Prix supporting race.

Even so this was to be an historic day, for the new Grand Prix car was to represent the great Torinese company which had dominated the scene until their sudden withdrawal, three years previously.

The great Pietro Bordino was to be driving the Fiat, and sure enough, he took his place on the wet starting grid for the race's first five-lap 50 kilometre heat. The Fiat looked low-slung and wicked, its exhaust note shrill and crisp. It looked every inch a winner.

But from the flag the Fiat was slow off the mark, running gently in mid-field as Bordino sought to run-in a brand-new engine and get the feel of the strange car on Monza's deceptive surface. After one exploratory lap he began to drive with all his renowned skill and fire, passing Campari's Alfa Romeo and Materassi's Bugatti, streaming into the lead and winning at 92.88mph, over half a minute ahead of Count Aymo Maggi's second-placed Bugatti.

The full Grand Prix followed, the taciturn Robert Benoist winning easily in his solitary Delage. His fastest lap of 94.31mph looked lame compared to Bordino's 94.96mph on a damper track, but the Delage was not to run in the second heat of the Milan GP and Bordino brushed off his opposition with disdainful ease, got the full measure of his new mount and stormed round the still wet Autodrome to record one staggering fastest lap at 96.49mph and win from Campari by over forty one seconds!

The huge crowd fully appreciated the new Fiat's potential, and dreamed of a free-for-all battle between that new Italian car and the haughty Grand Prix-winning French Delage. Some are still dreaming of such a battle today, for it never took place, and the Fiat 806 was never to race again. . . .

Fiat had a long competition history. As the Fabbrica Italiana Automobili Torino, the company had been founded in 1899 by Giovanni Agnelli di Bricherasio and Count Carlo Biscaretti di Ruffia, the gentleman who gave his name to Turin's fabulous automotive museum.

Their FIAT cars made their name by winning the Grand Prix, the Targa Florio and the Kaiserpreis in 1907. They never looked back, and re-entered the arena in 1921 with a three-litre straight-eight model followed by the super successful Bertarione-designed two litre 'six' which sparkled Louis Coatalen's splendidly wise dictum ' 'e ees a wise man 'oo copy wizout altair' as he pinched both Bertarione and his design for his later two-litre Sunbeams!

The Italian company, now rendering their name 'Fiat', introduced successful supercharged racing cars—a 1½-litre 'four' and a 2-litre 130bhp straight-eight which won the European GP—in 1923, and after a crushing defeat in the French Grand Prix of 1924 Senator Agnelli withdrew from racing in a huff. His company had been beaten by Alfa Romeo P2s designed by ex-Fiat engineers lured away to the rival company, and he saw no future in nurturing design expertise from which others were to draw the credit.

This withdrawal came as a bitter blow to those racing department engineers who remained loyal, notably Luigi Cavalli and Tranquillo Zerbi. The latter was largely responsible for the first supercharged engine when barely thirty years old, and now with his elder colleague he began working toward the time when Fiat would re-enter the fray.

In July 1925, Zerbi began work with engineers Sola and Treves on a design intended for the 1500cc Grand Prix Formula which was to run through 1926–27. They were attracted to two-stroke principles, and followed the phantom of reliable two-strokery for more than a year.

They chose a six-cylinder, twelve opposed-piston layout in a similar mould to the old 100mph Gobron-Brillié. The two crankshafts were geared together and the unit was intended to stand in the chassis with one crank vertically above the other. Bore and stroke dimensions were fixed at 52mm x 58.5mm, and typically Fiat roller bearing crankshaft and big-ends were adopted. A Roots-type compressor fed pressure air to the carburettor at a modest 1.37ata (5¼lbs psi) and the charge then fed through the inlet manifold to a series of ports uncovered by the upper pistons. The lower piston set controlled the exhaust ports.

A prototype engine was assembled and bench-tested, producing some vague power output between 150–170bhp, varying according to the reporting authority.

As with all engines of this type, piston crown cooling was a major problem. The brief opening of the inlet ports (virtually half that available with a four-stroke cycle), and the stark fact that one piston set was continually exposed to *all* the exhausting charges of incandescent gas, proved more than a match for the oil-cooling system applied to the exhaust pistons. Several spectacular failures occurred on the test bed, and the accompanying explosive noises issued from their test house quite regularly during 1926. So the back-up design was eventually brought out and dusted-off.

This was for a more conventional four-stroke engine, but one which was arranged in an unusual manner. It had twelve cylinders, arranged in two separate vertical banks of six, mounted on a common crankcase in which the two crankshafts were geared together.

Three overhead camshafts controlled inclined overhead valves, the outer pair operating six exhaust valves on each side and the centre shaft carrying twelve cams which actuated the inlet valves in both banks. A similar arrangement was to feature in Dr Porsche's V16 Auto Union engine which was to appear in Germany seven years hence.

The cylinder banks consisted of welded-up two-cylinder blocks, which was standard Fiat practice, but gone were the roller bearings they had earlier helped to popularise. Instead Cavalli and Zerbi used a Hirth-type crankshaft running in four broad plain bearings, and the six con-rods on each crank were formed in one piece.

A front-mounted Roots-type supercharger was driven by the engine's right-side crankshaft, and although this 'double-six' engine looked quite big and bulky, its weight was kept very low by the extensive and daring use of advanced alloys. Bore and stroke were 50mm x 63mm, giving 1,484cc and this unit, designated the type 806, scaled 381lbs. Compared to Delage's straight-eight, which was its main rival, this was extremely light, for the all-roller bearing French engine weighed fully 500lbs. It produced 177bhp, but that was no match for the new Fiat 806 unit which showed a shattering 187bhp at 8,500rpm on the test bed. Miller, Talbot and Bugatti were way out of court where this kind of power was concerned.

In May 1927 the 806 car was completed and was given a brief shake-down test on a deserted military parade ground in Turin. The cockpit was offset to the right-hand side to give the driver some room, even though the engine was itself offset to the left by three inches for the same reason.

In August serious testing began at Monza, with Pietro Bordino and Carlo Salamano doing the driving. Both complained of excessive steering vibration but Bordino forced the wicked-looking car round the ten kilometre Autodrome in 3 minutes 32.6 seconds, no less than 4.1 seconds inside the Grand Prix lap record which stood to American Pete Kreis's Duesenberg from 1925.

This was a most praiseworthy performance, but unfortunately it proved too much for the new engine, which broke. Obviously a sustained 8,500rpm in a hard-pressed chassis was more than the new unit's sophisticated alloy construction could stand, and another unit was built up at Turin with reduced boost pressure and capable of producing a more modest 160bhp at 8,000rpm.

Even this was sufficient to be competitive with the contemporary Delage, for the 806 weighed 1,477lbs complete, which was over two hundredweight less than the Delage and Talbot. Its maximum recorded speed of 149mph was thought to be over 15mph faster than the French car's best and it was clearly capable of winning a Grand Prix *if* it survived the distance.

Cavalli and Zerbi hoped to enter the car in the Italian Grand Prix that September, but Agnelli was not keen to place Fiat's reputation so heavily upon the 806's un-proven shoulders.

So a compromise decision was made, and the 806 was entered in the supporting race. Bordino took the car to Monza and was showing its fierce paces in practice when its fragile engine shattered once more.

In Turin the experimental staff had their hands full with aero engine work for the Schneider Trophy sea-plane race, but after a slow start they knuckled down to a crash building programme to get the 806 mobile in time for its race debut. They worked twenty-four hour shifts and in the small hours of race morning the last nuts were tightened, the levels checked and the new engine howled into life. The car was transported back to the Autodrome and in slick, damp conditions Bordino put up his great performances and announced to the Grand Prix world that Fiat were back.

After the Monza success there were rumours that a three-car entry had been made for the British Grand Prix at Brooklands, where the new overhead-cam front-drive Alvises were to appear, but Fiat of course had neither cars nor engines.

The 1½-litre Formula to which the 806 had been so carefully constructed effectively came to an end in the new year, when virtual free formula took over Grand Prix racing and the old two litre cars of 1922–25 were revived.

In Fiat's experimental shop the prototype 806 lay under wraps until the new year, and on January 14 Guido Fornaca—Fiat's very pro-racing managing director—died. As a new régime took over under Agnelli so racing fell from favour, and then came the inexplicable order to destroy the last Grand Prix car, to destroy its engines and all existing parts, and even its detail drawings. This orgy of destruction spelled the end to Fiat's noble Grand Prix career, and their ultimate racing car became just so much molten metal, bubbling in a cauldron in a Fiat foundry.

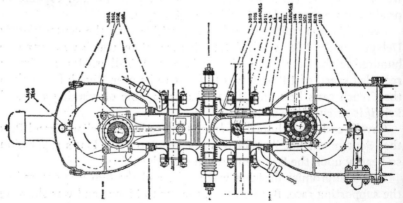

The 1926 experimental Fiat opposed piston 2-stroke (turned sideways).

16 'Marcel' Violet in his decidedly eccentric Sima-Violet 1500 Grand Prix car, 1926.

17 The Australian Chamberlain Special's front-drive system, 1935. This remarkably complex little sprint car used an eight-opposed-piston two-stroke engine; its eight-coil, twin distributor, eight-plug ignition system provided 64,000 sparks a minute!

18, 19   The radial-engined Trossi-Monaco. Top – a rare shot of Count Trossi rolling-out his car onto the drawbridge of his castle at Gaglianico. Bottom – Giulio Aymini tests the fractious beast at Monza, 1935.

8

Chasing the Chimera –
Two-Strokery in Europe, 1926-1939

The same bonuses of high power and mechanical simplicity which had sent Cavalli and Zerbi on a year-long wild-goose chase found many other devotees in motor racing's middle age.

One of the industry's most persistent two-stroke fanatics was Monsieur Achille (he preferred to be called Marcel) Violet in France. In the early twenties his cars were being built by the Société Industrielle de Matériel Automobile, of Courbevoie, and they were called Sima-Violets in recognition of the partnership.

Their 500 and 750cc cyclecars appeared with very low-mounted horizontally-opposed two-stroke motors, driving through a two-speed gearbox in unit with the back axle while suspension was generally by transverse leaf springs. Alcyon produced an identical half-litre model, and despite the design's strict non-comformity and late arrival on the cyclecar scene it scored some notable racing successes, and in consequence sold reasonably well.

Racing success with the 750cc cyclecars prompted Violet to contemplate Grand Prix racing under the 1½-litre Formula, for it would be a relatively simple task to double-up the existing twin-cylinder engine and produce a very lightweight car to do the job.

So he flung himself into the task, building a totally unconventional car which was extremely light and which incidentally disregarded the Grand Prix minimum weight limit!

His horizontally-opposed four-cylinder engine had bore and stroke dimensions of 74mm x 84mm, giving a displacement of 1,492cc. The air-cooling of the early cyclecar engines was gone, replaced by properly jacketed water-cooling, with each two-cylinder block casting bolted onto opposite sides of a box-like central crankcase. The

E

engine's reciprocating parts were all carried on roller bearings, and were arranged around a flat-plane crankshaft which allowed the front pair of cylinders to fire simultaneously, followed by the rearward pair to give near perfect balance.

Each horizontal cylinder block had a simple induction manifold mounted vertically on its upper surface, with a Solex downdraught carburettor on the top. Single spark plugs per cylinder screwed into the integral heads and were fired by twin distributors gear-driven from the rear of the crankshaft. Exhaust manifolding led away from the underside of the unit, and Violet made provision for the future addition of a supercharger.

His chassis was equally unconventional. The undertray and sides of the body were formed from folded steel sheet, carrying internal bulkheads to which the rest of the body-panelling was attached. This formed a kind of semi-monocoque structure in a manner vaguely reminiscent of the Grand Prix Voisins.

Then he adopted a kind of massively overgrown torque tube arrangement which carried a combined four-speed gearbox and differential assembly suspended from its rear end, and which ran the whole length of the car, passing clean along the top of the engine crankcase to connect with an articulated joint on which the front suspension's transverse leaf spring was mounted.

A separate propeller shaft ran rearwards from a multi-disc clutch on the engine flywheel, below the line of the 'torque tube', to mate-up with its suspended gearbox. Quarter-elliptic springs mounting within the body-chassis structure suspended the live rear axle-cum-transaxle, and there must presumably have been some kind of front-cross-member attaching that end of the body-shell to the linked rolling gear. In other words the greater part of this peculiar device's mass was unsprung weight.

Violet then mounted his car's radiator up in the scuttle structure behind the engine. Air entered through a conventional nose aperture, was ducted through the radiator core and then vented upwards through bonnet-top vents placed just ahead of the cockpit coaming. A large capacity fuel tank carried the normal two-stroke mixture of petrol and oil.

This very eccentric design produced a low and compact racing car with a six inch ground clearance and an overall height of 33½ inches. Its wheelbase was 7ft 10½ins and track 4ft 3ins. It scaled 500kg (1,102lbs) complete, which was praiseworthy but misguided in Grand Prix terms for the regulations specified a minimum weight limit of 700kg, or over 1,543lbs! To qualify as a Grand Prix entry, the Sima-Violet 1500 would have to carry over 400lbs ballast.

Since the flat-four engine gave less than 60bhp unsupercharged, the car was hard-pressed to exceed 87mph flat-out, and was obviously totally uncompetitive.

The Courbevoie company was apparently unconcerned, and entered three such cars for the 1926 French Grand Prix, which was to be run for the first time on Paul Bablot's desolate Miramas Autodrome in the flat Camargue country of southern France. The circuit was a dull 3¼mile loop with wide, low-banked turns at either end, and of the four teams entered (Sima-Violet, Bugatti, Talbot and Delage) only the three Bugattis actually started.

Instead, Violet himself drove the car in the 1,500cc class of the Boulogne GP des Voiturettes, and actually finished second behind George Eyston's Bugatti. It is significant that *nobody* appeared in third place. . . .

Violet was quite a brave man to race his own creations. 'Sammy' Davis—who was then a well known driver and sports editor of *Autocar*—recalls: 'Even the Violet cyclecar drivers would regard the whole thing as a huge joke. They knew their cars wouldn't go round corners and had no power to speak of, but they pressed on just for the hell of it!' Tony Gosnell, who owns the only Sima-Violet cyclecar in running order in Britain, points out that 'Violet's steering was incredibly direct, with only a third of a turn from lock-to-lock. The car tries to skip over its front wheels all the time, and any 'normal' steering motion will just flip it straight over . . . you certainly daren't sneeze while you're driving it. . . .'

Despite his critics, Violet was to be seen happily testing his low-slung and singular racer at Montlhéry in 1927, but he made no entry in the Grand Prix and it is very doubtful if the 'full team' of three cars was ever built.

The following year found Violet running his car in some national hill-climbs where the ballast could be discarded, but he had no success. Highlight of his sporting year must have been third place in the 1928 GP des Voiturettes at Comminges, which was for 750cc sports cars.

Violet left the Sima company some time in 1929, and moved on to build equally quirky two-strokes for Deguingaud-Galba, Leroy-

Violet and then Huascat and Donnet. During the thirties he was retained as a consultant by Peugeot's motorcycle division, and postwar
he popped up again with a supercharged four-cylinder two-stroke,
supposedly of 500cc, supposedly intended for Formula 3—which was
an unsupercharged class—and supposedly churning out 80bhp at
8,500rpm. It required a five-speed gearbox. Then again, in 1960,
Violet was back on the competition scene, attempting to launch a
three-wheeler racing formula in France!

The fate of his Grand Prix car is unknown, but there is a story that
it was sold to a British customer. What he did with it and where it
ended its days is another of motor racing's mysteries.

During the time that 'Marcel' Violet was wrestling with his ideas
on two-stroke design another, perhaps rather more gifted, engineer
was working along roughly similar lines.

He was Réné Cozette, a young Frenchman born in 1895 who had
joined the flying service on the outbreak of war in 1914. He was
injured and invalided out of the forces, then postwar put his aviation
engineering knowledge to good use and founded Carburateurs
Cozette. He tackled the problems of providing an aero engine with
efficient carburation at altitude, and decided to adopt supercharging.

This use of a compressor to force into an engine a greater volume
of gas than it would normally inspire had first been suggested, it
seems, by Louis Renault, as early as 1902. In that year he had
patented a system in which a centrifugal fan blasted air down the
throat of a carburettor, but little seems to have stemmed from this
basic idea.

Three years later, in Pottstown, Pennsylvania, the Lee Chadwick
company introduced their six-cylinder Type 15 road car to replace an
existing four-cylinder model. The new 'six' was quicker than its
predecessor, but not sufficiently so to satisfy Lee Chadwick himself
and his Chief Engineer, John T. Nichols.

By 1907 a Type 16 replacement model was released, using larger
inlet valves to increase power and performance, and this was shortly
followed by a Type 19 which actually had overhead valves of manhole-
cover dimensions . . . but still the expected power bonus did not
materialise.

So Chadwick and Nichols began working on a system to pressurise
the carburettor, to force more mixture into the engine than it could
ordinarily suck in unaided. Nichols took a belt-drive from the engine's

18 inch flywheel, and drove a single centrifugal compressor at nine times crankshaft speed. Results were very promising, and a more complex triple-stage booster system was then developed, driven by a leather belt, again at nine times crank speed. Two universal joints were built into the drive-line to allow belt adjustment, and the compressors themselves had ten inch diameter twelve-bladed impellers of varying widths to give the progressive compression, triple-stage effect. A trunking carried air up behind the radiator core to the carburettor. Curiously—in light of later cooling developments—this trunking was heated by water jacketing fed from the radiator. . . .

Works driver Willy Haupt drove this supercharged Chadwick in the Wilkes-Barre hill-climb on 30 May 1908, and won it—the first competition victory for the system. That October saw the Chadwick racing in the Vanderbilt Cup, and Haupt actually forced his way into the lead for a couple of laps before the car suffered magneto maladies. In the Savannah Grand Prize, the car failed due '. . . to the after effects of an accident which had taken place on the road prior to the race'; but in subsequent events the supercharged Chadwick achieved considerable American success, including a win in the Fairmount Park 200-Miles race in 1910.

Sufficient reliability was eventually developed for suitably detuned supercharged Chadwicks to be sold to the public, and these were cars capable of a genuine 100mph top speed. Lee Chadwick wound up his motor manufacturing business in 1911, and competition supercharging lay dormant for twelve years.

In 1923 Fiat successfully introduced supercharging to Grand Prix design, using a Wittig vane-type compressor. Cozette had chosen this design for his own units, and conducted all kinds of experiments which eventually attracted an offer from Albert Champion, the Franco-American spark plug manufacturer, for him to spend six months in America where he could also study the centrifugal high-speed supercharger just becoming popular for high-speed oval track racing.

Back in France he worked with racing driver Albert Guyot to produce the Burt McCollum sleeve-valve engined supercharged Guyot Specials which ran at Indy in 1926. After this experience with racing cars, 31-year-old Cozette set about building his own 1,100cc racing and record car, and it had to be sophisticated.

He quickly outlined the engine design, which was to feature opposed pistons and two-stroke operation. This was at the same time as the same features were leading Cavalli and Zerbi a merry dance at Fiat, and they were later to feature in a Causan 1,500cc design intended for a Dr Etchegoin's record-breaking speedboat.

Cozette's first opposed-piston two-stroke coughed into life in mid-1927. It was a four-cylinder, eight-piston unit, with 56mm bores and 55.8mm stroke for each piston. Like Louis Chevrolet's Frontenacs and Monroes of a decade before, the Cozette engine was formed entirely in aluminium with the exception of the cylinder liners, crank-shaft and con-rods.

There were two crankshafts, one on 'top' of the engine and the other at the bottom, both running in five main-bearings and being coupled together by a train of gears at the rear. A large Cozette supercharger drew from an equally massive Cozette carburettor, and was placed vertically in front of the engine and driven from the lower crankshaft. The induction manifold hooked round the right-side of the unit, with the exhaust manifolding on the other side.

Two Marelli magnetos supplied sparks and there were two plugs per cylinder, introduced into the combustion chamber space enclosed by the opposed pistons at their closest approach. There was one water pump and two oil pumps built-in, and efficient lubrication was ensured by a massive oil cooler placed in the system.

After some development work the 1,100cc Cozette proved very powerful, giving about 100bhp at 5,000rpm. Its constructor mounted it in the front of a very slender pure single-seater chassis, inclined rearwards to drop the propeller shaft well below the driver's seat, where it passed to a double-reduction back axle. A four-speed gear-box was fitted, and with a figure-hugging light alloy body shell the result was a very pretty early European single-seater.

Cozette had some backing from the Rumanian Prince Ghika Cantacuzene, like Prince Djelalledin an emigré domiciled in Paris. He drove the 'Cozette Spéciale' on its first tests at the Montlhéry Autodrome, south of the French capital, and after some good private results Cozette arranged official timing by ACF officials, and Cantacuzene made a tilt at the official 1,100cc records.

The raucous little car howled round the empty, echoing Autodrome to great effect, breaking seven records from five kilometres to 100 miles in distance, at speeds ranging from 110-112mph, and raising the shortest distance record by over 10mph. The Rumanian went on to cover 103 miles in an hour round the speedbowl. The Spéciale was very fast for its size, and *worked* which is more than could be said for the basically similar two-stroke engine with which Fiat had been experimenting in Turin.

After this success the car was taken to the famous tree-lined record road at Arpajon for a speed meeting, but there it was up against André Morel with a special six-cylinder supercharged Amilcar, and he simply flew through the flying kilometre to set a new 1,100cc outright record at 206.894kph, over 128mph. Casse's single-seater Salmson 'four' followed this up with an 18.19-second run to record 197.856 kph, nearly 123mph.

In the midst of this orgy of speed, the Cozette wailed through the measured kilometre in 18.76-seconds, recording 191.846kph, or just over 119mph. This was a good performance in Cantacuzene's relatively inexperienced hands, and Cozette himself was delighted with this performance.

Recalling his stay in America he decided to modify the car and enter it for the Indianapolis '500'. It was returned to his works at Courbevoie, closely neighbouring those of Sima-Violet, where work began on producing an enlarged 1,500cc engine intended to produce about 130bhp at 5,000rpm.

In July 1929 the Spéciale returned to Montlhéry for an extensive test session, and Réné Cozette himself powered it round the bankings at over 130mph. This was decidedly promising, and on 20 August 1929 Cozette returned to the Autodrome for further development testing.

During that day the Cozette's distinctive exhaust note was howling round the Autodrome when those present heard it waver abruptly, then cut-out. Rescuers ran to the scene and found the Spéciale lying wrecked far from the road with its gifted designer-driver fatally injured. . . .

The car had an unusual steering system, partly composed of chain links, and it has been suggested that these failed and sent it careering off the track. The Cozette was so dreadfully smashed that the full truth of the disaster was never established, but this accident robbed France of one of her most talented racing engineers.

The two-stroke engine was acquired by someone from the Midi, who built it into a Derby single-seater raced locally by a driver named Boucly.

Cozette had many advanced projects planned when he died at the age of only 34, including a fabulously powerful aero engine and a three-litre engine for sports-car racing. Cantacuzene took to flying, record-breaking and air-racing, and a Cozette motor appeared at Le

Mans in 1929 powering a front-drive Tracta designed by Pierre Fenaille and carrying an all-enveloping aerodynamic body. The famous Tracta cars used a sophisticated front-drive system perfected by J. A. Grégoire, who did more than any other engineer to make the Christie – Gregory – Alvis – Miller system 'socially acceptable'.

Meanwhile, the two-stroke cause continued its fatal fascination for competition car designers. . . .

The year which saw poor Réné Cozette's fatal accident also saw further two-stroke developments a world apart. Taking them alphabetically, 1929 saw the birth of the Chamberlain Special in Australia, and considerable competition successes for 'Z' in Czechoslovakia.

Allan (better known as 'Bob') Chamberlain was co-proprietor of a light-engineering works, and in 1929 he built a racing car with a welded tubular chassis, all-independent suspension (by transverse spring and wishbones at the front and swing-axles at the rear), and with front-wheel drive. Early in its career this astonishingly advanced little car used motorcycle air-cooled engines, including a special unit built up from two Model 18 Norton barrels mounted on an American Harley-Davidson crankcase, with chain drive to the front wheels. At one stage it was supercharged with a blower borrowed from a four-cylinder Mercedes, but sometime in 1934 Chamberlain crashed it heavily in a Victorian hill-climb and broke his leg.

His brother, William, took over the bent remains and then read a description of an English Jameson engine. This was a two-stroke unit in which the cylinders had two bore sizes. The larger bores were at the lower end of the unit, occupied by conventional con-rods and pistons, while the upper cylinders were very much smaller. They housed special pistons and con-rods which produced very little piston movement during the power stroke, but which gave very rapid movement during the part of the cycle when the piston controlled the inlet ports. This gave very large effective port openings, while the conventional lower pistons controlled the exhaust ports. The upper pistons and crankshaft provided very little motive power, leaving the lower set of pistons and crank to propel the vehicle. A Roots compressor was used to scavenge the unit, which had eight plugs, eight coils, two distributors and four sets of points, all of which combined to provide 64,000 sparks a minute, long before the days of easily-obtainable transistor ignition!

The Chamberlain was only used for sprint work, but in 1935 when the new engine was completed there were no plugs capable of handling a high-output two-stroke. Large throttle openings always blew a hole in a piston.

During World War Two improved plugs were produced and the Chamberlains made up their own, and with these in place the 1,100cc unit gave something variously recorded as 'nearly 100bhp on the dynamometer' or '84bhp at 4,500rpm *at the wheels*' on a rolling road!

In this trim the car proved capable of covering the standing-start quarter-mile in seventeen seconds with the wheels spinning furiously all the way. The Chamberlains' company produced everything from tractors and pistons to naval torpedoes before being absorbed into Geoffrey Russell's Repco empire, which subsequently became involved in a much more grand form of motor racing.

I understand that another Chamberlain Special was planned to carry a special two-litre engine mounted amidships in Auto Union style, but was finally completed with a Ford V8 engine in 1938. Both cars are still in existence today, the two-stroke in the Chamberlain family and the later model in the aviating Hawker family, also in Australia.

While these curious goings-on were taking place in the far-off Antipodes, the 'Akciova spolecnost Ceskoslovenska Zbrojovka' were producing two-stroke racing cars of their own in Brno. This was an armaments firm which found itself redundant after the Great War and turned to building cars designed by an engineer named Novotny.

He produced small rotary-valve two-stroke cars under first the DISK and later the ENKA title, until 1929 when his designs were adopted by the Aero aircraft factory. This left the Zbrojovka works to produce their own variants, and in 1928 their Zetka Z18 two-cylinder sporting cars won the team prize in the Austrian winter trial.

With this basis of reliability, the Brno design team tried a one-litre six-cylinder engine with opposed pistons, and then a 1.5-litre 'duplex' engine, in which a broad block carried eight cylinders side by side, connected in pairs by a common combustion chamber. One cylinder in each pair carried the inlet ports, the other the exhaust ports, and either Roots or Cozette compressors were used to scavenge the cylinders.

The crankshaft ran in plain bearings and there were four 'master' con-rods attached to it, each of which carried a shorter, articulated con-rod for its twinned piston in the adjoining cylinder. According to

Jerry Sloniger and Baron von Fersen, '. . . this engine was particularly sensitive to heat transfer or casting variations, and would deform on sight if it was not properly warmed before each start. It had to be started very carefully to avoid cracked blocks and seized pistons. . . '.

This decidedly delicate engine was known as the Z13, and it produced about 45bhp. It was mounted in a simple chassis frame with the front semi-elliptic leaf springs passing through eyes in the axle beam and with quarter-elliptics at the rear. The car made its racing debut at Brno in 1932, reputedly achieving a speed of 85mph, and although quite successful its activities were—perhaps sensibly—largely confined to Czechoslovakia.

The duplex cylinder arrangement of the Z appeared in another two-stroke racing engine built at about this time. In April 1934 details were released of the Zoller opposed-piston two-stroke engine, for which 200bhp was being claimed from only 1,500cc!

Berlin-domiciled Swiss engineer Arnold Zoller had been a designer for Horch before setting-up on his own and making his name with a wide range of superchargers. His compressors were used on the 175 and 250cc DKW and 750cc BMW world record-holding motorcycles at the time, and now he was hanging his reputation on the treacherously knotty problem of producing a high-performance two-stroke racing car.

His engine had an aluminium alloy crankcase and cylinder block, cast in one piece with twelve bores in two rows of six. Steel cylinder liners were used, and the detachable head casting carried common combustion chambers for each pair of cylinders.

The left side of the engine carried the inlet ports, and the right side the exhausts. The exhaust-side pistons had the 'master' set of con-rods, with shorter slave rods to the inlet bank. This system was arranged so that the exhaust pistons opened and closed their ports earlier than the inlet pistons, Zoller maintaining that this was one of the main advantages of two-stroke engines of this type, since it permitted efficient scavenging of both cylinder barrels and a high degree of supercharging.

Zoller's crankshaft ran in roller-bearing mains, with needle-rollers carrying the big-ends. Spur gears from the nose of the crankshaft drove two Zoller superchargers, arranged horizontally one above the other, and they drew from a dual-choke Solex carburettor through a tall divided manifold. The charge was delivered to the cylinders through a water-cooled trunking, and boost was set at 21psi, with two safety valves which operated above 28psi.

Bore and stroke were 43mm x 84mm, giving a displacement of 1,465cc, but the dualled cylinder arrangement was claimed to enable the engine to consume the amount of gas normally aspirated by a six-litre conventional unit.

Ignition was by single plugs and Scintilla Vertex magneto, and Zoller was also reported to be developing a similar short-stroke 750cc unit for the Austin–MG class of racing. *Autocar* mentioned that Zoller was said to have applied for regulations for the Isle of Man races, and that he was preparing a three-car racing team. . . .

What he needed now was a suitable chassis, and for this he turned to Röhr.

The Röhr Automobilwerke AG had been established at Ober-Ramstadt in 1928 by an ex-aviation engineer named Hans-Georg Röhr. He left in 1930 to go to Adler, but he left his old firm with the first swing-axled car – following in Rumpler and Benz footsteps – to reach full production.

His Röhr Typ R was based on a sheet-steel platform chassis with twin transverse leaf springs suspending the front wheels and outboard semi-elliptics at the rear springing swing-axles. With a 2½-litre eight-cylinder engine and four-wheel hydraulic brakes the car was something of a sensation, for it performed well in every department: going, stopping and cornering.

On the company founder's departure, a Swiss finance house took it over, and perhaps it was no coincidence that the Swiss supercharger designer with his two-stroke engine should adopt Röhr suspension layout in his new racing car.

This was intended to run in 1,500cc Voiturette class events, which were then being contested fiercely by cars such as ERAs and Maseratis.

The resulting Zoller two-stroke Grand Prix car was neat and pert in appearance, looking very much like a scaled down version of the contemporary all-independent Mercedes-Benz W25s, and three started at AVUS in 1934 driven by Gerhard Macher, Ernst von Delius and someone named Wimmer, but suffered burned-out plugs, fuel-feed trouble, a blown head gasket and eventual retirement caused by failing brakes. Two ran well in the Eifelrennen before savage over-heating claimed them. Unfortunately there was no third chance, for Arnold Zoller collapsed and died suddenly, and his unusual little racing car died with him. Gerhard Macher attempted to carry on the project completing a sports car with Zoller engine in 1938, but it was not developed in time to enter competitions and the outbreak of war spelled *finis*.

One final European attempt to produce a two-stroke-engined Grand Prix contender was perhaps the most incredible of them all. The car concerned was that built by *Ingegnere* Augusto Monaco for the wealthy Italian racing driver, Count Carlo Felice Trossi.

Augusto Monaco first came upon the scene in 1932 when, with Enrico Nardi, he built a very lightweight front-wheel drive sprint car which they christened 'Chichibio'. It had a front-mounted 998cc JAP vee-twin engine driving through a five-speed gearbox, and with 65bhp on tap and an all-up weight of only 672lbs it proved a potent device which did very well in Italian hill-climb events.

In fact it performed so well that Monaco was convinced that a very much larger, more powerful front-drive car could be a very competitive Grand Prix challenger.

Nardi having joined Lancia, Monaco joined forces with a fellow engineer and reasonably well-known competition driver named Giulio Aymini, and they planned a machine which was to look much more like a flightless aeroplane than any known racing car design.

Monaco's plans were complete in 1934 when the new 750kg Grand Prix Formula came into force, and he toured the Italian industry in an attempt to find a sympathetic ear. Surprisingly he found one at Fiat, where Senator Agnelli offered facilities to build a prototype Monaco-Aymini engine.

It was developed at Fiat's Lingotto plant, where on the test bed it proved to be an unsightly and unreliable beast beset by so many problems that Agnelli regretfully withdrew his support and left Monaco with a half-built engine, no car, no money, and supposedly no hope.

Monaco then took his scheme to the urbane, pipe-smoking Count Trossi, who was at that time President of the Scuderia Ferrari which prepared, maintained and raced Alfa Romeo's works Grand Prix cars. Trossi proved an attentive listener, and Monaco seems to have been a good talker, for the Count offered him full manufacturing facilities in his own workshops.

They were situated within his ancestral castle at Gaglianico, just outside Biella, and there Trossi and Aymini began to complete their prototype engine and constructed the chassis to carry it.

Thus was born the Trossi–Monaco, and after much speculation

about the security precautions at Gaglianico, and about what was going on behind its closed doors, the Italian press thrilled to hear that the new car was to be tested at Monza Autodrome late in July 1935.

Aymini was to drive it, and the few cognoscenti who were present were staggered when the covers were removed and the new car was unloaded from its wagon. It looked like an aircraft engine nacelle, somehow entirely divorced from airframe and with its radial engine arrangement looking bare without an air-screw!

The radially-disposed engine was mounted in the extreme nose, with its eight finned blocks positioned around a central crankcase. Each block carried twinned cylinders and pistons with common conjoining combustion chambers just as used by Z and Zoller. Inlet ports were in the rearmost cylinders, and exhausts in the forward set. The crankcase was machined from solid duralumin, and carried a three-piece built-up crankshaft in roller bearings.

There were two master connecting rods attached to the crank-pins, each one carrying seven other articulated rods in normal two-stroke duplex-cum-aero engine manner. Bore and stroke dimensions were 65mm x 75mm and the engine's capacity was 3,982cc, making it the biggest European two-stroke thus far in racing.

Behind this radial assembly was an ancillaries bay, in which were mounted two M160 Zoller superchargers drawing mixture from twin Zenith carburettors and which pressurised four blocks each. They fed at a modest 10psi, their induction impulse serving to scavenge exhaust gases out of the forward ports which were opened simultaneously with the inlets.

Ignition consisted of twin Scintilla high-tension magnetos firing single Marelli plugs per bank, set into the centre of each deeply-finned cylinder head. Exhaust gases discharged into aero engine-style four-pipe collector rings on the front of the engine, which then fed into two long tail-pipes running the length of the car's sleek 'fuselage'.

Output of this amazing unit was claimed to be 250bhp at 6,000 rpm, which compared very indifferently with 305bhp for the contemporary 3.8-litre Alfa Romeo, 375bhp for the 5 litre V16 Auto Union and 430bhp for the 3.99-litre Mercedes. Monaco was banking upon squeezing much more power out of his new engine with development, and installed in his lightweight chassis the whole thing was 40kg under the maximum weight limit.

Transmission was by a simple shaft straight through the gearbox to the clutch, then returned into the gearbox on a sleeve-type input shaft, then to the differential. Spur gears from the main power shaft drove the superchargers and magnetos.

Rearward-raked half-shafts connected the differential with front wheels, and they featured homokinetic universal joints of French Grégoire design as used in his Tracta cars. The steering was arranged with a short horizontal column operating a steering box mounted above the clutch housing, with an inverted Y-arm operating independent drag links to each wheel.

Hardly any less unconventional was Monaco's chassis frame, for he drew freely from aircraft experience and built a welded 'spaceframe' from manganese-molybdenum steel tubing of about one and a half inch diameter. Larger diameter cross-tubes at front and rear carried the horizontal suspension coil springs, which were operated by crank-arms attached to the lower of two delicately-proportioned wishbones. Siata friction dampers were featured, hydraulically adjustable by a cockpit control.

The 'spaceframe' chassis, perhaps the first of its type, was clothed in a well-proportioned streamlined bodyshell tapering down to a very long and pointed tail; the design being by Count Revelli, a friend of Trossi's.

The whole machine was beautifully made, with such features as jewel-like needle and roller bearings providing the wishbone pivots. Hydraulically-operated brakes were fitted, with the drums formed into the wheels, which were attached by Rudge Whitworth knock-off hubs. Front tyres were 5.25x31 with 4.40x27s at the rear. Wheelbase was only 7ft 6½ins and track was quite wide at 4ft 9ins. With its radial engine projecting well ahead of the front axle line, weight distribution was biased 75 per cent on the front wheels.

Aymini and Trossi both test-drove the car at Monza, where it ran without its aircraft-style Townend ring encircling the cylinder banks. They were certainly already well-shrouded by the exhaust collectors, and perhaps this contributed to cooling problems which the small team immediately encountered.

Trossi managed to force the car up to 155mph in one timed run, but cooling the paired combustion chambers and persuading the spark plugs to remain fit and active proved an apparently insoluble problem.

The Trossi–Monaco rapidly proved itself hopelessly unreliable with a voracious appetite for plugs, and I suspect it was quite a handful to drive in corners with its 250 horsepower and 75-25 weight distribution.

Trossi sadly cancelled his entry for that year's Italian Grand Prix, and laid up the car in the cellars at Gaglianico. He took to racing much more conventional and far more effective Maseratis, and finally became a much-valued member of the Alfa Corse team. He won the Italian Grand Prix for them in 1947 and added the European Grand Prix at Berne in 1948. He was second to the great Jean-Pierre Wimille in the Monza GP that year, but this was to be his last race for early in 1949 he died of cancer in a Milan clinic. His loss, added to the death of Achille Varzi at Berne the previous year and then of Wimille in a Simca–Gordini in Buenos Aires, persuaded Alfa Corse to retire from racing for the 1949 season.

Trossi's widow, the Contessa Lisetta, presented the Trossi–Monaco to the Biscaretti museum in Turin, and it is still there today, accompanied by the tiny 'Chichibio' which it could never emulate, and sharing eternity with its similarly virgin partner, Giulio Cappa's little Itala V12.

9

Depression-Bred –
Indianapolis in the Thirties

'Black Tuesday', 29 October 1929, was the day on which Wall Street's famous crash occurred. The Dow Jones trading index plummeted 48.31 points in the day, and was to fall to its all-time low of 41.22 points in July of 1932. World trade slumped 57 per cent between 1929 and 1936 and at its height the Great Depression wiped $125,000,000,000 off security values.

Despite financial chaos and disaster the relatively carefree motor racing world went on its way. There were changes, there were downgradings, but still the originality of thought bred only by fierce competitive pressure continued to shine through.

For the 1930 Indianapolis '500' the AAA raised their capacity limit from 91½ cubic inches to 366 cubic inches (5.99 litres). There were to be no superchargers allowed on four-stroke engines, no more than two poppet valves per cylinder, no more than two carburettor throats, a minimum weight of 1,750lbs was imposed, track width was set at between fifty-four and sixty inches, and body-widths were set at thirty-one inches with both driver and mechanic to be carried. This latter ruling was tragically to cost many lives during the reign of the 'Junk Formula', but the legislators were well-meaning in their attempt to cut the costs of buying and maintaining a racing car, and to attract the big manufacturers back into racing.

The new cubic inch allowance also allowed some adventurous 'special builders' to get to work, and the Formula's first 500-Mile race saw 1928 winner Lou Meyer in one of the most interesting of the new cars.

It was a 16-cylinder with two ninety-one cubic inch straight-eight Miller engines mounted in parallel on a common, twinned

20 Lou Meyer (driver) and car owner Alden L. Sampson in the 16-cylinder 'Sampson Special' at Indianapolis, 1932.

21 Leon Duray's amazing U16 two-stroke engine, raced at Indy in the Depression years. There were two sets of twinned cylinders in each of the four blocks. All alone on the Speedway it sounded like the rolling start!

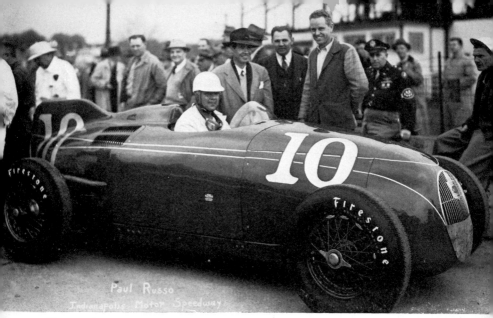

22 Paul Russo poses in the 'Fageol Twin Coach Special' at Indy in 1946. The car had an engine in either end, all four wheels were driven, and it qualified second fastest for the race . . .

23 Harry Miller introduces his four-wheel drive car to the press in Los Angeles, April 1932. He was an extraordinary man, an artist engineer whose aesthetic sense showed in every detail of his cars, as in the grill here.

crankcase. It was the work of Riley Brett, who had become one of American racing's most famous figures.

He had been Jimmy Murphy's mechanic back in the early twenties, the man who promoted the front-drive Millers. Then he had helped build the 'Black Hawk' Stutz Land Speed Record car for Frank Lockhart.

Lockhart himself was a towering figure in the development of American speedway racing. He had won the Indy '500' on his first attempt in 1926 and he ended the season second in the AAA Championship. He was the man who dreamed up the supercharging intercooler for racing use, intended to cool the charge before it entered the cylinders and improve performance. In 1927 his speedway winnings exceeded the season champion's by more than $15,000, and he invested it all in the Stutz in which he met his death at Daytona in April 1928. He was then only 25 years old, but his shadow stretched long over the racing scene.

His specially-modified pair of rear-drive Millers were the most potent cars on the speedway circuit, developed and refined by Lockhart's intuitive engineering skill coupled to the practical talent and experience of mechanic Ernie Olsen—the man who had been Murphy's riding mechanic on the day Duesenberg won the French Grand Prix for America.

After the Daytona tragedy Ray Keech bought one of the Lockhart Millers. The other was driven by Lockhart's ex-team mate Tony Gulotta at Indy, and it would have won but for minor troubles which allowed Lou Meyer to go ahead and stay there to the finish. Meyer invested his winnings in Gulotta's car, adding the services of Riley Brett, and in 1929 the two Lockhart Millers raced home first and second in the Indy '500', with Keech ahead of Meyer. Two weeks later Keech was dead, killed in his car on Altoona Board Speedway.

Later that year Brett contacted Leo Goossen, the guiding hand behind Miller's detail design, to draw him a sixteen-cylinder engine, using vertical downdraught inlet ports. Brett had a bee about this system, and so Goossen confected the double-eight unit which was to power Meyer's car in the 1930 '500'.

Truck manufacturer Alden L. Sampson owned the car, suitably named the 'Sampson Special', and its basically Miller 91 engines had been enlarged to 100.5 cubic inches each (1.65 litres) with bore and stroke dimensions of 2 5/16 x 3ins. Spur gears on the front of each crankshaft meshed with a central gear driving a long hollow

F

shaft which ran rearwards between the crankcases to a large central flywheel. The racing clutch and three-speed transmission from Meyer's 1929 car mounted against the rear of this unit.

Except for their fuel supply the two engines were individually plumbed, so that failure of one's ancillaries did not affect the other. Each had a downdraught Winfield carburettor and complex manifold, with its own exhaust piping feeding out into two large diameter tail pipes running along either side of the big car's body.

Each engine had its own oil system, drawing from individual tanks, and there were two eight-cylinder Bosch magnetos mounted crosswise at the front, driven by bevel gears from the main power shaft.

The crankshafts themselves were two inches in diameter, and the coupling gears were $6\frac{1}{4}$ inches in diameter and $1\frac{1}{2}$ inches thick. All this machinery was mounted in the front of a classical widebody speedway chassis, with a standard Miller tubular front axle and a new back-axle design with a strongly crosswebbed diff housing to which steel axle tubes were bolted. Wheelbase was 8ft 7ins, front and rear track 4ft 8ins and 4ft $8\frac{1}{2}$ins respectively, and the car's empty weight totalled 1,950lbs. The gas tank held 38 gallons, while nine gallons of oil and four of water completed the new double-eight's reserves of vital fluids.

This Sampson Special faced a horde of less sophisticated but fast and durable racing and stock models, including the supposedly fearsome 'Sedici Cilindri' Maserati from Europe. The Italian car will be examined later, but here at Indy its fangs were drawn by the mandatory removal of its supercharging.

Meyer's sixteen was the fastest car in the field, howling along the straightaways but nose-heavy and 'pushing' in the turns. He stole an immediate lead from the start but after two brief and glorious laps Billy Arnold bulleted ahead in his eight-cylinder Miller-Hartz, with which he was to score the first '500' victory for front-wheel drive.

The Sampson was running a close third until lap 23 when Meyer made a $4\frac{1}{2}$ minute stop to fix a broken throttle linkage. He rejoined in fourteenth place, battled his way up through the field and was back into fourth place at the finish. His winnings were $4,200.

For 1931 Brett adopted a new front-axle design to improve the car's handling, and with a change in the race regulations was able to fit an impressive array of *eight* Winfield downdraught carburettors.

It was not a good year for the several sixteens entered, and although Meyer started the Sampson from pole position (won at 113.953mph) he had to make a forty-second stop on the seventh lap and was out for keeps when an incurable oil leak was diagnosed on lap 28.

The 1932 race found Meyer out again in the further-modified Sampson, but he qualified slow and spun on lap 51 during which incident the car's drive-line seized (as cause or effect I am uncertain) and both crankshafts snapped in the 16-cylinder engine.

Lou Meyer forsook Alden Sampson's sixteen for 1933, took to the 'Tydol Special' rear-drive Miller and romped away to his second Indy win. Chet Gardner drove the 'Sampson Radio Special' into a strong and popular fourth place, and the following year found him running again, qualifying fast at 116.894mph and coming home ninth. Then the Sampson sixteen went into honourable retirement but without a success to look back on.

Meanwhile, the 1931 Indianapolis race had seen a very non-conformist vehicle joining the Sampson Special in the sixteen cylinder line-up. This was Leon Duray's two-stroke, a wondrous machine which brought a new, shrill and ear-splitting exhaust note to the historic Hoosier Bowl.

Born George Stewart to Irish parents, this showman driver based his name and initially his driving style on Arthur Duray, the American-born Belgian driver who campaigned those early opposed-piston Gobron-Brilliés and who was an early star of American motor racing.

'Duray' was at his height during the twenties when he campaigned his electrifying purple-painted 'Packard Cable' front-drive Millers on both sides of the Atlantic. In the early thirties he was without a car and so he began work on a project which was to take advantage of the Junk Formula paragraphs which banned supercharging to four-stroke engines, but not to two-strokes.

He needed backing to embark on such an ambitious scheme and there is some mystery as to its source. He was to enter two cars for the 1931 race, one for himself and the other for Cliff Durant, wealthy son of William Crapo Durant, the father of General Motors. GM had been experimenting with two-stroke engines in the late twenties and it would seem reasonable to assume that some tie-up stemmed from these unusual coincidences. But there is a strong story that the engine construction was in fact sponsored by the Champion Spark

Plug Company, through its head man, Bob Stranahan, and perhaps the truth lies mid-way between the two with one backing completion of the cars and running the Indy entries and the other handling the really expensive side of engine development.

Whatever the truth, the bulky, sinister, black-painted Duray which did appear at the Speedway for qualification was a sensational mystery car. Karl Ludvigsen has quoted one eyewitness as recalling 'During practice, all alone on the track, it sounded like the flying start, and if noise alone could win, the race was in the bag for Leon. . . .'

Duray's was the only car ready for '500' qualification, leaving Durant without a ride, and beneath that monstrously long bonnet there sat a U16 engine of similar type to those used by Zoller and Z and Monaco in Europe.

His engine was arranged in four almost square blocks of four cylinders each, with the left-hand cylinders containing the inlet ports and the right-hand ones the exhaust. Common combustion chambers linked each pair of cylinders, and internally there were similarly 'Veed' con-rods to those used in Europe. The blocks were cast in aluminium with steel cylinder liners, and an individual head on each block carried two Champion spark plugs in each combustion chamber.

Bore and stroke were 2 7/16-inches x 3 1/8-inches, giving a displacement of 233 cubic inches or 3,818cc.

A massive crankcase contained a simple eight-cylinder type crankshaft running in five main-bearings, and gears on the front of this complex unit drove two Bosch magnetos, two water pumps and a giant vertically-mounted Roots-type supercharger. This carried the name of Ralph de Palma, the great Italian-American driver of earlier years, but had been built by the American Cirrus Engine Company. It drew mixture from a single Winfield carburettor and supplied the engine through a lengthy induction manifold incorporating a delicately chiselled intercooler.

Duray's backing baulked at providing him with a decent chassis, and he bolted this mechanical monster into a modified stock chassis from a Willys-Overland Whippet. It had a 9ft 7in wheelbase, and was modified to carry a Ford transmission and back axle, Gemmer steering and Bendix brakes. It was something of a last-minute lash-up to get the two-stroke engine to Indy, and it certainly seems to have reflected this in its handling; bounding and twisting and shimmying around on the Speedway's bumpy brick-paved surface, and kicking fiercely whenever the throttle was opened and the engine happened to be firing on all sixteen!

The car actually qualified quite respectably, coming into the forty-strong field in 29th position at 103.134mph, but its practice periods had been fraught with trouble. It refused to cool adequately, one engine seized solid, and then came a spate of ruptured oil lines and snapping con-rods.

There was just an eighth-inch water passage between the neighbouring exhaust cylinders in each 'square' block, and it was here that heat would build up until the steel liners began to melt. Then a piston would seize and the engine's internals would tear themselves apart.

No way was Duray going to last 200 laps, or 500-miles of the Indianapolis Speedway, and after just six race laps the black car coasted into its pit, bubbling and steaming from another thoroughly cooked engine.

Duray swore he would be back with new blocks with better cooling, but come 1932 and he was back at the Speedway with a new sponsor, a new gimmick (a two-way radio) but no new blocks. He maintained he had traced the cooling problem to faulty water pumps, and that revision to the plumbing had solved all problems. An even larger Roots-type compressor was now used, mounted at the rear of the engine, and it was topped by an enormous downdraught Stromberg carburettor.

As the 'Mallory Special', the two-stroke Duray failed to qualify, and the impetuous Irishman finally unloaded it to a scrap merchant for a reputed $90!

In later years he returned regularly to Indy with a pair of these Willys-framed cars now Offenhauser-engined and entered for other drivers, and Mauri Rose brought his 'Duray Special' home second in 1934. In the three-litre Formula which took over in 1938 Duray produced another special powered by a four-cylinder Miller engine fitted with the long-gone two-stroke sixteen's De Palma supercharger, and Billy DeVore was tenth in this 'Duray-Barbasol' in the 1939 race. Postwar he mounted this same engine in a Kurtis chassis, making the race in 1947–48 and failing in qualification until Duray finally gave up the unequal struggle in 1951.

George 'Leon Duray' Stewart died in May 1956, but the Kurtis built car containing his last Indy engine and the supercharger from that long-lost two-stroke sixteen are still to be seen in Bill Harrah's incredible collection in Reno, Nevada.

As though doubled-up engines were not enough to come from the depths of a crushing and ruinous depression, Indianapolis in 1932 saw Harry Armenius Miller arrive with something really sensational.

On the crest of a wave after his great years in the twenties, Miller had formed the Miller-Schofield Company with financier George L. Schofield, in 1928–29, capitalised at $5,000,000 to produce a new type of aero engine and Miller automotive parts such as pushrod ohv bolt-on cylinder heads for the Model A Ford.

When the Wall Street crash came, Miller-Schofield was rocked and eventually fell in 1930, leaving Miller to set-up a small special works with Fred Offenhauser—his former works manager—and the inevitable Leo Goossen. The Miller name and Goossen's services had all been part of the Schofield deal, and the new more modest concern was christened the Rellimah Company in direct reversal of its founder's initials and surname. Miller himself had been a wealthy man before the crash, but his fortune was dribbling away and he was personally bankrupted in 1932.

As a marvellous final fling before the bailiffs moved in, the Miller team produced a pair of 307.9 cubic inch (5,045.6cc) V8-engined *four-wheel drive cars!* They were sponsored by the Four-Wheel Drive Auto Company of Clintonville, Wisconsin, which had been manufacturing four-wheel drive trucks to a basic design by an engineer named Otto Zachow since 1908. One of the new cars was entered for Gus Schrader as the 'Harry Miller Special', and the other for Bob McDonough as the sponsoring company's 'FWD Special'.

It was claimed that the new V8 engines produced so much power that four-wheel drive had to be used to prevent wheel-spin. The new units had internal dimensions of 88.9mm x 101.6mm, with four overhead camshafts and four downdraught Miller carburettors. The engine drove into a conventional gearbox, after which large spur gears were used to step the drive sideways where an offset differential powered propeller shafts to front and rear. De Dion axle beams were used at both ends in a kind of doubled-up Miller front-drive arrangement. The front-drive assembly was buried in a neatly streamlined oil tank, and the cars were classical in their tall, broad-bodied appearance.

Both these unorthodox cars qualified very quickly, McDonough's at 113.279mph and Schrader's at 112.03mph, but in the race the latter spun out and clouted the retaining wall after only three laps and McDonough was out on the seventh lap when an oil line burst.

After this anything-but-auspicious debut for four-wheel drive, one of the cars (Miller's own) was sold to Frank and Al Scully of Chicago, joining a four-cylinder rear-drive Miller which they owned, and early in 1934 both cars were shipped to Tripoli in North Africa for the annual lottery race on the super-fast Mellaha circuit.

Peter de Paolo and Lou Moore were to drive the cars, with Ernie Olsen as team manager, and they sailed for Africa on the SS *Saturnia* on 7 April 1934. When they arrived in Tripolitania they were warmly welcomed by the Italian Marshal Balbo, governor of the province, and De Paolo (who had been born in America of Italian parents, nephew to the great Ralph de Palma 'of supercharger fame') drove the Marshal round the Mellaha in his four-wheel drive car. Balbo later challenged De Paolo to a race, the Marshal's light plane against the racing Miller. The Marshal won – honour was satisfied.

When practice got under way the American contingent were staggered to find the European road racers like Chiron and Varzi a full nineteen seconds faster per lap in their Grand Prix Alfa Romeos.

They resigned themselves to a hopeless race, but finished respectably with De Paolo sixth and Moore seventh. Road racing was an utterly different world to speedway racing, and the Millers were out of their element. Moore returned to America to take part in the Indianapolis '500' while De Paolo took the remaining car to Berlin's AVUS circuit for the nearest Continental/European approach to a speedway race. He was running in a strong third place when two conrods let go and virtually sawed his engine in two.

Journalist W. F. Bradley arranged a Maserati 8CM ride for the little American champion in the Penya Rhin GP at Barcelona, but poor De Paolo up-ended the car very severely in practice while trying to avoid some wandering spectators and suffered serious head injuries which eventually invalided him back to America.

Meanwhile at Indy Frank Brisko brought out the FWD Special in the '500', but suffered further lubrication line failures in the 45th lap and retired, finally to be classified twenty-seventh.

The same driver was back in the same car in 1934, now fitted with a four-cylinder 255 cubic inch engine, and this time he qualified it quickly at 116.894mph and it held together until the finish when Brisko was placed ninth. In fact he had held the lead at one point, and ran in a strong second place for many laps until a pit-stop dropped him down to sixth and then beyond. Slowly the four-wheel drive system was proving itself on Indianapolis' rectangular, left-turn only Speedway and although the big-engined Miller was quite impressively (if not extraordinarily) fast along the straightaways it could maintain much of its speed through the turns, and came out of them like an express train.

Mauri Rose ran the big Miller in 1935, was again one of the fastest qualifiers and then went out of the race on lap 103, to place 20th overall. In 1936 things went better, and Rose brought the FWD Special thundering across the line to finish fourth at an average of 107.272mph for the 500 miles. In 1937 the four-wheel drive car was still around, and Tony Wilman raced it against the new generation of European road-racing cars finding their way onto the Speedway, and went out with a broken con-rod on the 95th lap, after qualifying at 118.242mph. He was classified 25th.

One futuristic-looking car which failed to qualify that year was Lee Oldfield's V16-cylinder 365 cubic inch (5,981.3cc) Marmon-based Special, which had a mid-mounted engine behind the cockpit, all four wheels independently suspended (by coils and wishbones at the front) and featured inboard rear brakes. It was a kind of grown-up Benz, or a poor Chinese copy of an Auto Union. In 28 years time a similarly laid-out car was to win the '500' for the first time. . . .

Meanwhile, by way of a brief diversion, Ettore Bugatti had produced a four-wheel drive sprint car in France. It was called the Bugatti Type 53 and appeared concurrently with Harry Miller's design in 1932.

He had spent two years building the prototype, and evidently failed to appreciate the need for constant velocity drive-shaft joints although Grégoire and Miller had been using them for years.

The four-wheel drive Bugatti was powered by a 4.9-litre straight-eight engine as used in the Grand Prix Type 54s, which was rigidly-mounted in the front of a simple and crude chassis frame. A short propeller-shaft drove to a mid-mounted gearbox, which had an integral driven shaft carrying a differential. An open shaft ran forward alongside the engine to a pair of bevel gears offset in the front end of the frame, while a similar shaft drove to an offset drive unit in what was otherwise a normal Bugatti live axle.

Bodywork was completely graceless and unprepossessing in a very unusual manner for Bugatti, but two of these 300bhp blivots were constructed. With the accent on acceleration away from slow corners they were intended very much for short-distance sprint and hill-climb work, and during 1932 Louis Chiron smashed the La Turbie hill-climb record in one.

This car was brought to England to run at the very short Shelsley Walsh climb late that year, but Jean Bugatti put it out of shape and crashed heavily into the earthworks. In 1934 there was news of the Type 53 running again, for René Dreyfus again broke the La Turbie hill record, exceeding 100kph for the 6.3km climb for the first time. One of these cars is said to be in the private Schlumpf Collection at Malmerspach in the Vosges Mountains, but the other of the pair is apparently missing.

While this rather poor 'European Miller' was charging up the La Turbie hill-climb in 1934, Harry Miller was beginning to stage his comeback in America.

His bankruptcy had been a savage blow, taken hard; he went East and began drinking heavily. Goossen and Offenhauser were together, using the old Miller drawings, patterns and machine tools to establish the legend of the four-cylinder, marine Miller-based 'Offenhauser' four-cylinder engine which was to rule Indianapolis with occasional interruptions way into the *seventies*.

While the Offenhauser Engineering Company was growing from strength to strength, Harry Miller became deeply involved with dynamic, dapper promoter Preston T. Tucker. He had been very appreciative of the stock-based cars' Indy performances, and realised that with proper factory backing and high-grade chassis engineering a production engine could win at Indy, and that would be worth millions to its manufacturer.

He approached Miller with the idea, whose fertile imagination was instantly fired and who came up with a practical scheme for Tucker to sell to Detroit.

Late that year Miller-Tucker Incorporated was formed. Miller went out to attract some drivers which was about as difficult as a magnet attracting iron filings, and Tucker tackled Edsel (son of Henry) Ford.

The plan was to build a team of new cars around Ford stock parts, using the production V8 flathead engines in a new Miller chassis. Tucker did his sums and priced the whole projected ten-car team at a staggeringly modest $25,000. I wonder if he realised that he was cooking up a scheme which was to keep Ford of America *out* of single-seater competition well into the sixties!

The Ford–Miller-Tucker deal was clinched with Henry's grudging approval in January 1935, and the final go-ahead for the building of the ten-car team was given on February 7—with only two months in hand before practice and qualifying began at Indy.

Tucker was very successful in talking the Ford publicity agents into arranging a deal whereby their Ford dealers across the nation contributed something towards the Indy project. This brought Miller-Tucker a further $50,000, but it could not bring them more time.

A crash programme was put in hand to build the cars, and there was nothing lashed-up about their specification. They were the lowest, most streamlined racers seen at the Speedway in years. They had a new front-drive system, and independent suspension to all four wheels. The whole mechanism was fared neatly away into a smooth low-slung body, and even the exhaust pipes were cowled neatly away in flat, broad tunnels let into the cars' undertrays.

They were the first all-independent, front-drive cars to appear at the Speedway, and Miller's legendary attention to detail finish was visible even in the neat aerofoil dural castings which enclosed the suspension links.

The engine was a production Ford flathead V8 with bore and stroke of 3 1/16 x 3 3/4 inches giving a swept volume of 220.4 cubic inches. Modifications included raising the compression ratio to 9.5:1, the addition of light-alloy cylinder heads and high-lift racing camshafts. Some cars used four single-choke carburettors and others two double-chokers, but power output could only be described as modest at around 150bhp at 5,000rpm. In a typically ad agency-orientated stunt there were no rev counters fitted, only 160mph speedometers.

To keep the smooth bodies as slim as possible, Miller had set the riding mechanic's seat slightly behind the driver's, with a hole in the bodywork where the mechanic could tuck his arm to keep clear of his partner's busy elbows.

The fact that any cars were built in time for the race still staggers me, but the first 'Ford-Miller' was delivered to the Speedway on May 12. Practice had been under way for two weeks by this time, and the drivers signed-up by Miller were running low on patience.

Pete De Paolo had been one of Miller's first recruits, and when the first enthusiastic batch of Ford dealers arrived to see 'their' car run on May 15 he was the man who drove it.

After two laps he came gingerly into the pit lane, and brought the new car to a halt. The steering was beginning to stiffen-up—there was a basic design fault in the cars which carried Ford's hard-won reputation. . . .

Without his faithful and watchful old team around him, Miller had mounted his new cars' steering box close beside the bulky V8 exhaust system. As temperature built-up around the exhaust piping so the steering box casing heated-up, drying its oil and eventually swelling until its delicate gears began to warp. De Paolo brought his car in to pronounce it unsafe after the steering had tightened on him in one of the turns and his car had made an unscheduled dive towards the infield.

De Paolo bowed out of the team, as did Hollywood stunt man and long-time Indy driver Cliff Bergere. Their departures left a choice of George Bailey, George Barringer, veteran Lora Corum, Wes Crawford, Dave Evans, Ted Horn, Johnny Rae, Bob Sall, Johnny Seymour and Billy Winn as pilots.

The project had gone off at half-cock. The public had been told that the cars were Fords, and dealers all over the country had been loudly predicting a Ford walkover in the famed '500'. Panic ensued at Dearborn as a rush began to complete the team of cars, and there began such a crash programme to build cars that there was no time to test or develop them adequately although at least one major short-coming was now known.

At Indy the cars proved fast despite their low power, for they could be held virtually flat-out all round the Speedway while the chassis' good handling and fine stability made their cornering speeds astronomical by contemporary standards. But there was no time for proper suspension tuning, and the drivers just drove the cars as and when they were delivered.

Ted Horn and Johnny Seymour made the race on May 27, when they qualified at 113.213 and 112.696mph respectively. Bailey and Sall made it on the last day at 113.432 and 110.519mph. Four of the ten cars were in the race, the image was dented, Henry Ford didn't want to know, and Edsel was getting hell for mixing the company up with something as insecure as motor racing.

Bob Sall's car was the first Ford V8 out of the '500'. He stopped after 22 laps to add water since his engine was overheating. As the car sat on the pit apron so heat soak swelled the steering box gears and the steering locked solid. To remove the car to the garages they had to jack up its front end on a trolley jack, and drag it away. Bailey went out on lap 65 with the same problem. Horn went out after 145 laps with the same problem. Seymour had stopped on lap 71 with the front-drive casing apparently swelled from similar causes. Ford's four-car result read 16th, 24th, 26th and 29th, no cars running at finish . . . and *everybody* knew.

Under Henry Ford's personal orders the Indy cars were taken from Miller-Tucker Inc and locked in a back store at the Highland Park plant. They lay there disregarded and despised until late in 1937 when it was discreetly put about that 'friends of the Ford Motor Company' could buy the cars if they so desired.

Lew Welch, the spares king, and Lou Fageol, manufacturer of the famous underslung chassis 'Fageol Safety Coach', bought most of them, and they now embarked on a second and much more fruitful Speedway career.

Welch replaced the old flathead Ford engine with an up-to-date Offenhauser four-cylinder, and in 1938 Herb Ardinger drove one such car for him, qualifying in mid-field at 119mph and finishing sixth in the race at an average of 109mph, making the most of the low, compact and good-handling Miller chassis. The same car returned in 1939 with top-ranking driver Cliff Bergere—the man who had walked out of the original deal in 1935—at the wheel.

He qualified at 123.835mph and placed third, on the same lap as Shaw's winning Maserati, at 113.698mph for the whole distance. Come 1940 and Ralph Hepburn had the old car but in a strange throwback to earlier behaviour the steering reportedly failed and he spun into the infield on the 47th lap.

This was the signal for Welch to go to Offenhauser in search of more power, and his chief mechanic, Bud Winfield, specified the basic layout for a three-litre supercharged V8 engine which Leo Goossen subsequently designed. Just like the old flathead Ford, the new engine's cylinder banks were to be staggered, and Welch christened it after the Michigan town where he lived. This had been the sixth stop on the old Detroit-Lansing toll road, and its name – No VI – had remained, although rendered Novi by its modern inhabitants.

Thus the nerve-tingling centrifugally-supercharged Novis came into being; the cars which were to remain the sentimental favourites of Indy crowds well into the sixties. In 1941 Hepburn drove the first V8, still with its Miller chassis, through the '500' to take fourth place. The old chassis was absorbing 300 more horsepower than it had ever been intended to carry, but perhaps predictably it was lapping slower than it had with a more mundane power unit the previous year.

It was in 1940 that some of the other Miller-Ford cars began to re-appear. George Robson's 'Keller Special' ran 67 laps to be classified 23rd and Lou Tomei finished 11th in the same car, renamed the 'H-3 Special' in 1941. That year saw Lou Fageol enter Mel Hanson in a similar Offenhauser-powered car, in which he qualified at 124. 599mph, a record for the type, but which went out after only eleven laps with a rod through the block.

Four years of war failed to kill off Harry Miller's old chassis, and 1946 saw Anthony (Andy) Granatelli make his debut in one fitted with a Mercury V8 engine and named the 'Grancor V8 Special'. Danny Kladis took over the car for the race, and perhaps marked the beginning of Granatelli's Indianapolis luck, being towed and dis-qualified from the race on the 46th lap. In 1947 Henry Banks took another Miller-based car, the Federal 'Engineering Special', round the Speedway for 36 laps until all the oil dropped out of its Offy engine, and Pete Romcevich in Granatelli's 'Camco Motors' Mercury V8-engined car was classified 12th after retiring with a ruptured oil line.

But to my mind the most striking postscript to the story of Harry Miller's '35 Fords was seen at Indianapolis in 1946, in the first post-war '500'. It was the 'Fageol Twin Coach Special', which used front-drive units from the eleven-year-old project mated to midget Offen-hauser engines in either end of the frame, driving all four wheels!

The car was described by Peter De Paolo—then a racing columnist for the *Indianapolis News*—as '. . . one of the most beautiful racing cars that will face the starter in the 500-Mile race May 30. . . .'

Lou Fageol's entry was anything but beautiful to modern eyes, bulbous and bulky with a tiny high-sided cockpit exactly amidships and a muted head-rest faring down the tail to kick up into a small aircraft-style vertical fin. The body-panelling was smooth and evidently nicely made, broken only by two rows of neat intake louvres on either side of the tail, feeding into the rear engine bay. Large air ducts, similar to those '. . . found on P47 Army fighter planes . . .' supplied the superchargers at front and rear.

The midget-racing Offy engines had a nominal capacity of 97 cubic inches (1.59 litres), but they had been modified with an eighth-inch shorter stroke to give a 90 cubic inch (1.47 litres) capacity. This doubled-up to produce a total of 180 cubic inches which brought them just within the supercharged limits. Fageol selected Roots lobe-type compressors for his new car, borrowing directly from European road racing practice. Most American speedway cars used centrifugal superchargers which delivered high boost at very high engine speeds, but which were woefully lacking in mid-range 'punch'. This is one of the shortcomings which ruined the notorious V16 BRM programme.

The only connection between the two engines, front to rear, was a coupled throttle linkage, and provision was made for either unit to be disconnected and the car to be driven as either a front-drive or a conventional rear-drive machine.

The idea behind this twin-engined special was to equalise weight distribution front and rear and to make full use of four-wheel drive's tractive capabilities. Fageol felt that a four-wheel drive car with a single engine must have been wasting some traction at the 'light end', and although his 'Twin Coach Special' was heavy at 2,520lbs his West Coast team approached the '500' optimistically.

Paul Russo was signed to drive the car, and in practice he expressed himself very satisfied with its performance and stability. Paul Weirick, mechanic and car constructor, also did some laps in the car and then Fageol himself took over and put in some shattering laps which had Chief Steward Jack Mehan running into the Fageol pit, flagging him in and presenting an excited reprimand for going so fast when he hadn't even taken his mandatory 'driving test'. Fageol was unrepentant, smiled from the cockpit, and said of his new creation 'What a sweetheart!'.

Russo proved how sweet when in qualification he punched it into second place on the front of the grid with an average of 126.183mph.

Then, in the race, he was running well in contact with the leaders until the 16th lap, when he lost control in the northeast turn, the well-balanced Fageol rotated like a top and smashed into the retaining wall. It was written-off, and Russo was carefully lifted clear with a broken leg. On that same lap an Alfa Romeo retired in its pits with a bad fuel leak and two laps later a rejuvenated Sampson sixteen (of which we will hear more) dropped out with its oil leaked away. Perhaps Russo lost his unique car on a slick of fuel and oil, or perhaps something caused the twin engines to go out of synchronisation. Whatever the truth, the Fageol Twin Coach Special was the most enterprising idea at the Speedway since Miller himself had vacated the scene; but it shared his luck . . . and that was always against it.

As a postscript to the story of these interesting and unusual Indy cars, there came perhaps the most peculiar of them all in 1948.

The third post-war '500's most interesting entry failed to appear in Indiana that spring; the two-cylinder front-drive 'Suttle Steamer' from Detroit, which was claimed to include only sixteen moving parts! In its place, all attention was focused upon the incredible six-wheeled 'Pat Clancy Special'.

Rear-end of this device was a maze of chassis tubing, axles and propeller shafts, with two Midget-type back axles 'connected by a universal joint'. A conventionally nose-mounted 270 cubic-inch Meyer-Drake engine was used, and it was claimed that the four-rear-wheel layout gave better traction and improved handling over less well-endowed designs.

Bill DeVore qualified the car 20th on the grid at an average of 123.967mph and ran reliably and smoothly through the race to be flagged off after 190 laps, being classified as 12th place finisher. It wasn't a performance which set designers gnashing their teeth, junking their contemporary cars and starting again on a six-wheeled base, but the Pat Clancy Special remains a brave attempt at something new.

It was relatively rare in being an unconventional odd-ball which actually survived Indianapolis and raced in other events in the oval track season. A week after the 1949 '500' the six-wheeler was out in a 100-miler at Milwaukee, where Jackie Holmes actually brought it home in fourth place. Milwaukee was still a dirt track in those days – maybe that had something to do with the high placing.

Its next race was at Trenton, New Jersey, in another 100-miler. Mack Hellings drove it, and was well placed right at the end when a last-lap accident claimed the car. It was classified ninth in the results.

Repairs were made in time for a very busy weekend which saw the Syracuse and Detroit 100-Mile races on successive days—the tracks being 700 miles apart '. . . and no freeways . . .' as USAC statistician Don Davidson tells me.

Jimmy Davies made his championship debut in the six-wheeler at Syracuse, finishing eighth, and at Detroit the next day brought it home for another reliable sixth place. Right at the close of that 1949 season Davies actually won the Del Mar 100 in a 'Pat Clancy Special', but this was a conventional four-wheeler. It was suspected at the time that Clancy had converted his remarkable sextuple special but evidently it was a brand-new car. So perhaps the oddest of all Indy's odd-ball cars passed into limbo, but it had a marked advantage over most of the non-conformists. It proved very reliable, and was consistently a good finisher, and to win a motor race one must first finish. Pat Clancy was most of the way there. . . .

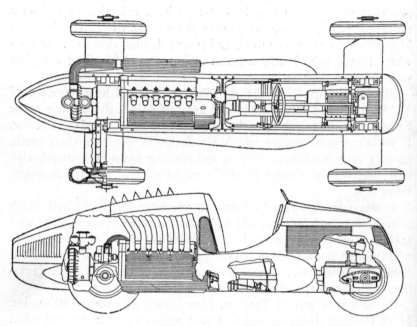

Four-wheel drive—original scheme of the 1938–39 Gulf-Millers.

24 Why not try six wheels? The 'Pat Clancy Special' in Gasoline Alley, Indianapolis, in 1948. It proved quite successful!

26 Twinned – the 16-cylinder Maserati's two straight-eight engines, mounted side by side complete with their crankshafts geared together.

25 Luigi Fagioli waits impatiently in the 'Sedici Cilindri' Maserati V5 as a wheel change is completed during the 1932 Coppa Acerbo at Pescara.

27 Nuvolari in the Alfa Romeo Tipo A – Jano's variation on the twinned-engine theme used two 1750cc straight-sixes, mounted side by side complete with their individual gearboxes and drive lines. The driver had a gearlever on either side of him . . .

28, 29 The immortal Alfa Romeo 'Bimotore' – Nuvolari in full tyre-destroying flight at the AVUS track in Berlin in 1935 and Austin Dobson examining his newly-acquired sister car at Brooklands, in 1937.

10

Why not Try Two Engines? –
Europe and America, 1928-1946

Two years before Riley Brett, Leo Goossen and Alden Sampson put together their sixteen-cylinder 'twin' engine in America, Ettore Bugatti had toyed with similar ideas in his Molsheim works, near Strasbourg, in Alsace.

During the Great War he had produced a sixteen-cylinder aero engine design subsequently taken up by Duesenberg on behalf of the US Government. In 1928 he produced his first sixteen-cylinder car, using an engine confected in similar style.

He took two existing 60mm x 84mm, 1,900cc straight-eight cylinder blocks and mounted them side by side, with their individual crankshafts coupled together in much the same manner as the first Sampson Special of America's Depression years.

The two blocks were joined by steel structures at front and rear, the rearward one housing spur gears which united the two crankshafts. Gear-trains on the back end of both blocks powered camshafts, magnetos and superchargers, and a forward-facing central shaft took drive to the front-mounted water pump.

Each crankshaft ran in eight roller-bearings plus a single central plain-bearing, all of which were mounted in housings hanging down from the huge block casting. A gigantic unstressed sump pan was then bolted up underneath, common to both eight-cylinder blocks.

Bugatti's original sixteen-cylinder aero engines had suffered persistent lubrication problems which were eventually cured by Charles B. King, Duesenberg's chief engineer, much against the *Patron's* wishes for he evidently hated anybody challenging his designs! Great care was taken with the new racing engine's lubrication, and there were three pumps driven by worm gearing from the crankshafts—one

G

scavenged the sump, another gave a low-pressure feed to the cam-shafts and coupling gears and the third forced very high-pressure lubricant to the crankshaft bearings.

Drive was taken through a multi-plate clutch from the centre coupling gear, and a short propeller shaft led back to a gearbox located below the driver's knees. Another short propellor shaft then drove to a lightweight back axle. Both engine and gearbox contributed materially to the light chassis frame's torsional rigidity, and suspension was by semi-elliptic leaf springs passing right through a typical beautifully-made Bugatti tubular front axle, and by quarter-elliptics at the rear. Combined capacity of this new double-eight was 3,801cc, and it is thought that it produced about 250bhp. It certainly weighed around 500lbs, and the completed cars (which were absolutely archetypal Bugatti despite their voluminous exhaust systems) were given the Type 45 classification. A road-going Type 47 was projected, with an intended displacement of 2,986cc, but before prototype work could be completed, the whole programme ground to a sudden halt.

Three Type 45s had been built for the French Grand Prix, but when that event was downgraded to become a handicap race for sports cars at Comminges the sixteen-cylinder Bugattis were all dressed up with nowhere to go.

The redundant trio were subsequently entered in hill-climbs and other minor speed events, but according to *Bugattiste* Hugh Conway the crankshaft coupling gears proved a source of continual trouble. The cars were consequently retired, and after lying derelict for many years I understand that one is now in America, and that the other two are in the private Schlumpf Collection in France.

On 1 July 1929, a brand-new Maserati racing car appeared for the first time, being entered for a race on the very fast 25-mile public road course at Cremona, in Italy.

Baconin Borzacchini was recruited by the Maserati brothers to drive the low-slung, vicious-looking beast, and when it howled through a measured ten-kilometre section of the Cremona course at 152.9mph, its construction seemed fully justified. This was the fastest speed ever recorded on a road circuit at that time, and was also claimed to be the first international record to be set on Italian soil. The 'Sedici Cilindri' Maserati had proved itself the fastest road-racing car in the world.

Maserati was a famous name in Italian racing. The brothers from

Bologna, Carlo, Bindo, Alfieri, Ettore and Ernesto, had links with the
dawn of motor sport when Carlo had raced on both two-and four-
wheels. He had died in 1911, and during the Great War the remaining brothers began a business making Maserati sparking plugs. In the
early twenties Alfieri acted as racing engineer and driver for Diatto,
and in 1925 he built a pair of two-litre Grand Prix cars for the Turin
company. When Diatto withdrew from competition in 1926 Alfieri
took over his Grand Prix designs, modified them to 1½-litre form and
reproduced them as the first Maserati cars.

In the late twenties these cars and their derivatives began to prove
very popular with private entrants, and for 1929 two wildly different
models were offered at the top and bottom of the Maserati range.

One was the 8C-1100 with a supercharged twin overhead-cam-
shaft straight-eight engine of 1,078cc, and the other—since the
original eight-cylinder Diatto design could not be enlarged effectively
—was the doubled-up Sedici Cilindri double-eight.

The brothers took two of their two-litre engines, and mounted
them at a very slight vee angle upon a cast light alloy coupled
crankcase. The vee between the two blocks was just sufficient to give
clearance between the cam boxes. Block castings were in iron, and
the heads carried two inclined valves per cylinder set at an included
angle of 90 degrees and actuated by twin gear-driven overhead
camshafts. Bore and stroke were 62mm x 82mm, which doubled-up
to produce a total capacity of 3,961cc.

The left-hand block was in virtually standard trim, while the right-
hand unit had been modified with the inlet and exhaust ports
reversed to bring the exhaust manifolding to the outside of the
assembly. Two individual Roots compressors were mounted on the
front of this composite, each being driven from its respective unit's
crankshaft, and they drew mixture from a single Weber carburettor
each.

Bosch magnetos were used to fire single plugs per cylinder, and
light-alloy pistons were mounted on con-rods machined from the
solid. It is said that each rod and piston assembly weighed 1.84lbs
with rings. Blower pressure was quite modest, under 15psi. There
were two gear-type oil pumps, an oil cooler fitting in the nose beneath
the normal water radiator with its divided cores, and there were two
centrifugal water pumps, one mounted above each compressor and
driven from the timing gears. The *Officine* claimed 305bhp at
5,200rpm, and the Cremona speeds seemed to confirm it.

After Borzacchini's maximum speed record in the new car, which had been confusingly titled the Maserati V4, Alfieri took over for the Cremona race, averaging 124.4mph for fastest lap but failing to survive to the finish.

The Italian Grand Prix should have been held at Monza later that year, but a Formule Libre Monza Grand Prix was run in its place, using a 2.8-mile version of the Autodrome circuit.

Alfieri Maserati drove the raucous V4 there, and set another lap record, this time at 124.2mph. He was beaten by just 0.2 of a second in the first heat by August Momberger's unlikely Mercedes SSK, but later in the day the V4 went off song and eventually retired. It was clearly the fastest car of its day, but that was no recompense for its continued inability to finish races.

In the following season Maserati were to have a good year, their cars winning seven major races and the brave Borzacchini bringing victory to the V4 at Tripoli when he won at an average of 91.05mph. The car was then shipped across the Atlantic to compete at Indianapolis, but with the new 'Junk Formula' regulations in force it had to run minus its twin superchargers and performed poorly, qualifying at an indifferent 95.213mph and retiring after only seven laps with apparently incurable electrical trouble. It was to be another nine years before Maserati rang the changes at the Speedway, and won the '500'.

Back in Europe Ernesto took over the V4 at Pescara, shattered the lap record on one madly-adrenalised lap, and finished behind his new driver, Achille Varzi, in one of the new 8C-2500 cars.

For 1931 René Dreyfus took Varzi's place at Bologna, and Ernesto continued racing V4, and *won* the Gran Premio di Roma on the steep-banked Littorio circuit. In the first heat of the Monza Grand Prix later in the year he trailed home in last place, and this marked the end of the trail for the four-litre car.

In 1932 a larger V5 Sedici Cilindri was built-up, using an engine of similar type to the original but with 8C-2500 components giving a capacity of 4,905cc and an output of over 330bhp at 5,200rpm. This power was demonstrably too much for the very basic chassis frame in which the engine was installed, but with a suitably courageous driver the latest Sedici Cilindri was clearly going to be a potent road-racing car.

Luigi Fagioli, the granite-hard driver-cum-spaghetti-manufacturer, was just the man for the job, and he shared the new V5 with Ernesto Maserati (briefly) in the 1932 Italian Grand Prix.

The race was held in June, and with a five-hour duration it should have been Maserati's all the way so long as the new car could last the pace. But the Trident team's pit-work was pathetic in comparison to that of Alfa Romeo with their brand-new P3 Monopostos, and all the advantage which Fagioli gained by sheer bullet-like speed out on the Autodrome wasted away on the pit-apron. Fagioli was 2½-3 seconds per lap faster than Nuvolari in the new Alfa but he just could not quite catch him.

Fagioli wrung the utmost out of his car in a wild final attempt to close on the single-seater Alfa Romeo, but the V5 could do no better than come howling home in second place, with a new lap record of 112.2mph for the revised circuit.

Soon afterwards 'The Abruzzi Robber' gained just reward in V5, by winning Maserati's third consecutive Rome Grand Prix, and then the car was entrusted to René Dreyfus who ran it in the AVUS-Rennen in Berlin and came home with a new lap record at 130.87mph despite something failing within that complicated engine and putting him out of the race.

Back at Monza in September for the circuit's own 'Grand Prix', Fagioli and Nuvolari had a terrific wheel-to-wheel battle in their heat which ended when the Alfa Romeo evidently found itself shouldered off the track. Nuvolari's car bounded over a low wall, slewed wildly across a narrow grass verge and then rejoined the race with a buckled wheel and bent axle. He still managed to finish second to Fagioli's winning V5, which had averaged 106.3mph.

Fagioli's driving very nearly led to Alfa Romeo withdrawing their fleet of P3s on the spot, but they did run in the final which saw Fagioli's car suffering ignition troubles and running badly.

Later that month there was one final event at Miramas in France, but again V5 misbehaved and could do no better than stagger home sixth in this Marseilles GP on a circuit which should have suited it.

With the racing season ended, the *Fratelli* decided to mount an attack on the World's One Hour and other records at Montlhéry, but instead of using the rugged Fagioli's services once more they arrived at the Parisian course with a young driver named Ruggieri. He had considerable experience of racing Maseratis, but they had been small ones.

The Sedici Cilindri was a very different kind of motor car, and unfortunately V5 got away from Ruggieri at high-speed and hurtled off the Autodrome course, thundering off banks and trees and ending up a total wreck with its unfortunate driver fatally injured.

This was a tragic blow at the close of a hard season, and followed closely upon the natural death of Alfieri Maserati himself. He had been working on a front-wheel drive racing prototype in recent months, which seems to have been something of a personal pet and which was dropped after his demise. I contacted Pete Coltrin—an American living in Modena who is a great Maserati authority—to obtain more details of this mysterious front-drive car. His reply was brief and to the point; 'Re the front-drive car – it didn't work'. Thus history is written.

Despite these losses the surviving brothers embarked for 1933 upon their most ambitious racing programme yet, but V5 was rebuilt as a low-priority project. This was the last season of Formule Libre racing, before the new 750-Kilogramme Formula was to come into effect, but the Sedici Cilindri was not to appear until the following year when only a few events remained for it to contest.

In 1934 the rebuilt V5—now much more like a normal production 8CM single-seater but with at least 350bhp beneath its tall bonnet—was entrusted to Piero Taruffi for the very fast Tipoli Grand Prix on the Mellaha desert circuit.

In the first four laps of the race Taruffi found his car's front brakes overheating consistently into one corner at the end of a very fast straight. He was reaching towards 165mph along that straight, and on the fifth lap his front brakes locked solid and remained locked as he took his foot off the pedal!

In his autobiography he wrote; 'I still have a clear picture in my mind of the front wheels motionless and clouds of smoke pouring from my tyres as they melted . . . I thought the car would never stop. . . .'

In basic terms, it didn't. It speared off the outside of the slightly banked corner, arched through the air, bounced hard on its wheels, shattered a hoarding advertising beer and then somersaulted end-over-end, finally coming to rest upside down with its unfortunate driver pinned underneath. He was dragged out with a broken arm and severe shock . . . but it was the end of Maserati's sixteen-cylinder.

In later years the smaller V4 engine reappeared in a most desirable road-going tourer owned by a Dutchman named Verkade, but the larger V5 appears to have been far beyond resurrection.

Alfa Romeo also had their twin-engined cars, the famous *Bimotore* cars of the mid-thirties, and the Tipo A of 1931. This car followed on naturally from Maserati's remarkable showing with their double-eight, but Vittorio Jano (Alfa's famous ex-Fiat designer) decided on a slightly less exotic double-six.

He took two existing 1,750cc supercharged 'sixes', and mounted them side by side in similar style to the preceding Maserati V4. The two engines were 'handed', placing their inlets together on the inside of the 'U' and their exhausts on the outer sides. The two crankshafts revolved in opposite directions, to counter each other's torque reaction, and on the rear of the units were two individual gearboxes although the cranks were geared together as in other doubled-up engines we have seen. Both clutches were linked to a single pedal, and there were two gear-levers also linked so that the driver could change with either hand. Two parallel propeller shafts ran to individual bevel-gear final drives for each rear wheel.

This 3½-litre ensemble was mounted in a conventional channel chassis with semi-elliptic leaf springing. Steering was by two separate drag links with no track rod, and to bring this rather heavy vehicle to a stop were massive dural drum brakes with steel liners, measuring a full 18 inches in diameter and 2½ inches in width. They were rod-operated.

The car carried genuine Monoposto bodywork with a single central seat, and the twin rev counters mounted on the dashboard were to become a familiarly anachronistic feature of the single-engined P3 Monoposto which was subsequently developed from this proto-type.

Cylinder dimensions were quoted as 65 x 88mm, giving a total twelve-cylinder capacity of 3,504cc, and power output was about 220bhp at 5,000rpm, although at least 300bhp was claimed at the time. Wheelbase was 9ft 6ins and track 4ft 9ins, and the Tipo A scaled 2,570lbs which was in fact only six pounds lighter than the much bigger, much more powerful Maserati V4.

As Grand Prix regulations asked little more than that race duration should not be less than *ten hours*, the Italian Grand Prix that year was brought forward from its normal September date to be run on May 24. It was there that the new Tipo A made its debut.

Unfortunately, Luigi Arcangeli was killed in the car during practice. He was trying to better Giuseppe Campari's times (set in the new wide-body 2.3-litre Alfa which was to win its 'Monza' name tag in this race) when he lost control in the deceptive bends at Lesmo, the Tipo A rolled over and threw him out.

The car itself was barely damaged and Jano had it rebuilt and entrusted it to Nuvolari for the race. Borzacchini, the ex-Sedici Cilindri driver, was to be the Mantuan's partner, but neither seemed very keen on the idea and the car proved a pig to handle.

Nuvolari was running a rather unhappy third in the Grand Prix when Jano called him in after 33 laps to take over one of the 2.3-litre cars in an attempt to reel-in the leading Bugattis. Nuvolari succeeded in this task, sharing with Campari, and won the race.

Later in the season the Tipo A reappeared, this time in a better-developed and more manageable form. Campari actually won the Coppa Acerbo race on the fast and arduous Pescara circuit on the Adriatic Coast, and after this success two Tipo As were entered for the Monza Grand Prix to be handled by Campari again, and by Nuvolari.

Unfortunately Campari's car suffered some kind of trouble with one of its gearboxes, and when Nuvolari's ran into tyre problems it was the end of the double-six Alfa story. They were never to be raced again, but performed yeoman service in pointing the way towards the classic P3 Monoposto which was to dominate Grand Prix racing until the advent of the German teams.

In 1933 the Alfa Romeo works officially withdrew from participation in racing, leaving the private Scuderia Ferrari to uphold their honour. This Enzo Ferrari's team succeeded in doing, and with the advent of the 750-kilogramme Formula the cars carrying his legendary prancing horse symbol fought a gallant rearguard action against German might.

Work at Alfa's own Portello factory was slow in producing an effective answer to the new all-independently-suspended silver cars, and Ferrari's own engineering staff began to work on some prospectively money-making but fearsome 'specials' of their own.

Technical director of the Scuderia Ferrari was Luigi Bazzi, and after the Scuderia's annual banquet – on 16 December 1934 – he suggested that a very powerful racing car could be built in a very short time by taking two existing engines and mounting them both in a suitably-modified existing chassis.

His calculations indicated that the resultant car would be over the 750-kilogramme Grand Prix weight limit, but it could still earn useful funds in the predominantly Italian-organised Formule Libre events. He was determined not to run into the twinning complications experienced in the Bugatti and Maserati double-eights and the original Alfa Romeo double-six, and so he envisaged his two engines being completely separate, with one at either end of the car to create an even weight distribution.

A team under Bazzi and another engineer named Arnaldo Roselli began work in Ferrari's Modena works with the cautious approval of Enzo himself and Jano. They took a new Monoposto chassis, lengthened it by six inches and then boxed it for extra rigidity. The Dubonnet-type independent front suspension then being adopted on the 1935 Grand Prix cars was grafted onto the modified frame, but since both front and rear engines were to drive the rear wheels (Bazzi not being drawn into four-wheel drive) the rear suspension was much more complex.

Since the rear engine would be in the way, the normal tubular beam axle of the existing Monoposto had to be discarded, and in its place Bazzi adopted very wide-based fabricated wishbones (resembling the claws of a pair of coal tongs in plan view) which carried the individual bevel drives for each rear wheel. These wishbones were as long from front to rear as were the semi-elliptic leaf springs, and they mounted inside them on the same chassis cross-members.

Bazzi turned the rear engine around in the chassis, so that it drove forwards towards the front engine. This unit retained its normal P3 clutch housing and gearbox, with the differential mounted on the gearbox output shaft. Bevels took drive from this differential, and then powered two propeller shafts which diverged towards the rear of the car to provide a vee drive to the individual bevel-box final drives attached to each hub. This was standard practice in the P3 design, but now a second drive from the rear-mounted engine had to be introduced.

Bazzi adopted a hollow gearbox main-shaft, and drive from the rear engine passed right through it and on through the clutch centre where it engaged with an internally-toothed union.

There was a simple dog-clutch introduced into the drive-line from the rear engine so that it could be disengaged by the driver to leave the car with only the front engine driving the rear wheels.

Final major departure from Tipo B layout concerned the fuel tanks.

which could no longer reside in the tail cowling and so were slung
pannier-fashion on either side of the chassis frame. This feature
served to concentrate the vehicle's mass even more within its wheelbase, and meant that its handling should not be altered materially
as the fuel load was burned off.

There were two separate radiator cores, one for each engine,
mounted in the nose, and massive Ariston drum brakes were fitted
all round, with hydraulic operation and an extra mechanical hand-
lever operating on the rears. Wheelbase was 9ft 2¼ins, track 4ft 6½ins,
height 4ft 6¾ins and overall length 13ft 7½ins.

Two of the cars were assembled, one using the latest 3,165cc
straight-eight supercharged GP engines and the other two of the
earlier, provenly reliable, 2,905cc units. The larger engines produced
270bhp each at 5,400rpm to provide a total of 540 horse power in
the larger 'Bimotore'. The smaller units were rated at 260bhp at
5,400rpm, to total 520 horsepower. Both sizes of engine shared a
100mm stroke, the larger being bored out to 71mm as against the
earlier dimension of 68mm.

The two cars were bodied in aluminium sheet, formed in classical
lines over dural bracing, and with the suspension carefully cowled at
front and rear and a prominent tail fin extending from the head
fairing, Ferrari's new 'specials' were very striking in appearance. Dry
weight was quoted as 2,205lbs, rising to 2,888lbs fully-laden.

The smaller car was completed in only three months, and on
10 April 1935 it was tested on a closed section of the Brescia–
Bergamo Autostrada by the Scuderia's chief tester, Attilio Marinoni,
and Tazio Nuvolari. The champion driver was timed at 175mph on
one run at 4,500rpm, and then he booted the new prototype to a
brief near-rev limit 5,300rpm on the return run and recorded
210mph! That afternoon the car was taken to Monza Autodrome
where it completed quite a long session mechanically trouble-free and
apparently quite pleasant to handle. The rear tyres began to show
certain signs of distress with sustained high-speed running, and
Bazzi instantly realised that this would be a problem when it came to
racing the car.

Ferrari and Jano both gave their full support at this juncture,
and—while the Tunis GP was allowed to slip by—the second, larger-
engined car was completed and a two-car Bimotore entry made for
Tripoli.

The fast North African race took place on May 12, and the two brand-new Bimotori took their places on the 28-strong starting grid with Nuvolari in the latest 6,330cc model and Louis Chiron in the original 5,810cc prototype.

Mercedes and Auto Union were present in force, and from the flag Caracciola and Fagioli rushed into the lead with Nuvolari hanging onto their tails with the big Ferrari Alfa. He forced his way past Fagioli into second place, but at the end of his third lap he brought the Bimotore swerving into the pits for new rear tyres!

After four more spectacularly rumbustious laps Nuvolari was back again to replace rear tyres worn through to the canvas, and so it went on. He eventually changed eight tyres during the race while Chiron's smaller car had to change six. They were not alone, tyre-changing being an integral part of top-class motor racing in those days, but their consumption was much higher than the opposition's and it cost them dear. Nuvolari was finally placed fourth and Chiron a troubled fifth, but although immensely fast along the Mellaha's straights neither car could match the German cars' nimble handling and meteoric lap speeds. Caracciola won, and his best lap of 136.77 mph in the Mercedes compared admirably with Nuvolari's fastest at 133.78mph. The Bimotore was clever, but far too crude in this company.

Europe's fastest race, the AVUS-Rennen, followed two weeks later, and practice saw Nuvolari watching open-mouthed as his tyres stripped before his eyes, whenever he attempted to hold more than 175mph along the narrow straights. Stuck's Auto Union was a whole twenty seconds quicker while the Italian car consumed its rubber, and yet Nuvolari was not to be cowed by this disconcerting habit and kept his foot hard on the floor in the first five-lap heat. He made his first stop for tyres on the second lap, eventually finished sixth and failed to qualify for the final.

Chiron took things more calmly, treating his car's tyres as though they were made of paper, and he qualified for the final by tip-toeing into a comfortable fourth place in his heat. He drove very intelligently in the ten-lap final and while the faster German cars stopped to change tyres he just kept going, easing his way round the corners and feathering the throttle on the straights. Fagioli's Mercedes won, but the Bimotore boomed home in second place with one rear tyre completely devoid of tread.

This was the end of the Formule Libre season, and so the Scuderia turned to record-breaking with its twin-engined cars. On February 14

Hans Stuck had set a new flying mile record for Class C (3-5-litre cars) of 199mph in his Auto Union on the Florence–Viareggio Autostrada—actually using the level eight-kilometre section between Lucca and Altopascio.

Although the big Bimotore was in Class B (5-8 litres), Tazio Nuvolari set about raising the German record on Italian soil. There was little doubt that the car would shatter its strict class record (then held by Doré's Panhard at only 137mph on the Arpajon road) but that was purely a secondary target.

Early on the morning of July 15, the big 6.3-litre Bimotore was wheeled from its transporter onto the Lucca road. It had been modified with a slick head faring and disc covers for the rear wheel spokes. The pannier tanks had been removed and 50kg weight had been saved simply by removing the big tail-mounted oil tank. Dunlop tyres were fitted in place of the original Engleberts, these being 6.50 x 32 rears and 6.00 x 19 fronts.

Bazzi was on hand with his team of mechanics, Carlo Pintacuda was cooling his heels as spare driver and the Duke of Spoleto was spectating. It was intended to try for the record in the cool, still, morning air, but on a preliminary run Nuvolari found the oil pressure was fluctuating and so had the oil tank replaced.

The best time of the morning was past when he got going again at 9.30, thundering away down the arrow-straight Autostrada towards Altopascio. The red car disappeared from sight long before its twin-engine exhaust note stilled in the air. A 200-yard battle for control left its legacy in glaring tyre marks just after an over-bridge where the Bimotore was caught in a sudden cross-wind, but Nuvolari simply wheeled round at the end of the run and came howling back again, correcting another vicious side-swipe to return to a relieved, and soon elated, Ferrari depot.

The timekeepers announced that the Bimotore had taken the flying mile record at 200.77mph, the flying kilometre at 199.92mph and that its peak recorded speed through a special trap had been 208.91 mph . . . The flying kilometre figure bettered the former record set by Caracciola's Mercedes at 197.35mph on the Gyon Highway, in Hungary.

Next morning the Autostrada again shuddered to the Bimotore's passing, but the wind had risen and after five increasingly desperate runs Nuvolari gave up. The big car was taken back to the Scuderia Ferrari workshops in Modena, where its engines were removed and it was put into a back stores beside its similarly demobilised smaller sister. One of the chassis was subsequently scrapped, while the other (generally accepted as being the Chiron car) was bought in 1937 by British amateur driver Austin Dobson for national events at Donington and Brooklands.

Ferrari installed a pair of 2.9-litre engines for their new client, replaced the Dubonnet front suspension with a more modern trailing-link set-up and shipped the rebuilt car thankfully to England, having made some return on the project at long last.

Dobson's appearance with the Bimotore caused great excitement in British motor racing circles, and after discovering that the big car was right out of its element on the twisty road course at Donington Park he broke the Class B lap record at Brooklands' Mountain Circuit, taking it to 77.84mph. He shared the wheel with Fairey Aviation test pilot Chris Staniland in the BRDC's 500-Kilometres race, and the latter lapped the outer circuit at 132.8mph. The Bimotore was placed sixth in this event on corrected handicap.

At the close of the season Dobson decided that perhaps the car was not for him, and he sold it to the Hon. Peter Aitken. He decided to modify it for English racing, and had it cut virtually in two, the rear engine removed along with the transmission and rear suspension, and replaced by an ENV pre-selector gearbox with a new back axle mounted on quarter-elliptic springs.

This emasculated special was renamed the 'Alfa-Aitken', and it was not completed until the middle of 1939 when it appeared with a brand-new bodyshell with bulbous farings completely enclosing front and rear suspensions, and an odd almost circular radiator grille high-mounted on the nose.

After some brief appearances the Alfa-Aitken was retired for the duration of the war, during which its owner was killed, and postwar it passed to R. V. Wallington who won in it at Gransden Lodge aerodrome in Britain's first postwar race meeting.

Wallington sold the car to Major 'Tony' Rolt—one of Colditz Castle's glider manufacturers when a prisoner-of-war—and he had it modified by F. W. Dixon who removed its twin superchargers and fitted eight SU carburettors to make it eligible for what were then 'Formula A' races. Dixon enlarged the surviving engine to 3.4 litres and Rolt raced the resulting 'GP car' quite widely in the late forties.

This 'Monomotore' Alfa eventually found a buyer in New Zealand where it was further abused, winding up with a GMC truck engine installed. It is now in the good hands of Gavin Bain in Christ-church.

Meanwhile the original rear engine from the car had been acquired by Lord Ridley, of Ridley Special fame (see pp. 50–51), and later came to the Hon. Patrick Lindsay who fitted it into an engineless Tipo B Monoposto chassis which he had bought from Australia. This chassis (No 5002) was reputedly ex-Nuvolari, and after its emigration to Australia it had been variously powered by 4.3-litre Alvis, six-cylinder side-valve GMC truck, and Chevrolet Corvette V8 engines . . . at least it, and the remaining Bimotore, have survived!

While the circuits of Europe were echoing to twin-engined exhaust notes of Bugattis, Maseratis and various Alfa Romeos, perhaps one of the most interesting and impressive power units of 'speed history' was lying in storage in America.

It was the 'double-eight' engine from Frank Lockhart's Stutz Black Hawk record car—once again Lockhart, Indy winner at 23, dead national hero at 25, was throwing his long shadow across American motor racing.

On 4 February 1927, Malcolm Campbell had covered the flying mile at 174.224mph on Pendine Sands, and on March 29 Segrave's Sunbeam had broken the 200mph barrier and pushed the Land Speed Record to 203.79mph at Daytona. On April 11 Frank Lockhart wheeled his little Miller '91' Speedway car out onto the crusty salt of Muroc dry lake and recorded a two-way average of 164mph and a one-way best of 171mph with less than one twenty-eighth of the 1,000hp Sunbeam's cubic capacity.

This feat staggered the motoring world and fired Lockhart's imagination. On a longer course, such as Ormond Beach at Daytona, his Miller could have pulled a higher gear and travelled much faster. With more power he could become the fastest man on earth.

Lockhart was a visionary, an instinctive engineer whose imagination boiled and buzzed with schemes. He had already won the '500', he was already the biggest money-earner in speedway racing, but he wanted something more, something which would give him the stature to turn all his dreams into hard, successful, mechanical fact.

He approached Fred Moscovics, head of the Black Hawk, Indian-apolis-based Stutz Motor Company, to support the building of a Land Speed Record car. Moscovics was enthusiastic, raised around $35,000 in outside sponsorship and put Stutz's facilities at Lockhart's disposal. In return the car was to be named the Stutz 'Black Hawk'.

Lockhart conscripted the Weisel brothers, gifted young aviation engineers whom he had met on the West Coast, to design his record car. He wanted to mount two of his special Miller '91' engines side-by-side with the crankshafts geared together in similar style to the Bugatti-King aero engines of the Great War.

Zenas Weisel drew on Duesenberg's experience, perhaps not knowing that in Alsace the Bugatti works were building a similar engine at the same time, and for the still modest power which this double-Miller would produce he advocated a slender torpedo-shaped body with separately fared wheels to reduce frontal area.

The engine combined Miller, Lockhart and Stutz parts, with the two '91' straight-eight dohc blocks and crankshafts mounted in a thirty degree vee on a common casing. The crankshafts were geared together and two centrifugal superchargers with attached Zenith carburettors ran at $3\frac{1}{2}$-times engine speed off the rear of each block. This three-litre twin-crankshaft V16-cylinder produced 385bhp at 7,500rpm.

Less than eight months after its initiation the project was complete and the Stutz Black Hawk rolled out in February 1928. It had already swallowed all the original cash float, and during those months Lockhart had been pursuing a furious racing programme to keep the project solvent.

Weisel's body shape was wind-tunnel tested to suggest a potential maximum speed, with the modest power available, of no less than 330mph – at a time when, on February 19, Campbell was just pushing the record up to 206mph on Daytona's sands.

At Daytona the Stutz initially disappointed. It couldn't do better than make a few faltering runs at under 180mph, but the bugs were quickly combed out and on a dull, drizzly day with a cold wind knifing inland off the grey Atlantic Lockhart eventually went through the traps at 225mph!

Suddenly the tiny white car ran into a rain squall, blinding its driver who unwittingly veered into soft sand. The Stutz kicked its tail in the air, and abruptly tumbled over, bounced into the sea and planed crazily over the breakers to sink in shallow water. Lockhart's unconscious form was almost submerged, but Moscovics himself was first on the scene and held the driver's head above water until the car was dragged ashore.

Lockhart's injuries were not serious and as he recovered in hospital so the car was rapidly rebuilt back in Indianapolis. In mid-April the team returned to Daytona, but Lockhart was looking for every possible way of making money, and he had some free tyres fitted whose manufacturers had offered $20,000 should he take the record.

At dawn on 25 April 1928, Lockhart warmed the car in a gentle southerly run along the level beach. He returned, and then wheeled into another run to the south which was obviously in earnest as the superchargers wailed piercingly away into the distance. His speed was announced as 198.29mph, and then the Stutz was spotted on its return run, rocketing into the measured mile at around 220mph and still accelerating rapidly.

It was bulleting along the beach when there came a spout of sand and shredding pieces from the right-rear tyre, the car appeared momentarily sideways-on then blurred into the air, pounding end-over-end down the beach to end up in a heap of tangled scrap. Lockhart was hurled out to his premature death, and the great project was over . . . a clam shell had split that tyre.

Riley Brett, who had worked on the car at Stutz, bought the V16 twin-crank engine and put it away in store until perhaps there would be some use for a three-litre racing unit.

Time passed, Brett's Sampson Special sixteen-cylinder was built and raced and faded away, and then for 1938 the AAA announced that Indianapolis rules were to be brought into line with Europe's Grand Prix Formula, and that eligible engines would be of up to three litres supercharged, or $4\frac{1}{2}$-litres unsupercharged. Brett now had a use for the old ex-Lockhart engine, and with backing from Alden Sampson he asked Leo Goossen to design him a chassis.

Brett had been in Europe in 1937 and he had seen the W125 Mercedes-Benz in action with its wishbone front suspension and torsion-bar suspended De Dion-axled rear end capable of transmitting much of its mighty excesses of power.

Goossen laid out a similar chassis, the first in America to use torsion bar suspension. The arched De Dion tube carried a ball stud at its centre, which rode in a vertical slot formed in the rear of the diff-housing. This allowed vertical movement of the wheels while tying them together laterally, and short universal-jointed half-shafts drove to them from the chassis-mounted diff.

The gearbox was in unit with the differential and both were dry-

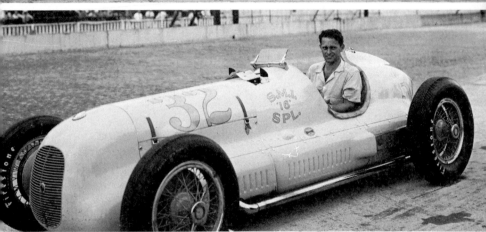

30, 31 The wreckage of Frank Lockhart's Stutz 'Black Hawk' record car after its first accident at Daytona, in 1928. After his second, fatal crash in this car, the twin-crank 3-litre V16-cylinder engine was stored for ten years before powering Bob Swanson's Sampson-owned 'SMI Special' at Indy in 1939.

32 A grim-faced Raymond Sommer takes the CTA-Arsenal out for a practice run at Lyon in 1947. It was a French national failure.

33 A rare photograph of the Dommartin, Emile Petit's 1948 resurrection of his mysterious 1934 SEFAC. Dommartin's publicity claimed 'abnormal' attributes – it was right.

34, 35 Maurice Trintignant in the Bugatti 251; on test at Entzheim Aerodrome and holding a vicious slide at Thillois Corner, Reims, during the 1956 French GP.

sumped and pressure-fed from a separate lubricant reservoir. Long, drilled radius arms ran forward from the wheel hubs to locate them fore and aft.

An engineer named Gordon Schroeder built the car with Brett and in the short space of five months they completed the chassis, modified the old engine in the light of modern experience and had it in race-worthy tune in time for the 1939 Indianapolis '500'.

The new 'SMI Special' was something new and unusually scientific in the American speedway world of the late thirties, and Sampson signed up Bob Swanson to drive it.

He qualified on the outside of the front row of the grid behind Jimmy Snyder and Lou Meyer with an average of 129.431mph. Unfortunately the back axle failed after only 19 laps, and Swanson later relieved Ralph Hepburn in the 'Hamilton-Harris Special'. On the 107th lap this car was involved in a multiple collision which killed Floyd Roberts (winner the previous year) and which put Swanson and Chet Miller in hospital for a long time.

In 1940 Swanson returned to the Speedway in the wailing sixteen-cylinder and this time round he had a steady run into sixth place, the last fifty laps of the race being run under a yellow caution flag due to falling rain. Later that year Swanson died in a midget car accident on the Fort Miami Speedway in Toledo, Ohio, and in 1941 Deacon Litz drove the Sampson 16, but slowly, and went out after 89 laps with some kind of oiling problem, being classified 22nd. That December saw Pearl Harbour.

With the return of peace in 1946 Indianapolis was revived, and in Los Angeles Gordon Schroeder wheeled out the sixteen-cylinder Sampson and fettled it up ready to race again. He attracted sponsor-ship from Spike ('Tea for Two', with raspberries and whistles) Jones, and hired Sam Hanks to drive the car at Indy as the 'Spike Jones Special'.

Hanks found it a very good-handling car, but with its centrifugal superchargers it was very docile and sluggish at low engine speeds and then the power came in at about 4,000rpm and it would sit-up and take-off like an artillery shell.

He qualified at a modest 124.762mph (Ralph Hepburn's Novi V8 having qualified quickest at no less than 133.944mph) but became an early retirement when that old lubrication problem reared its head again after only 18 laps. The car was classified 31st, and this was its last appearance in the '500'. Schroeder decided that the beautiful

H

beach car engine would have to be entirely redesigned to suit the different conditions of Speedway racing, and today the car and its historic engine are displayed in the Indianapolis Speedway Museum; Frank Lockhart's memory lives on, though in failure.

11

C'est pour la France –
National Racing Cars, 1934-1956

Motor racing was born in France. It began in a humble way with the Paris–Rouen Reliability Trial of 1894, and then came the Paris–Bordeaux–Paris race of 1895. The Automobile Club de France founded the Grand Prix in 1906. Motor racing meant much to the French, and it hurt their national pride when first Italy, and then Germany took dominance from them.

As the start of the 750 kilogramme Formula approached in the early thirties, strong rumours were filtering out of Germany concerning new and advanced Grand Prix cars of untold power and speed. In France the Bugatti works announced that they were retaining their beautiful Type 59 cars for their team's exclusive use, and private entrants despaired of finding a good car in their own country. Many went to Maserati at Bologna, and to a small faction in French racing this was a pitiable state of affairs. To put matters right they organised the construction of a radically new car to redress the balance.

The group included Raymond Sommer, the wealthy and capable racing driver; a youthful industrialist named André Parant; M. Raymond Brault; and designer Emile Petit, the man who had been responsible for Salmson's long and successful line of competition cars. They called themselves the *Société d'Etude et de Fabrication d'Auto-mobile de Course*, or SEFAC for short, and Petit laid out a most unusual engine design intended for a chassis being prepared by a colleague named Edmond Vareille.

In April 1934 details of this patriotic project were released under headlines such as 'The SEFAC Mystery Car', and it was revealed that Petit's Grand Prix engine was a 'parallel-eight' with two vertical banks of four cylinders arranged side by side with their individual crankshafts geared together and rotating in opposite directions to counter torque reaction.

The right-hand crankshaft drove a vast Petit-designed vane-type supercharger drawing from twin Solex carburettors, from its rear end, and a water pump from its front. This left the other crank to drive the four-speed Wilson pre-selector gearbox, which was of course offset to the left side of the car. This complicated system allowed the propeller shaft to pass along that side of the cockpit and enabled the driver's seat to be very low-mounted. This produced a nice low-slung profile, but made the car's centre-section unduly wide.

Each four-cylinder engine block showed great Salmson influence with twin overhead camshafts giving a semi-desmodromic (positive closing) action to the inclined valves. Gear-driven camshafts featured, with the exhaust shafts driving Vertex four-cylinder magnetos from their front ends, and there was one spark plug per cylinder. Vital dimensions were quoted as 68mm x 90mm, giving a swept volume of about 2,600cc. No claims were made for the engine's power output.

Vareille's chassis was a hefty channel-section structure with peculiar independent front suspension by long forward-facing radius arms with coil springing. The rigid rear axle was also coil-sprung and steering was by individual drag links to each front wheel. A boxy and decidedly ugly body-shell clothed the car, which sat low and heavy between its Rudge-type wire wheels. Petit made great play of some six-segment drum brakes he had designed for the car, and an entry was made for the French Grand Prix to be run on the Parisian Autodrome at Linas-Montlhéry.

The car failed to materialise, and was considered as something of a 'phantom' into 1935 when a public subscription was being raised in France in support of her *Grandes marques de course*—a list including Bugatti, Delage, Talbot, and Delahaye, with the SEFAC tacked on very much last—and least.

Another entry was made in the French Grand Prix, which was again being held at Montlhéry where the ACF stooped to the iniquitous practice of introducing tight straw-bale chicanes to slow down the German cars from Mercedes and Auto Union, and supposedly give Bugatti a chance.

This time the SEFAC actually appeared in practice, driven by Marcel Lehoux. This veteran Algerian driver had replaced Raymond Sommer who was long gone in search of a sensible Grand Prix ride.

Some modifications had been made to the car's prototype specification, with the engine enlarged to 70mm x 90mm to give a swept volume of 2,760cc, and with a French electro-magnetic Cotal gearbox in place of the original British-made unit.

The car was shrouded in secrecy at Montlhéry, with photographers being discouraged and reporters given non-committal answers. Lehoux drove it briefly in practice where it showed no great promise, and then the SEFAC entry was abruptly scratched from the race. The *pesage* had apparently revealed that it was 175kg *over* the maximum weight limit!

When Mercedes finished 1-2 in the Grand Prix the French press howled. 'Never Again' screamed their stentorian headlines; France had been made an international laughing stock, partly by the failure of Bugatti but particularly by the SEFAC's disgraceful withdrawal. They demanded that the growing national fund be used to build a really first-class Grand Prix car, or that international regulations should be changed and the French Grand Prix scrapped!

In 1936 and 1937 the ACF followed the latter course, running their race for sports cars only and seeing the Bugatti and Talbot works triumphing under the tricolour.

During this period the SEFAC was laid up, but in 1938 the AIACR introduced their new Grand Prix Formula which called for 3-litre supercharged or 4½-litre unsupercharged cars, the ACF revived their proper Grand Prix race on the very fast Rheims circuit, and Petit modified the old car to suit.

The SEFAC appeared at Rheims with a neat streamlined nose cowling which made a tiny attempt to present a more modern image, and Petit put sports car driver Eugène Chaboud behind the wheel. Even though the car was now four years old it was still shrouded in unusual security, and there were rumours that it had turned in some very fast laps during testing at Montlhéry. Nobody treated it very seriously when compared to the new V12 supercharged cars from Mercedes-Benz and Auto Union, and even a new single-seater Bugatti, but perhaps its weight of 931kg revealed at the *pesage* was illuminating in view of its sorry debut in previous years.

Chaboud actually started the race, from a poor grid position, but on the third lap the SEFAC expired in clouds of blue smoke out at La Garenne and was 'thought to have blown-up'. Petit's red-faced crew recovered the car before the race was finished, and were on their way home by the time Mercedes achieved their 1-2-3 finish.

Early in 1939 the SEFAC ran in the Pau Grand Prix, driven by another sports car man named Jean Trémoulet. Again, it failed to last the distance. An entry was made for the Grand Prix at Reims, but even the ACF were wise to the SEFAC and a note beside its name in the programme read dolefully, 'Départ Improbable'. The car failed to materialise.

Six years of war should perhaps have seen the end of this sad project, but in 1948 something familiar flitted across the pages of the motoring press. 'New French GP car—Unorthodox Design Has Duplex Engine Driving an Offset Propeller Shaft', read the headlines. It was named the Dommartin, and this company announced themselves as being dedicated to the construction of racing cars, aero engines and a new 500cc two-stroke air-cooled racing engine.

Emile Petit was named as designer of the new Dommartin Grand Prix car, which featured details transparently recognisable as his fourteen year-old SEFAC. It had a new bore and stroke of 80mm x 90mm to give a capacity of 3,619cc, but the parallel four-cylinder blocks, the contra-rotating crankshafts, semi-desmodromic valve gear and Cotal gearbox were all the same as in the thirties. Even the six-segment drum brakes were retained, described innocently by Dommartin's press release as having '. . . abnormal power, abnormal equality of force and abnormal cooling properties. . .' Yves Giraud-Cabantous was to drive the car, but perhaps thankfully it was never to appear.

In this final form as the Dommartin, the car carried quite an attractive sweeping single-seater body, but I believe the great lost hope of French motor racing rotted for years in a lock-up beneath the tall bankings at Montlhéry. It is now long gone from there, but whether scrapped or still in existence I have been unable to discover.

While the SEFAC became a designer's nightmare, the French still maintained a peculiarly Gallic ambition to produce a successful national racing car.

In 1946 the *Centre d'Etudes Techniques de l'Automobile et du Cycle* (or CTA for short) initiated design studies into what they described as a 'high-speed research vehicle'. They obtained a Government budget for the work and were given facilities in the state arsenal at Châtillon to construct the car.

CTA employed Albert Lory as designer, who had achieved undying fame in the twenties for his all-roller bearing straight-eight Delages which had totally dominated the 1½-litre Grand Prix Formula.

He decided to build another roller-bearing engine but this time chose the compact installation offered by a 90-degree V8 layout. He wanted to use very large diameter inlet valves and so chose iron block castings with non-detachable heads, since there would be no room for valve inserts in a similarly compact block if he had it cast in alloy.

Then the cylinder banks were staggered so that the big-end roller bearings could sit side-by-side on the crankshaft, which was itself carried in five roller-mains. There were two overhead camshafts per bank, driven by spur gears from the front of the crankshaft, and they actuated steeply inclined valves through short finger tappets. There were two spark plugs in each hemispherical combustion chamber, fired by twin BG magnetos driven from the inlet camshafts. BG, strangely, refused to guarantee their magnetos for engine speeds in excess of 6,000rpm, so Lory arranged a cut-out device to protect them from such dizzy heights.

Cylinder dimensions were 60mm x 65.6mm, giving a displacement of 1,482cc, and although no claims were made for power output it seems to have been around 266bhp at 7,500rpm – despite those magnetos.

Two-stage supercharging was used, with Roots same-size compressors at the front of the engine running at different speeds. Their combined boost was about 24psi and they drew mixture from a huge Solex carburettor bolted to the primary stage unit. Two long sweeping manifolds carried the charge into the middle of the engine vee.

Lory mounted his engine inclined rearwards at eight degrees in a simple welded chrome-steel tubular ladder frame. The driver sat astride the propeller shaft which dived down under his seat to a double-reduction back axle. Suspension was independent all round, with torsion bars mounted parallel to the chassis side members at the front and transverse at the rear. The wheels were carried on slides in railway-style axle boxes, which came as something of an eye-opener, and Lockheed two-leading shoe hydraulic drum brakes were fitted.

The whole assembly was clad in a very pretty slipper body, with a neat little radiator grille, tucked-down tail, low cockpit sides and a prominently fared head rest.

Raymond Sommer was to drive the new car, and in tests at Montlhéry early in 1947 he found it far from raceworthy although a rather non-committal mention was made of the CTA 'travelling at

124mph' at the Autodrome. Whether this applied to its maximum speed or its lap time round the speedbowl is not clear. In any case, Sommer thought it hopeless as a Grand Prix car and in need of considerable development.

Unfortunately CTA were under government pressure to make a showing in the ACF Grand Prix at Lyons, and again it was a case of an untried, undeveloped and complex racing car being forced to appear ahead of its time.

During practice the blue CTA-Arsenal was in all kinds of trouble. 'More bits seemed to be off the CTA on the Friday before the race than most people would regard as reasonable . . .' wrote one observer. It was still being bolted together!

Out on the circuit Sommer found it weaving badly on the straight, and freely admitted that it would finish only by a miracle in its present state.

On the line for the 34th *GP de l'ACF* Sommer watched the French tricolour raised, hesitate and fall. Clutches slammed home, wheels spun, tyres burned away along the road, obscuring the starting grid in clouds of acrid blue smoke.

As the smoke wafted away the CTA-Arsenal's pert shape could be seen dribbling to a halt. Sommer climbed out. Crestfallen mechanics inspected a snapped half-shaft, and the small crowd jeered France's latest national racing failure.

No more entries were made that year, although in November a CTA V8 engine was to be seen in the Grand Palais at the Paris Motor Show. The *Autocar* show report commented; 'France's national racing car, the CTA-Arsenal, is still very much in the development stage. So much is freely admitted by its sponsors. . . .'

Another car was completed at Châtillon, and both were entered in the 1948 French Grand Prix at Reims but were withdrawn on the first day of practice as being 'unready'.

That was the end of this extravagant piece of Gallic governmental enthusiasm, and CTA was reorganised to become the *Union Technique de l'Automobile et du Cycle* and occupied itself with more mundane matters.

Talbot-Lago eventually bought the cars, engines and what spares were available and they laid in the Suresnes works while the company's racing department toyed with development ideas and continued to race their own unsupercharged 4½-litre cars.

When Talbot-Lago felt the pinch and withdrew from racing the

CTA-Arsenals remained for years at Suresnes, and were finally abandoned in that famous store beneath the Montlhéry bankings. They were still in this kind of French racing Valhalla in the late fifties/early sixties but today only one car's whereabouts are known as it trails round the French motor museums, rather beaten and battered, and very sad.

As a postscript to the CTA-Arsenal's sad saga, it was Raymond Sommer who gave the famous 1½-litre centrifugally-supercharged V16 BRM its equally disastrous debut in the International Trophy meeting at Silverstone in August 1950. As Tazio Nuvolari dropped the flag to start the second heat, Sommer found the transmission gone in Britain's brand-new national hope, and was simply left motionless on the back row of the starting grid.

Not that Sommer should be regarded as a car breaker, for he was a driver of considerable stature who simply loved to have a go in anything unusual. It was in 1950 that he was awarded the French *Légion d'Honneur*, but tragically he lost his life late that season when his 1,100cc Cooper overturned in a minor race at Cadours. At the close of 1973 two more French drivers were awarded the *Légion*. Henri Pescarolo and Gerard Larrousse had played a major part in winning the World Championship of Makes for Matra-Simca; the team had considerable French Government backing, which had at last paid off.

Six years after the BRM's failure before disappointed British eyes, the French saw Bugatti's sorry final fling in Grand Prix racing.

In 1945 the return of peace to Europe found Bugatti's Molsheim works virtually untenable, and although the marque achieved instant success when Jean-Pierre Wimille won the first major postwar race in the Bois de Boulogne the story was almost at its end.

Ettore Bugatti died in 1947, leaving his son Roland to run the business. A half-hearted racing project resulted in the 1½-litre supercharged Bugatti Type 73C single-seater, which is now in Tom Wheatcroft's Donington Collection, housed on the site of Britain's prewar Grand Prix circuit and open to the public.

Then, in the early fifties, the fabled name of Bugatti began to be heard again in connection with Grand Prix racing. A new 2½-litre Formula was coming into effect in 1954, and persistent rumours filtered out of Alsace during that year, concerning goings on at Molsheim.

This project had been planned by Monsieur Boloré, the famous 'cigarette paper king' who had married Madame Bugatti and gained control over the company. The new Grand Prix car was to be an advanced and unusually sophisticated machine, acting as a prestige project with which Bugatti's re-entry into the quality high performance touring and sports car markets was to be identified.

The Molsheim works had been refurbished with the aid of the French railway company, whose oil engines were maintained there, and as the Indo-China war had flared towards its violent climax in the early fifties, Bugatti had existed largely on Government contracts to produce engines and parts for armoured fighting vehicles.

Work had started on the Grand Prix project in 1953, and the original programme called for the construction of six cars to be running during the following season. France's military reverse at the battle of Dien Bien Phu, and the subsequent partitioning of independent Vietnam on 22 July 1954, brought the Indo-China war to an end. This was received with relief by the people of France, but the inevitable cut-back in military expenditure hit Bugatti badly. Under former works driver Pierre Marco, the factory showed a £1,700,000 turnover in 1953, and now a major source of revenue had disappeared at a stroke. The Grand Prix project had swallowed £60,000 of hard-earned cash, and its future—before it had even run in anger—began to look sombre. However, work went ahead . . . though slowly, and development dragged on through 1955.

On 21 November 1955 members of the motoring press were invited to the bleak, windswept expanse of Entzheim aerodrome, close to the Bugatti factory, to see the radical new '251' Grand Prix car.

It was the work of Gioacchino Colombo, an ex-Alfa Romeo, Maserati and Ferrari engineer, who had laid out one of the first mid-engined Grand Prix cars since Cisitalia in the forties (see page 134), but with an added unique feature in that the engine was mounted *across* the frame.

The car shown that day at Entzheim was very much a prototype, intended more for development testing than for serious racing, and similarly its first engine was a test unit running in a very mild state of tune.

It was intended to prove the chassis design without niggling engine troubles causing delays. Once the chassis was considered ready to race then full competition versions of the unusual new engine could be prepared and installed.

Colombo's daring engine design had eight cylinders in line, arranged effectively as two four-cylinder units connected end to end. A train of gears ran from the division between the two crankshafts to provide drive to the gearbox and for the twin overhead camshafts. Each crank ran in five main-bearings, and Colombo contended that they could be bolted together in different planes to alter the engine's torque characteristics to match differing circuits. On a tight course such as Pau he could provide plenty of mid-range punch, while for a very fast course such as Reims or Spa the engine could produce the bulk of its power higher up the rev range.

Bore and stroke dimensions were 76mm x 68.5mm, providing a displacement of 2,430cc, and with twin plugs per cylinder and four Weber carburettors an early 7.5:1 compression engine was credited with 230bhp at 8,000rpm. Colombo predicted that a further developed 9:1 compression engine would be capable of 275bhp which would be very competitive with the contemporary Maseratis, Mercedes-Benz and Lancia-Ferraris.

Transmission was via a five-speed gearbox with Porsche-designed all-synchromesh internals. This in itself was prophetic, for the Matra-Simca team were to win Le Mans as recently as 1973 using similarly Porsche-devised gearboxes in their French-blue cars.

The gearbox and final drive were both mounted in unit with the engine to form a very compact assembly sitting ahead of the rear axle line. Each four-cylinder 'half' of the engine fed separate exhaust expansion boxes which then exhausted rearwards in single tail-pipes. On the front of the engine were two magnetos driven from the central gear-train, plus the Weber carburettor array which drew air from a large collector box formed beneath the head faring. Air entered a scoop just in front of the windscreen, then fed through two large-diameter flexible pipes which ran along either side of the cockpit into this collector box.

A lightweight multi-tubular spaceframe chassis was used, but true to Bugatti tradition it retained rigid axles at front and rear. Both were De Dion affairs, with the wheels joined by a lightweight hollow tube and located by twin radius rods—running to chassis pick-ups within the wheelbase—at either end.

Vertical push-rods rose from the De Dion tube at each hub, to operate rocker arms pivoted on the upper chassis rails. The inboard members of these arms actuated long suspension coil-springs inclined across the frame to mount on the lower chassis rail on the opposite side. This arrangement provided a kind of St Andrew's cross of suspension springs at either end of the frame, and was dictated by the mass of machinery occupying the areas normally reserved for mid-frame members which would serve to brace more conventional spring mounts.

The car's stumpy, tubby aspect was completed by its pannier fuel tanks slung between the wheels on either side of the chassis. This feature would maintain even handling characteristics as the fuel load was consumed. Bodywork was nicely formed from aluminium sheet, with a prominent head faring on the rear engine cover and large air scoops to duct cooling air onto the exhaust piping. A detachable access panel clipped onto the scuttle, and a full-width nose cowl carried a broad and attractively formed radiator air intake with a horseshoe motif carrying the famous 'EB' monogram.

Due to the unusual component layout radiator piping was difficult to devise, and Colombo ran coolant through the tubular chassis longerons. His car's nose cone carried cooling ducts for the front brakes, which he intended to be of disc type made by Bugatti, but this development ran out of time and ordinary two-leading shoe drums were finally fitted.

Meazza, racing director of Lancia's now-defunct racing division, was recruited by Colombo to organise the new Bugatti's initial test programme. Maurice Trintignant was signed up as works driver and in extensive tests at Entzheim he found the short prototype car quite a handful. An entry had been made for the 1956 *Grand Prix de l'ACF* at Reims in July and as the date approached Colombo's technical team felt the car was not really ready to race while Bugatti's management and publicity people insisted that it should, to keep faith with an expectant public.

Trintignant tested the prototype car at Reims a week before the race, but found little to lift the gloom now descending upon Bugatti whose overall financial position was in rapid decline.

Two Bugatti 251s arrived for the Grand Prix, the later car being hastily bolted together and featuring several detail modifications plus a longer wheelbase to provide improved stability.

Trintignant found the prototype car had terrific traction with so much of its weight on the driven wheels. It accelerated like a bullet out of the slow hairpin corners at Thillois and Muizon, but the front end tended to lift and wander and the steering felt very vague and failed to impart much confidence. There was also a lot of work to be done before the eight-cylinder engine would come up to scratch, and Trintignant's best time was 2 minutes 41.9 seconds compared to Fangio's pole position time in the Lancia-Ferrari V8 of 2 minutes 23.3 seconds.

Trintignant had the later engine from the second chassis installed in his familiar prototype frame overnight, and in the race he was trundling round at the back of the field when he found the throttle beginning to stick and came into the pits. The mechanics found that the carburettor air-box had forced dust and grit into the delicate throttle mechanism and so the car was withdrawn.

Bugatti took the two cars back to Molsheim where a further development programme was planned, but before this could come about the company ran out of money, and various internal political problems called a halt to the racing programme.

Colombo's two 'cross-engine' cars were never raced again, and when the Molsheim works was cleared they were auctioned and bought—I believe by Bugatti enthusiast Fritz Schlumpf for his vast private collection at Malmerspach. They are still there today— France's final fling in the era when good Grand Prix cars had their engines in the front, and national colours meant something in inter-national motor racing.

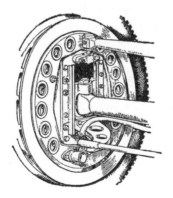

The unusual—and—unsuccessful—suspension arrangement designed for the CTA-Arsenal.

12

Odd Things from Alfa –
Italy, 1938-1953

Twin and single-crank V16s, Italian versions of the Auto Union, aerodynamic sports-racing coupés and Grand Prix cars with the driver riding behind the back wheels—these are some of the unusual and interesting designs which flooded from Alfa Romeo's prolific racing shops in this period.

In 1938, by decree of Ugo Gobbato—Director-General of Alfa Romeo—Scuderia Ferrari relinquished control of Alfa's racing programme to a new organisation known as Alfa Corse. It was formed out of the old Scuderia, and Enzo Ferrari himself stayed on as manager for a short while before moving on to form Auto Avio Costruzioni – the forerunner of his postwar success. Alfa Corse were based in the old Scuderia works in Modena until early in 1939, when they moved to brand new premises in Milan.

Vittorio Jano had left to join Lancia, and the Spanish engineer Wilfredo Ricart was now design director. He had run his own Ricart and Ricart-España companies in Spain before coming to Alfa Romeo via Nacional, and he had a good team working with him including Gioacchino Colombo, and Luigi Bazzi of 'Bimotore' fame.

The new three-litre supercharged Grand Prix Formula came into effect in 1938 and Alfa Corse attacked it with eight twelve and sixteen-cylinder designs while mounting a serious assault on Italy's own 1½-litre supercharged Voiturette class. Here at least they stood every chance of winning, and late in 1937 Ferrari had laid-down basic specification for what was to become the immortal 'Alfetta'.

Colombo produced this Tipo 158 design, and for his sixteen-cylinder Grand Prix engine Ricart decided to adopt the Voiturette blocks, cranks, rods, pistons and valves, mounted in two sets on a common casing with the crankshafts coupled to form a sixty-degree vee. Bore and stroke were identical to the basic 158 at 58mm x 70mm, but while this unit was being assembled the first Voiturette engine was test-bed run and found to produce about 180bhp at 6,500rpm. This doubled-up to give the new 2,958cc sixteen a potential output of only 360bhp which was clearly going to be no match for the German Mercedes and Auto Unions which were to exceed 400bhp. After some development the straight-eight engine gave 195bhp at 7,000rpm, but still the doubled-up engine would be hard-pressed to better 390bhp.

Alfa Corse pressed on, with detail design in the hands of Alberto Massimino, and their first twin-crank V16 ran on the test bed in January 1938. It was quickly pronounced raceworthy, and installed in a new low-chassis car with independent suspension all round by coil-springs and low-pressure damper units at the front, and transverse leaf-spring at the rear with swinging half-axles and a four-speed gearbox in unit with the final drive.

The new Alfa Romeo 316 scaled 2,030lbs and it was tested at Monza late in April and entered for the Tripoli Grand Prix on May 15. Clemente Biondetti was to drive it and he lapped the Mellaha at 136.75mph in practice only to find his car's new engine persistently overheating. The 316 had to be withdrawn from the race, and lay fallow in the works at Modena while the 158 made its startlingly successful Voiturette debut in mid-season.

Come the autumn and two 316s were hastily prepared to show the flag in the Italian Grand Prix at Monza. Giuseppe Farina joined Biondetti to drive them, and while the German armada uncharacteristically broke up, Farina came home second to Nuvolari's Auto Union with Biondetti fourth.

Alfa Corse laid plans for a six-car fleet of 316s for the 1939–40 season, but only the Belgian Grand Prix saw the twin-crank car run again and this time with an unusual and ugly streamlined body in place. Farina was the driver and he actually led away from the start in a superb burst of Latin enthusiasm, but despite low mist and rain the German cars could use their power and Dick Seaman pulled well ahead in his Mercedes Benz and was miles in the lead when he suffered his fatal accident. Farina had fallen back in the field when the 316's supercharger drive failed, and the outbreak of war in September was to put an end to further development.

Meanwhile, Ricart's department had laid out a completely new

Grand Prix design with a 135-degree V16-cylinder single-crankshaft engine. Its cylinder dimensions were 'square' at 62mm x 62mm to give a displacement of 2,995cc, and there were twin overhead camshafts per bank operating four valves per cylinder. Ricart made extensive use of lightweight elektron alloy in the crankcase, and added aluminium cylinder banks with steel liners.

The crankshaft ran in ten main-bearings and carried its con-rods on roller big-ends, while the camshaft drive train came from the centre of the engine and doubled up to power two-stage Roots-type superchargers for each bank. These four compressors drew mixture from two triple-choke Weber carburettors. There were similarly duplicated magnetos to spark eight plugs each and five pumps pressured and scavenged the engine's oil, fed from a 42-litre tank.

This monster was bench-tested in November 1939 and was found to produce 490bhp at 7,800rpm. Ricart was aiming for 560-590bhp at over 8,000rpm, but this was sufficient to start with!

Consequently the big V16 with its mass of ancillaries was installed in a welded-up tubular ladder frame chassis, with similar independent front suspension to the 316 but a De Dion set-up replacing the old transverse leaf-spring at the rear. Torsion bars were used to spring this axle, and the car was clad in a very attractive bodyshell closely resembling the 'Alfetta' Voiturette.

The new 162's vital statistics included a wheelbase of 8ft 7¼ins, front track 4ft 6ins, rear track 4ft 8¼ins and a dry weight of 2,370lbs. It carried 68 gallons of fuel in a tail and two pannier tanks, and Alfa Corse's founder Ugo Gobbato ordered that six cars should be built for the 1940 season.

Despite the outbreak of war Alfa Corse's development went on at Portello, Milan, and the prototype 162 was rolled out on 18 April 1940. Attilio Marinoni, the pop-eyed chief tester who had three consecutive race wins in the gruelling Spa 24-hours to his credit, gave the bare chassis its basic shake-down on a closed section of the Milan–Gallarate autostrada.

Everything appeared to operate satisfactorily, and further autostrada tests in May convinced Ricart and his engineers that they had the equal of anything the Germans possessed. There was more testing in June but suddenly Mussolini entered the war on the side of the Axis and a halt was called to further development. The 162 never had a chance to demonstrate its paces in public, or to run in anger.

There was a sequel to the big sixteen's story, as before Alfa Romeo

36 The works mock-up of Alfa Romeo's projected Tipo 162 GP car. It was to use a 3-litre 16-cylinder engine with four superchargers, giving a projected 590bhp.

37 Alfa's 316 twin-crankshaft V16 engine was raced in 1938-39, but the planned six-car team was never completed.

38 Italy's Auto Union — the flat-12 1.5-litre engined 512 was intended for Grand Prix racing in 1941 . . .

39 'Like a plump country chicken . . .' – the 1939 Gulf-Miller four-wheel drive car with George Bailey at the wheel and Harry Miller alongside. The bulbous, exposed fuel tanks ruptured in poor Bailey's fatal crash here at Indianapolis in 1940.

40 George Barringer's modified 1941 version, during qualifying at the Speedway.

41 The incredible Porsche-designed flat-12 Cisitalia.

began to concentrate on military contracts Ricart ran a study on aerodynamic sports car construction starting in January 1941.

He outlined a scheme for a mid-engined sports coupé fitted with a very lightweight aerodynamic bodyshell and powered by an unsupercharged version of the big three-litre 162 engine. Colombo detailed the design, and produced a tubular chassis frame clad in a very thin and light aluminium alloy streamlined shell. It had two doors and side-by-side seating, while the 162's front suspension was adopted with a De Dion system at the rear using coil-springs in place of the Grand Prix car's torsion bars. Experiments were made to adapt the engine to eight twin-choke carburettors, in which state of tune it was expected to produce at least 240bhp. One engine was test-run sometime in 1941 and returned only 190bhp at 7,400rpm but it was thought there was more to come.

Progress was slow with no competition calendar to force development, and the coupé was almost complete by the end of 1942. The following year saw Italy's position in the war becoming perilous and the Alfa Corse shop was closed down, and all its cars, spares and plant were taken into the hills northeast of Milan and walled up for safe-keeping in a remotely situated cheese factory!

There they survived intact but the move had come too late for the prototype 162 and at least one of the 316s for they were destroyed by Allied bombing of the Portello works. The engine of Farina's Italian Grand Prix 316 survived and is in Alfa's wonderful museum today, while the hulk of the 163 coupé was unfortunately and inexplicably scrapped as late as 1953.

Meanwhile, Portello had been working hard on other projects— the most daring of which was the 1½-litre supercharged flat-twelve Tipo 512.

Gobbato had directed Ricart to produce an advanced concept car for the 1½-litre supercharged Grand Prix Formula which was confidently expected to replace the three-litre regulations in 1941. The Italian teams of Alfa Corse and Maserati had been securely complacent in their Voiturette class until Tripoli in 1939 when Mercedes-Benz suddenly arrived with two completely unheralded 1½-litre W165 versions of their all-conquering Grand Prix machines.

Driven by Lang and Caracciola the two tiny V8 cars simply ran away and hid from the chastened Italians. Auto Union were also known to be working on a 1½-litre project, and this thought gave the directors of Alfa Romeo considerable cause for trepidation.

I

At Portello development followed three avenues of approach. One was to apply two-stage supercharging to the normal Alfetta. Another was the design of a new rear-engined chassis which placed the engine more or less over the driven wheels and so reduced the tendency to spin the rear wheels which had troubled the lightweight front-engined cars. Thirdly, a flat-twelve cylinder engine was to be designed and built.

Once again Colombo was entrusted with the detail design, and he used a bore and stroke of 54 x 54.2mm which would give the new engine $42\frac{1}{2}$ square inches of piston area against 41 square inches for the W165 Mercedes-Benz and a modest 29 for the English ERAs which were still competing.

The Auto Union $1\frac{1}{2}$-litre V12 project was known to have had 9,000 rpm as its target crankshaft speed. It was to have had cylinder dimensions of 53 x 56mm and with a supercharger pressure of 28psi it was intended to produce no less than 327bhp!

Clearly the straight-eight Alfetta engine was going to be outclassed with only 225bhp at 7,600rpm. So Colombo set about his new design and he departed considerably from former Alfa Romeo practice by dropping the integral cylinder blocks and heads as on the 158 and instead used separate heads and new-type valves with finger rockers and hairpin valve springs.

The main crankcase-cum-block casting was split on its vertical centreline and was also formed in separate three-cylinder units per bank. A gear-train taken from the clutch end of the engine drove twin overhead camshafts per bank, and the crankshaft itself ran in eight main bearings – seven of them needle roller type and one of plain white metal. Needle-roller big-end bearings were used.

At the other end of the engine there were power take-offs to drive the two-stage superchargers and magnetos, which were mounted on top of the unit and so spoiled any idea of using its low profile to build a nice, low-slung motor car.

Colombo used Bosch magnetos, similar to those seen on the W165 Mercedes-Benz, and between the magneto mounts there passed a drive shaft which ran to the small secondary compressor of the supercharger system. Another drive was taken from the back end of this compressor's input lobe to power the larger primary blower, which had to be offset to the right-side of the engine to preserve its correct direction of rotation. On top of this compressor there sat a huge triple-choke Weber carburettor.

Complete with all ancillaries the new flat-twelve scaled 449lbs, which was less than the Alfetta unit it was to replace but it is worthwhile remembering that it was still vastly overweight compared to Zerbi's Fiat 806 twelve-cylinder of thirteen years before!

The engine was bench-tested with a 6.6:1 compression and 32psi supercharge, and returned a flash reading of 370bhp at 9,000rpm and an average of 335bhp at 8,600rpm. It was beyond sight of Auto Union's targets, and that was considered a triumph.

Meanwhile the mid-engined chassis had been prepared, and this naturally owed a lot to Auto Union practice, particularly of the 1934–37 period, for the fuel tank was located squarely amidships, forming round the driver's seat back. This feature forced the driver far forward into the nose, a driving position which had long been blamed for the Auto Union's notoriously difficult handling. It was said that the driver was always one step behind in sensing an incipient tail-slide, but with 600 horsepower being applied to swing-axle rear suspension I think the car would have been a handful wherever the driver was posted.

Alfa adopted another Auto Union feature in placing their five-speed gearbox outboard, behind the back axle unit, and they based the whole car on a very narrow twin-tube ladder frame with very Teutonic-style elliptical-section main longerons.

The 512 featured the first pure wishbone front suspension system to appear in a GP Alfa Romeo, and at the rear a De Dion system was used with a Watt linkage locating the beam laterally and two massive drilled radius arms running rearwards from the hubs to pick-up on a frame extension around the gearbox.

Link systems at front and rear operated longitudinal torsion bar springing, and three leading shoe drum brakes were mounted all round.

Workmanship on the 512 was of a very high order, with the front wishbones immediately catching the eye. The car was clad in a striking but bulbous light alloy bodyshell, incorporating an immediately identifiable grille design and with a high headrest behind the far-forward cockpit, faring into a spine over the engine cover and down onto the flat, louvred tail section.

Development of the car dragged on through 1942 with Italy getting deeper into the war, and yet Alfa Corse still found time for testing in 1943! Some of the trials were made on an empty autostrada during a formal visit to the works by King Michael of Rumania, and then it was taken to Monza where several established Alfa drivers tried it.

Reports vary as to how it behaved, although Carlo Pintacuda has been quoted as having been 'lyrical about its road manners and general manoeuvreability. . . .'. Sadly, it could still be pushed too far, for I believe Attilio Marinoni was killed in a 512 during a test.

However, the rear-engined car was among those walled into the famous cheese factory, and in 1946 Alfa Romeo announced full details of the car to a surprised motoring world. While their 158–159A cars totally dominated Grand Prix racing in the late forties it was often said 'Just you wait until they're beaten—they'll bring out the 512'. They maintained their unbeaten record until 1951, and *never* brought out the 512.

Colombo had joined Ferrari and given them a 60-degree Vee version of his flat-twelve with which they made their GP debut.

The Alfettas had a considerable fight on their hands to stave off the Colombo-designed supercharged V12 Ferraris, and with the threat of the Cisitalia-Porsche being bandied about it was perhaps obvious to Alfa Romeo that some others had done their sums equally well. So they concentrated on the lengthy development of the straight-eight design which had started the whole thing—remember the twin-crank sixteen-cylinder of 1938?—and when finally beaten in 1951 they hung on until Juan-Manuel Fangio had won his first World Championship and then retired gracefully from the scene.

It was rumoured that the flat-twelve engine had been tried at some time in the front of an Alfetta, but that it had upset the weight distribution to such an extent that the chassis could not easily be tuned to compensate.

Then in 1953–54, with a new 2½-litre Grand Prix Formula on the way, it was said that Alfa had been testing at Monza with a brand new flat-twelve 2½-litre engine mounted in a sports-racing chassis.

It seems that this was a development of the 512 unit, with a bore and stroke of 68 x 57mm and twin overhead camshafts per bank gear-driven from a roller-bearing Hirth-type built-up crankshaft. The block was very light, being cast in magnesium alloy, like the contemporary Sacha-Gordine (see page 139) in France.

The company intended to use this engine in a remarkable large diameter backbone-chassised single-seater. The engine seems to have been a stressed member, carrying a bridge-piece to which coil-and-wishbone front suspension was attached, while a De Dion back axle was suggested, similarly coil-suspended and located fore and aft by long radius arms which swept back from pick-ups mid-way along the central backbone. Schematic drawings were issued, showing a complex four-wheel drive transmission, apparently with a dog-clutch to disengage the front-drive system as the driver saw fit.

The bodywork was very low and sleek, and formed into a cockpit behind the back axle with the driver sitting in a shaped fuel tank-cum-tail section!

I believe that one of the Alfettas was lashed-up with a prototype dragster-style cockpit, cantilevered out behind the back axle for driver-acceptance trials. This was not the first time such an unusual arrangement had been used in a racing car, for at Brooklands in 1924 Ernest Eldridge had evolved a similarly uncomfortable-looking seating position in his 949cc Gwynne.

Consalvo Sanesi, mechanic turned works Alfetta driver, tested the mock-up car at Monza and despite acute discomfort in a turbulent slipstream which tore his goggles off he found the whole unlikely set-up remarkably controllable and lapped in very respectable times.

Alfa Romeo had already established their reputation and were rapidly developing into prestige car manufacturers of a very high order. If they were to return to racing they would have to return with something good. Evidently this projected Tipo 160 was not quite good enough for it largely remained a paper project . . . the last of Alfa's little-known single-seaters.

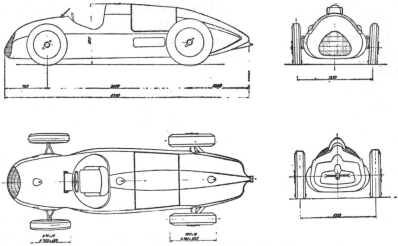

Alfa Romeo's 'Auto-Union': the Tipo 512.

13

Harry Miller's Last Fling –
Indianapolis, 1938-1948

After the disastrous failure of Miller-Tucker Incorporated's 1935 Indy programme with the flat-head Fords, Harry Miller was in the wilderness. When the AAA adopted European-style Grand Prix regulations for the Indianapolis '500' in 1938 they opened the flood-gates to invention and non-comformity, and Miller's ageing, often deeply unhappy, yet staggeringly fertile mind snapped back into gear.

In March he arrived at the Speedway with the first unit of a planned five-car fleet, an aluminium-coloured front-engined 'four' as slim and upright as his Ford cars had been low-slung and rectangular three years before.

His new car's engine was a 3,778cc unsupercharged four-cylinder with bore and stroke of 108 x 114.3mm, allegedly producing 225bhp at 4,500rpm. It was mounted in a 95-inch wheelbase, rear-wheel drive chassis, and in original form cooling was arranged through a system of fine tubes woven around the arching, streamlined nose cone.

Test sessions with Billy Winn in the cockpit soon saw this changed in favour of more normal radiators, mounted flush with the bonnet *sides*. Streamlined outrigged fuel tanks mounted on either side within the wheelbase were a feature, while suspension was independent all round on a system similar to the '35 Fords and Miller used four-wheel disc brakes. There were hydraulic driver-adjustable dampers with a control on the dashboard (31 years before McLaren arrived at the Speedway for optimistic testing of a similar system!) and since the regulations demanded onboard self-starters and Miller didn't favour the weight of conventional automotive types, the engine was fired by an aircraft-type Coffmann cartridge starting device.

Another of these cars appeared at the Speedway later that spring, but already they were of no interest to their designer, his butterfly mind having conceived of a more advanced idea into which he threw all his energies.

The 'fours' were not to qualify as the old man concentrated on his other car, a car which many 'railbirds' saw as his ultimate heresy. It was a design hailed in Britain by the headlines 'America Builds an Auto Union'.

Like Lee Oldfield's 1937 special, the new Miller had a mid-mounted engine behind the cockpit and all-independent suspension, but it added four-wheel drive, a canted engine installation, well oversquare short-stroke engine dimensions in a manner prophetic of all modern high-performance engines, side fuel tanks to promote consistent handling, and again there were disc brakes on all four wheels . . . It was a technical *tour de force*, but again it was too far ahead of its time.

Miller had put his scheme before the Gulf Oil Corporation, and they had sponsored his translation of these striking ideas into metal. Four cars were being built at Gulf's Harmarville, Pennsylvania, research centre when the prototype made its Indy debut.

Gulf intended the cars to publicise the efficacy of their 81-octane No-Nox Ethyline petrol and Gulfpride oil, and although Ralph Hepburn did some laps at the Speedway that year he was too late, the car was not properly developed (again) and he failed to qualify.

In this original form the Gulf-Miller had twin overhead camshafts, and bore and stroke dimensions of 89.1 x 79.6mm, giving a displacement of 2,957.9cc. A twin-intake centrifugal supercharger was used, running at 4.8-times engine speed and giving 20lbs boost. It was mounted behind the rear final drive unit, in the car's tail, while the whole six-cylinder engine was itself offset $3\frac{3}{4}$ inches in the frame and inclined at 45 degrees to lower the centre of gravity.

This feature also served to place the exhaust ports on the upper face of the engine, on the car's centreline, and tall curving manifolds fed into an unusual exhaust system. Air inlets let into the body just aft of the cockpit fed into a large diameter collector funnel which accelerated the air through a fat pipe into which the manifolds led, so providing an extractor effect. The tail pipe terminated in a deep fishtail forming a vertical slot in the car's tail through which the gases escaped.

Transmission was taken from the front of the engine via a short propeller shaft to a four-speed gearbox centrally mounted beneath the driver's feet. This was somewhat reminiscent of Bugatti practice in earlier years.

The gearbox drove almost directly to a front final-drive unit coupled through jointed half-shafts to the wheels, and there was a second propeller shaft driving back from the gearbox parallel to the primary shaft and then passing alongside the engine to a lockable rear differential. All four wheels were independently sprung by transverse leaf springs, tucked neatly away inside hingeing streamlined farings.

Miller's disc brakes were not of the familiar modern calliper type, but resembled a conventional transmission clutch in that a ring of friction material was forced hydraulically against a steel disc, the whole assembly being housed in a static drum carrying extensive cooling fins.

Once again a Coffmann starter was used to save a little weight and every major mechanical component on the car was lavishly supplied with cooling fins.

Bulbous aluminium fuel tanks hung pannier fashion on either side of the car, and if only it had two-wheel drive it would have looked as fierce and potent as Europe's Auto Unions. Unfortunately, the necessity to seat the driver above fore-and-aft transmission lines pushed him well into the air, and with sixteen inch wheels giving the car a giant ground clearance it looked instead like a plump country chicken sitting contentedly on a clutch of eggs.

Tazio Nuvolari, newly signed for Auto Union, was in America at the time and expressed himself most impressed by the new Miller— despite its non-qualification.

But there were some penalties. It was a heavyweight at 2,155lbs, and the six-cylinder engine produced only 245bhp at 6,400rpm while Miller's own four cylinders (now built and developed by Offenhauser) were good for 300bhp. Gulf's standard petrol was the trouble, for their publicity campaign naturally fought shy of the alcohol brews being used in competitive Offy-engined cars.

Despite the rush to get one car to Indy, and then the rebuff of having it not qualify, Miller had another chance, and in the latter part of the season there was considerable European speculation on Gulf-Miller shipping a team to Europe to enter Grand Prix racing. It came to nothing, perhaps mercifully in view of their minuscule power output, and then in 1939 a full team of three Gulf-Millers entered for the '500'.

Drivers were listed as George Barringer, Zeke Meyer and George Bailey, and they settled down to the task of learning all about four-wheel drive. Barringer was given a salutary lesson when his car got away from him in practice, spun like a top and thundered into the retaining wall, rupturing one of those vulnerable pannier tanks. He was very lucky to escape as the Gulf-Miller burned to a crisp.

With the sight of that huge, glittering fireball in his mind Meyer failed to qualify, and so it was left to Hudson works tester George Bailey to put a Gulf-Miller in the race—averaging an unabashed 125.821mph to qualify eighth quickest in the field of 33. Unfortunately, only 47 race laps were enough for the car, which retired with valve trouble to classify 26th.

Going into 1940 Harry Miller was a sick man. The relative failure of his latest designs didn't help him, a casual thorn prick on his face was slowly developing a killing cancer, his heart was ailing, he was diabetic . . . but he still had good friends and followers and one of them—Eddie Offutt—entered his four-wheel drive cars in 1940.

Now the luck really ran out, for in practice brave George Bailey put in a very fast lap at 128.5mph, then tried perhaps too hard, lost control, careened into the retaining wall and was killed as the Gulf-Miller's fuel tanks again burst and the wreck burned out.

There were only two cars surviving now, and in an attempt to salvage something from the project Gulf took George Barringer to Utah for an attempt on the International Class D (2–3 litre) records.

His car behaved itself, bellowing round a long circular course laid out on Bonneville Salt Flat's glaring surface for about four hours and smashing 14 World records in the process.

Barringer's figures included 158.446mph for the flying five kilometres, 150.242 miles in the hour, and the 500-miles Indy distance at 142.779mph. They shattered the existing records by an average of some 20mph, but it was all relatively meaningless, for there was not the public attention focused on Bonneville which Gulf had been courting in Indiana.

There was to be one last try at the world's richest race, and in 1941 the four-wheel drive Millers were back at the Speedway with the happy Bonneville outing beneath their belt. After the fiery disasters of the two proceeding years the AAA had banned exposed pannier tanks, and the cars were modified with bulky box-section side frames of stainless steel, carrying two internal fuel tanks on either side cushioned by felt pads.

George Barringer and one-legged Al Miller (no relation) drove the cars, and for the first time both qualified, in 14th and 15th positions with Miller quicker at 123.478mph.

Still fate took a hand. . . .

On race morning Barringer's mechanics were fuelling his car in the garage block when there was a terrifying flash of flame and the car began to blaze furiously! Sparks from a welding torch in an adjoining garage had ignited fumes drifting along the block, and while the Miller crew beat a hasty exit there was a mad panic as cars were wheeled out of the blazing area, boxes of spares and stacks of tyres were salvaged and the fire-fighters went to work.

When the blaze was quelled fourteen garages had been reduced to smouldering heaps of rubble, as had Barringer's car and two others which had failed to qualify. Thousands of dollars' worth of tools and tyres and spares had also gone up in smoke. The Miller luck, they said. . . .

The start was delayed for an hour, but Gulf's shocked crew were able to bring Al Miller to the line in their lone surviving car. He ran quickly in tenth place for 25 miles but then the six-cylinder engine began to misfire, he stopped twice for plugs and finally went out with the gearlever seized solid after 22 laps. That was virtually the end of the story. Seven months later came Pearl Harbour.

Harry Miller died during the war, in 1943, a broken and dispirited old man but a colossal figure in motor racing history. The Indianapolis '500' was revived in 1946, and a four-wheel drive Miller was on the grid once more.

Faithful George Barringer was the driver, and the car was entered by Harry Miller's old associate Preston T. Tucker, of Ypsilanti, Michigan. He named his car the 'Tucker Torpedo Special' to publicise his latest promotion; an utterly revolutionary American saloon car.

He had gathered together some of the American industry's most imaginative engineering brains and amassed impressive financial backing for the innovative new Tucker Torpedo. The car was to have a rear-mounted flat-six engine of no less than 589 cubic inches (or $9\frac{3}{4}$ litres!), with hydraulically actuated valves, a sealed cooling system, torque converter transmission, all-independent suspension, disc brakes and such forward-thinking safety features as a pop-out windscreen and breakaway driving mirror. Tucker had extensive crash padding built in to form a 'crash basement' into which the occupants could dive in emergency but only after his publicity agents had advised him against fitting seat belts (remember this is 1946!) on grounds of 'bad customer psychology . . .'.

At Indy, Barringer succeeded in putting his Tucker Torpedo *née* Gulf-Miller in the field at an average of 120.628mph, but after 27 laps he was out with transmission trouble for a miserable 29th place overall. It was poor Barringer's last Indy ride, for he was killed in September that year at Lakewood Speedway, Atlanta.

In 1947 Tucker persuaded Al Miller to give the nearly ten-year old car another try, and he got into the '500' at 124.848mph, and was out after 33 laps with magneto failure—placing 25th. In 1948 the old car was out one more time, and during its qualifying attempt it came cannonballing down the main straightaway when a con-rod snapped, exploded its way out of the engine in a spectacular shower of flying white hot fragments, and with a streaming trail of smoke and steam to mark its passing the Miller fishtailed to a halt with all four wheels locked solid. The dream was over.

Tucker's dream went the same way on 3 March 1949, when his Torpedo works were put under distraint by Federal trustees. In October he was charged with conspiracy to defraud, and the ensuing four-year battle which eventually proved his innocence took its toll of his health and reputation and killed the Torpedo stone dead. He died, another unhappy, unfortunate man, in 1956. Few people recall his name.

14

The Postwar Auto Unions –
Europe, 1946-1953

While the Tucker Torpedo, the Fageol Twin-Coach and the Spike Jones Special were being campaigned at Indianapolis, the CTA-Arsenal was being planned in Paris, and Alfa Romeo were blowing brick-dust and cheese rinds off their Alfettas at Portello, 'something big' was stirring in Turin.

That 'something' was the growing Cisitalia company, founded by Commendatore Piero Dusio. He had been Italy's champion amateur racing driver prewar with a blown 2.5-litre Alfa Romeo and he was a capable and astute businessman in addition to being a great racing enthusiast.

After the war ended in 1945, Dusio rightly calculated that the European public would be thirsty for any kind of sporting spectacle. He gauged the time to be right for the production of a cheap but efficient proprietary racing car.

He approached Dante Giacosa, designer of Fiat's famous Topolino, to devise him a car which must be capable of being built very quickly, and in large numbers.

Giacosa immediately decided to use the Fiat 1,100 production engine, and modified it to produce 60bhp in place of its normal 32 and then converted it to dry-sump lubrication so that it could be mounted lower in the frame.

This frame was one of the earliest multi-tubular spaceframes—pre-dated in racing by the Trossi-Monaco already examined—and prompted both by Giacosa's aviation experience and by the fact that Dusio had a clandestine source of otherwise almost unobtainable chrome-molybdenum tubing!

Giacosa grafted Topolino front and rear suspensions onto this tubular structure, added a double-reduction back axle to drop the propeller shaft low down beneath the driver's seat, and then clad the whole thing in a neat slipper body.

Although the car would be hopelessly out-gunned on fast circuits it would be a fine competitor on tight, twisty courses, and in any case Dusio was planning a 'Cisitalia Circus' in which the top drivers of the day could compete against one another exclusively in his tiny new racing cars.

Dusio engaged Piero Taruffi as test driver, and the Cisitalia D46 was soon in full production with orders flooding in. Dusio himself won an early D46 race at Turin's Valentino Park in which Nuvolari competed and walked home waving his steering wheel which had come off in his sinewy hands.

The Cisitalias raced everywhere around the Mediterranean, even making one abortive sortie into Egypt. Giacosa was commissioned to build a two-seater sports version, with which Nuvolari very nearly won the 1947 Mille Miglia, and Dusio became acknowledged as one of the new lions of Italian motor racing. These successes were all grist to the mill, for he already had a Grand Prix project under way, and for his design he had gone to the very top—to the Porsche Design Office.

After severing his connections with Auto Union in 1937, old Dr Porsche had been responsible for many Nazi projects although he was a completely apolitical animal, the complete engineer, immersed in his work.

He had perfected the original Volkswagen 'people's car', and for Daimler-Benz he had designed an aero-engined $2\frac{3}{4}$-ton six-wheeled record car with which Hans Stuck was intended to attack the world's Land Speed Record at Bonneville. The war put paid to these German plans to achieve 400mph on land, and the car is now engineless and bitter in the Unterturkheim museum of Daimler-Benz.

During the war Porsche's military designs included the vicious Tiger tank and the Ferdinand SP gun, and culminated in the ultimate land tank—the Mouse. This behemoth was a terrestrial battleship, weighing 180 tons, carrying 250mm armour and packing an 18cm artillery piece. It was so heavy there were no military bridges which could carry it, so Porsche blandly waterproofed the thing for a depth of forty feet and enabled it to wade any river. Porsche's Stuttgart office also designed military and agricultural tractors at this time, and then came Germany's military collapse and orders to move the office to Gmünd in Austria.

After the occupation, the 70-year-old Dr Porsche and his son Ferry were held on their estate at Zell-am-See while Chief Engineer Karl Rabe held the business together in Gmünd. In June 1945 the old man was taken to Hessen for interrogation by the Americans, and later that year the French took him, Ferry and son-in-law Dr Piëch to Baden-Baden. They wanted the family to cooperate in the design of a French people's car, and took them to Paris where Renault were developing their 4CV.

Meanwhile Louise Piëch – the Doctor's daughter – and Rabe kept the business going by repairing VWs, while news came from France that the three senior executives had been interned. In response to chivalrous appeals from Raymond Sommer and the French motoring journalist Charles Faroux, the two younger men were shortly set free and returned to Zell-am-See.

While this was going on, Dusio had travelled to Austria to see Rabe, and had signed a contract with him for four Cisitalia designs. They were to be the Porsche type 323 11hp tractor, the Type 370 1,500cc sports car, the Type 385 water turbine and the Type 360 Grand Prix car.

Dusio attached top priority to the GP design, allowing only three months for the schematic drawings to be finalised and planning to complete the prototype by September 1947. He demanded assurances that the Doctor's absence in internment at Dijon would not delay development, and that the office did *not* have the 1½-litre Auto Union stashed away somewhere, ready to bring out in competition at a later date!

He was assured on both counts, and his fat cheque was used by Ferry Porsche to meet the savage ransom being demanded by the French authorities for his father's release. In August 1947 Dr Porsche was in Austria, giving his approval to Rabe's plans for the new car, but in postwar Europe there was no way the prototype could be completed and running by that September.

Despite the shortages and delays in gaining clearance for even the most mundane functions, Rabe's design team had laid down a bold Grand Prix car, bristling with unusual features.

It was to have a horizontally-opposed twelve cylinder engine, with 56 x 55.5mm bore and stroke to produce a displacement of 1,492.6cc. In Italy Gioacchino Colombo was at this time laying out his 1½-litre supercharged Ferrari V12 engine, which was to introduce similarly 'oversquare' engine dimensions into Grand Prix racing for the first time since 1907, at the end of which season cylinder bores had been limited in size. Both Austrian and Italian designs had been pre-dated by the Gulf-Millers.

A Hirth-type built-up crankshaft was to be used, running in roller bearings, and the twin overhead camshafts in each bank were to be shaft-driven. The original scheme called for three Roots-type super-chargers, but this was later amended to two Centric compressors, operating in parallel. Rabe projected a rev limit in excess of 10,000 rpm, and an output of 300bhp at 8,500rpm.

Naturally, this engine was to be mounted amidships, but drive was to be to all four wheels and so the gearbox was inserted between the engine and the rear final-drive mechanism. Porsche had formerly mounted their gearbox outboard, behind the final-drive and this new location was dictated by the need to take power forward to the front wheels.

The gearbox itself was a five-speed unit, unusual in that its gears were in constant mesh and changing entailed pushing the selector lever backwards and forwards in a straight line, in motor-cycle style. The original design also called for research into a foot-operated change, and the gearbox is historic in that it used the first Porsche ring-type synchromesh.

Step-down gears at the engine's rear powered the gearbox, and were used to set the forward propeller shaft low down in the car, as it ran forward under the engine. Drive was stepped up to a simple chassis-mounted final-drive unit between the front wheels. A limited-slip diff was used at the rear.

This complex mass of mechanism was mounted in a true multi-tubular spaceframe chassis of enormous bridge-like dimensions formed in welded chrome-molybdenum steel. Suspension was by torsion bars front and rear with hydraulic shock absorbers, and absolutely gigantic two-leading shoe drum brakes were specified, deeply-finned for cooling. Wire wheels with 17-or 18-inch diameter rims were projected, and an 8ft 4½in wheelbase was chosen with track of 4ft 3ins. Aluminium pannier tanks were slung on either side of the chassis, containing twenty-one gallons each, and the large nose-mounted radiator carried five gallons of glycol. Compression ratio was as high as 15:1 to accept alcohol fuels and the dry weight of 1,583lbs was distributed roughly 758lbs on the front wheels and 825lbs on the rear.

Rabe designed a sleek slipper body for the car, and predicted speeds through the gears on fast-circuit ratios of 80mph in first, 102mph in second, 127mph in third, 157mph in fourth and 210mph in fifth!

While the design office were working hard on the detail drawings, it was obvious that Dusio's late '47 target date was impossible to meet. Rabe called in ex-Auto Union designer Dr Eberan von Eberhorst to assist with his meticulous calculations, while the first parts were being made at Cisitalia's Turin plant where engineers Hruschka and Abarth (later to become famous for his own range of performance cars) were based.

Dusio had laid down a very comprehensive programme, calling for the construction of six cars with sufficient spares to run them in a full Grand Prix season.

Not until November 1948 was the first prototype near completion, and its construction had proved so expensive that Cisitalia were in a poor financial condition. During that same month Dusio announced that he had been in negotiation with the Argentinian dictator, Peron.

He had a scheme to establish a company in the Argentine to develop high-performance and commercial vehicles, drawing heavily on Porsche design skills, and with Peron's blessing and backing Auto Motores Argentinos was founded, the name being contracted to 'Autoar'.

In February 1949 Cisitalia's creditors obtained a temporary court injunction for the payment of 240,000,000 lire debts and simultaneously the Cisitalia employees sued Dusio for 25,000,000 lire arrears in pay. Dusio fought an appeal which served to delay the axe's fall, and in March photographs were leaked to the press showing Nuvolari in the cockpit of an apparently complete car.

This was not true, the transmission was not complete, and in mid-summer Dusio concluded his deal with Peron, who covered his company's debts in return for Dusio taking the whole Cisitalia project south of the equator. His wife sold their Turin home to satisfy major creditors, and with the 420-strong labour force made redundant, Dusio took off.

On 14 March 1950, the Porsche office was about to return to Stuttgart from Gmünd, and they ran a complete inventory of the Turin works which revealed one car complete, plus enough parts to assemble a near-complete second car. Only parts of the other four cars were in existence, not enough to assemble into anything worth-

42 The Cisitalia space-frame chassis with its pannier fuel tanks attached in the Turin works, 1948-9.

43 Ing. R. Martinez de Vedia of Autoar pondering on Cisitalia engine problems in a Buenos Aires test house, 1952-3.

44 The author examined the Cisitalia quite closely – Schloss Wolfegg Museum, West Germany, April 1974.

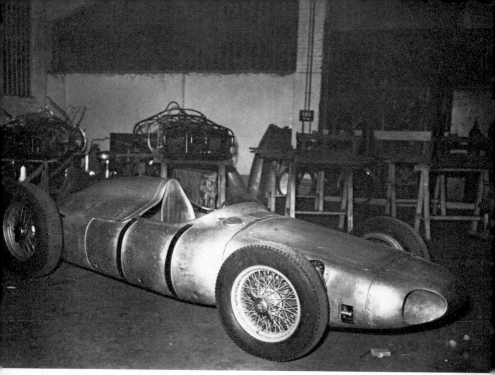

45 A rare photograph of the nearly complete Sacha-Gordine with four other chassis under preparation in the French film producer's Parisian workshops.

46 The low-slung Sacha-Gordine with (left to right), engineer Perkins, M. Gordine himself, and engineer Vigna.

while. Later that year Dusio had the complete car shipped to Autoar, never having run in its native land.

Meanwhile, the 1,500cc formula to which it had been built was on its last legs, and at the close of 1951—during which year the Cisitalia-Porsche had lain dormant in Buenos Aires—the Grand Prix organisers began to lay plans for the new year. Early in 1952 they announced that since Alfa Romeo's retirement, they felt that Ferrari versus the V16 BRM in Formula 1 would make no contest, and therefore the World Championship events of 1952–53 would be run for two litre unsupercharged Formula 2 cars.

The daring stroke—'the most fantastic racing car the world has ever seen'—had run out of time.

Late in 1952 Dusio returned to Turin, trying to get going again. Cisitalia was revived, and in a huge works mainly devoted to the rag trade—making military uniforms to Government contract—Dusio began production of more modest, non-Porsche-designed, motor cars. He tried to persuade Porsche to develop a 2-or 2½-litre engine for the existing Grand Prix chassis, but perhaps predictably they were not interested.

Meanwhile things were stirring in Buenos Aires, where Autoar dusted-off their unique car, painted it in blue and yellow national racing colours and entered it for the Formule Libre Buenos Aires Grand Prix at the Municipal Autodrome in January 1954.

The engine was stripped and rebuilt, bench-tested at 275-280bhp and then mounted in the car which was tested at San Isidro, just outside the city. Its suspension proved far too soft, with the car bottoming badly. Right at the close of practice for the Grand Prix the electrifying-looking car rolled out onto the Autodrome with pipe-smoking Italian driver Felice Bonetto at the wheel.

Autoar had discovered that the car had different final drive ratios at front and rear during the San Isidro test, and attempted to compensate by fitting odd-sized tyres. This was no car to be treated so lightly, and after one lap Bonetto was at the pits with the car lost in a dense cloud of blue smoke. An oil pipe had parted, it was fixed, and then local driver Clemar Bucci took over to see what he could do. He found himself consistently barrelling into corners to find the gearbox selecting neutral (which was present between each gear) and eventually advised that the car be withdrawn because it was totally unraceworthy.

Both drivers praised the car's road-holding, but it was obvious that

K

too many years and too many miles separated its complex systems from the engineers who had devised them. Early in 1953 Autoar were said to have produced over 360bhp from the flat-12 engine, and Bucci was asked to attack the South American flying kilometre record in an attempt to salvage some prestige.

The record was old, forgotten and virtually meaningless, having stood at only 140mph for many years. Autoar's calculations indicated that their car should push it up to a respectable 187mph, but they chose to make their attempt in July, which is the depth of the Argentinian winter.

Bucci found the engine running cold and sooting its plugs on a bitter morning with a howling knife-like crosswind. He managed one misfiring run at 146.6mph, testing the car up to 7,000rpm, and then wheeled into a second more serious attempt. The engine cleared and was pulling well until an oil pipe ruptured, a piston burned-out, and the engine cut abruptly as Bucci coasted past the timekeepers to record 142.2mph. The two-way average of these curtailed runs was a laughable 144.7mph, but still enough to take the record.

This spelled the end of the Cisitalia's mobile career, and in the late fifties Porsche sports car driver and team manager Huschke von Hanstein found the car in the Autoar garage, while in Buenos Aires for a 1,000km endurance race.

It was in a sorry state, having been under deep flood waters for some time the previous winter. Ferry Porsche managed to acquire the rotting remains in 1959 and shipped them back to Germany, where the Cisitalia-Porsche 360 was completely rebuilt and today occupies a proud position in the company's car collection.

Curiously enough, the uncompleted second car was discovered somewhere in Switzerland in about 1970 by some Italian enthusiasts, and dealer Corrado Cupellini sold it to Tom Wheatcroft in Britain for the public Donington Collection of Single-Seater Racing Cars.

It arrived as a collection of rusty parts, some of them unmachined castings, but with a complete chassis frame and two transmission sets. It was completed with a replica bodyshell in the Wheatcroft workshops and today has pride of place among the collection's unique display of seven four-wheel drive Grand Prix cars. The system was not revived in Grand Prix racing until 1960–61, by Ferguson, and then again in 1964 by BRM, and in 1969 by Cosworth, Lotus, McLaren and Matra. It didn't work in later years, but the front-engined Ferguson driven by Stirling Moss actually won the non-

Championship Oulton Park Gold Cup race in September 1961.

The Cisitalia-Porsche story had an early sequel in the fifties. An engineer named Vigna had studied at the Porsche Office, and he gained backing from the French film producer Sacha Gordine to build a series of major-Formula racing cars, which he based on Cisitalia experience.

Sacha Gordine was an extremely wealthy man. He was then in his early forties, and had made his name as a film producer after shooting his first movie clandestinely during the German occupation. Post-war he made films with stars such as Simone Signoret and Jean Gabin, and two of his perhaps more famous titles were *La Ronde* and *Black Orpheus*.

He was a great motoring enthusiast and was a regular rally competitor with his wife. He wanted a modern Grand Prix car which would put France back on the racing map, for although Amédée Gordini's cars were performing miraculous feats in comparison to their shoestring budget, their French blue was very much subordinated to Italian red.

So Gordine set-up his racing car company at 154 Rue Danton, Levallois-Perret (Seine) and to avoid confusion with his compatriot, Gordini, he hyphenated his names to christen the project Sacha-Gordine.

Simultaneously the French government were back on their national racing car bandwagon, Messrs Chaban-Delmas, Flandin, Puy and Gaubert urging a 250,000,000 franc budget for the construction of a French car '. . . capable de représenter nos couleurs et de défendre nos intérêts dans les compétitions internationales, *avec une chance sérieuse de succès . . .*'. After the SEFAC and the CTA-Arsenal they were choosing their words well!

Sacha-Gordine, however, was self-financing, and in January 1953 the first car was virtually complete and the press were shown round the Levallois workshops.

Vigna's design owed much to the ill-fated Cissy's layout, but it was much lighter and smaller, creating a sensation at the time because hardly any part of the bodywork stood higher than the tyres!

The Sacha-Gordine chassis was a very simple ladder-frame, with two straight tubular side members joined by cross-pieces and carrying a light superstructure of thin tubing to support the body panels.

Front suspension, like the Cisitalia, was by parallel trailing links, sprung by transverse torsion bars mounted in the chassis cross-members. A De Dion axle was used at the rear, sprung on longitudinal torsion bars housed within the main chassis longerons.

Vigna seems to have had a free hand with the budget, for he used extremely expensive magnesium castings everywhere in the engine and transmission, and all over the rear suspension.

The De Dion tube was itself in magnesium, was located by a ball joint riding in a vertical slide housed in the magnesium final drive casing, and was located fore-and-aft by twin cast magnesium radius arms running forward to the chassis on either side. Even the brake back-plates and air-scoops were formed in magnesium.

The engine was a 90-degree V8 unit with cylinder dimensions of 70 x 64mm giving a Formula 2 capacity of 1,970cc. The crankcase, base chamber, cylinder blocks and heads were all cast in magnesium alloy, and the steel wet liners were extensively finned just like an air-cooled cylinder barrel.

Combustion chambers were hemispherical, carrying two valves at an included angle of 90-degrees actuated from twin overhead camshafts per bank. Again in similar style to the Cisitalia, the camshafts were shaft driven.

A one-piece crankshaft was used running in Vandervell shell bearings, and dry sump lubrication was employed with a double oil pump in the engine's extensively finned base chamber. In unsupercharged Formula 2 trim the Sacha-Gordine carried four double-choke carburettors. Single spark plugs per cylinder were fired by a single Vertex Scintilla magneto, and glycol cooling was used with twin pumps driven from the camshafts.

The mid-mounted engine drove rearwards through a twin dry-plate clutch (in a magnesium housing) to a five-speed gearbox mounted transversely accepting drive through a central bevel pinion. A splined output shaft carried a transfer gear in a separate casing which could easily be changed to match the final drive ratio to any given circuit. Jointed half-shafts drove from a differential assembly to the rear wheels. Like the Cisitalia a motorcycle style gearchange was used, with each gear being engaged in sequence, if only momentarily, as the driver changed up or down.

Nostril intakes formed in the car's bodywork fed air into two large ducts which fed through two small radiators and then discharged through outlets just behind the front wheels. An oil cooler, oil tank, rack-and-pinion steering gear and glycol header tank filled the front end of the chassis, while massive pannier tanks were slung on either side of the cockpit offering a combined capacity of 66 gallons. Each tank was attached by two straps and could be easily detached from the chassis to give maintenance access.

Vast drum brakes were mounted on the wheels, sixteen inches in diameter at the front and fourteen at the rear, with four leading shoes and operated by independent hydraulic circuits front and rear. The wire wheels were themselves seventeen inches in diameter with an optional eighteen inch size at the rear, and the new car's smooth, flat bodyshell with its nostril air intakes and thrust forward, eager appearance (heightened by the stub tail being tucked down between the rear wheels) looked terrific, slung low between those tall Dunlop tyres.

Vigna and development engineer Perkins (a Frenchman of Siamese descent) were also working on 1,500cc, 2,500cc and 4,500cc versions of the V8 engine, with the $1\frac{1}{2}$-litre carrying twin Roots superchargers for Formula 1. A Le Mans car was projected, to use a special three litre version of the Sacha-Gordine engine, and a twin-tube chassis frame was mocked-up for this mid-engined vehicle, alongside *five* single-seaters!

Claims were made that the $1\frac{1}{2}$-litre Formula 1 engine was to have a 22:1 compression ratio, which would require 'iso-octane' fuel. Boost pressure for this engine was claimed to be 57lbs but I believe the unit was never to be completed. Vigna also intended to adopt a Hirth-type crankshaft with roller bearings in each of his engines. Power output for the virtually complete Formula 2 car was quoted as 191bhp at 8,000rpm, and the new Sacha-Gordine's dimensions were released as wheelbase, 8ft $5\frac{1}{2}$ins; front track 4ft $5\frac{1}{8}$ins; rear track 4ft 4ins and dry weight 1,400lbs. Vigna hazarded a Formula 1 supercharged engine output of over 380bhp at 8,000rpm.

This staggeringly ambitious project had two cars virtually complete in early 1953, and one was entered for the Pau Grand Prix at Easter, but suddenly Sacha Gordine realised that his fortune was fast dribbling away—he wrote off the whole project as a tax loss and it foundered as abruptly as it had begun.

Denis Jenkinson tells me that for years there was a story that the two virtually complete cars were stored in a factory park on an island in the Seine, and if one could find the proper vantage point the cars could be seen clearly. Evidently the story died a natural death about ten or twelve years ago, and nobody now seems to know where the Sacha-Gordines disappeared to.

With the collapse of Vigna's project, the Cisitalia-Porsche story could be said to have come to its end.

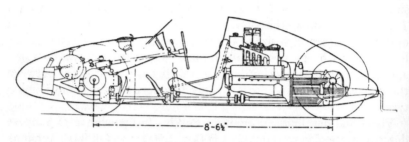

The Cisitalia-Porsche.

15

But the Engine was in the Front –
Italy and America, 1958-1961

Caracas, Venezuela, 3 November 1957. The last round of the season's World Sports Car Championship was being held on a tricky 6.12-mile circuit laid out in a park and along an autostrada on the outskirts of the Central American capital.

General Marcos Jiménez had brought big-time sports car racing to his country in 1955. Fangio won the race but the meeting lost a bundle. The grandstands were full of 'invited guests' and nobody could extract admission from the hoi-polloi out for an innocent Sunday stroll in the sun. In 1956 Moss won the race and the AC de Venezuela again made a terrific loss. This championship race was to be the event's make or break. If the club lost money once more their brief love affair with international motor racing would be over.

During that 1957 sports car season a titanic battle had raged between the 4-litre Ferraris and Maserati's monstrous 4½-litre V8s. Both teams arrived in Caracas in force to settle the issue, and the World Championship. Maserati trailed Ferrari by 25 points to 28 and their trio of V8 cars looked certain to close that gap in the Central American sun.

Maserati's misfortune began immediately in the race. Masten Gregory's private Temple Buell-entered V8 thundered into the lead as the two works cars stalled on the line, but almost immediately he misjudged a tricky corner, cannoned into a sand-bag barrier and over-turned into the road. Bystanders lifted the silent wreck and Gregory crawled out, bleeding from a cut over one eye.

Jean Behra's works 450S had burst into life and he knifed through the field to third place, trailing the Ferraris of Hawthorn and Collins with Moss making similar progress in his sister car some way behind.

By lap 16, Moss and Behra were running first and second. By lap 32, Moss was two minutes in the lead, thundering around the deceptively fast course at over 101mph, average. On the next lap an American amateur driver named Max Dressel failed to see Moss's bulleting Maserati tramping up behind him, and his AC-Bristol veered into its path. This was on the fastest part of the course and the 450S thundered into the AC's tail, hurled it into a lamp standard where it disintegrated, and itself slithered to a halt with its front end completely written-off but Moss escaping with shock.

Fate had not finished with Maserati, and four laps later Behra brought in his leading 450S for fuel and had it catch fire as he restarted. The Frenchman baled out with slight burns but was too shocked to drive on, so Moss leapt into the smoking cockpit and swept back into the race!

One lap later he returned for the seat was still alight, and Harry Schell took over to force the big car back into contact with the Ferraris. He put his heart into a wonderful drive, forcing the big Maserati back into the lead and then on one lap he came up behind Jo Bonnier's three-litre Maserati and pulled out to pass him.

At that moment the smaller car burst a tyre and slewed into Schell's path. The two red cars smashed together, Bonnier's bouncing away to run head-on into another lamp standard while Schell's cannoned into a wall tail-first, ruptured its fuel tank and exploded into a sea of flame. Both drivers luckily escaped miraculously lightly hurt, but all the Maseratis were out and as Ferrari came home to finish first, second and third the World Championship was theirs.

This chain of Maserati disasters was too much for the company to bear, for it was already over-extended financially and the loss of so much exotic and valuable racing equipment was virtually the last straw. A new three-litre sports car Formula was being introduced at short notice for 1958 and there was little chance of recouping the V8's development costs.

Soon after the tattered team's return from Caracas, Signor Omer Orsi announced that his company would be withdrawing from racing. It was not quite a final withdrawal, for in the French Grand Prix the following June a special lightweight 250F Grand Prix Maserati appeared, giving Juan Fangio his final race appearance. The great five-times World Champion brought it home in fourth place, and with that the Maserati works team was no more.

The team's chassis and transmission engineer during the latter part of the long 250F programme had been Valerio Colotti, and at the time of the company's withdrawal he had a new 'super-lightweight' 250F on his drawing board ready to combat the light and nimble mid-engined Coopers then rapidly becoming a force to be reckoned with.

After the Maserati withdrawal, Colotti left the company to form his own Studio Tecnica Meccanica design and engineering firm in Modena, taking many of his drawings and of course his ideas with him.

Giorgio Scarlatti—a well-known amateur racing driver—approached Colotti with an offer of backing to build the ultimate in lightweight 250Fs, and Colotti reviewed his ideas for the new car in the light of latest experience.

He scrapped the old De Dion rear suspension system, replacing it with a lighter transverse leaf-spring and wishbone location, mounted on a new spaceframe chassis welded up from small-diameter lightweight tubing. Girling disc brakes replaced the well-finned drums which had been such a familiar feature of the classic 250Fs, and an ex-works 2½-litre six-cylinder engine was to be acquired.

Consoli, an ex-works mechanic, built the car for Colotti, working in the living room of his modest home near to Modena's combination 'auto-aerodrome'. When a proper workshop was later provided for the job the embryo 'Tec-Mec F415' was wheeled out through his French windows.

In the meantime Hans Tanner, a Swiss motoring journalist and entrepreneur, had become involved with the project. He had been on the Modenese racing scene for years, being particularly closely involved with Maserati, and he enlisted financial backing from a Floridan racing enthusiast named Gordon Pennington who was at that time living in the Reale Hotel in Modena, a hostelry which was virtually motor racing's version of London's Piccadilly. Stand there long enough and you'd meet everybody you had ever known!

Pennington was intending to buy and race some kind of Italian car, and Scarlatti sold out his interest in the Tec-Mec project to him. Colotti, meanwhile, had left the 'Studio' to establish himself in partnership with Stirling Moss's famous ex-mechanic Alf Francis as Gear Speed Development SpA, with plans to build Colotti racing gearboxes.

While all these moves were taking place, Consoli had completed the new car late in 1959, and the engine (no 2523) had been taken from an old-nail 250F which Jo Bonnier had been hawking around Italy as a 'rent-a-drive' car for club competitions.

Under the Pennington-Tanner aegis, Studio Tecnica Meccanica had changed its name to Tec-Mec Automobili, and it was under this mantle that the car was tested at Modena by the American driver Bob Said, by Piero Drogo, Jo Bonnier and Scarlatti. It was diabolical at first, refusing to do anything properly, but then some extensive chassis tuning resulted in a marked improvement in its behaviour.

Unfortunately the whole programme had run out of time, for while Tec-Mec had been stumbling along in their amateurish 'backyard special' manner the Cooper mid-engined cars had taken over Grand Prix racing in no uncertain manner and Jack Brabham was well on the way to his first World Championship in one of the Surbiton cars.

Tec-Mec hastily began lashing together a bread-and-butter racing car to earn some money, taking what was basically Prince Bira's famous old 1954 250F chassis—then actually owned by Ross Jensen in New Zealand—cutting it about, installing a 4.9 litre fuel-injected Chevrolet Corvette engine and selling the result (as the Tec-Mec 2) to Johnny Mansel—also in New Zealand!

Meanwhile the 1959 World Championship season was closing with the first title-qualifying United States Grand Prix, run on the Floridan Sebring airfield circuit in December.

As this was virtually in Pennington's own back yard the Tec-Mec F415 was shipped across the Atlantic and entered for the Grand Prix to be driven by the Brazilian Fritz d'Orey. He qualified seventeenth out of the nineteen starters and the snub-nosed red car lasted seven laps before retiring with oil gushing from an unspecified engine failure.

With this failure repaired the car was later taken to the new Daytona Speedway for some kind of record attempt, but the engine threw a rod and then d'Orey was injured in an accident in another car, Pennington lost interest and the little Tec-Mec concern folded-up, though forgetting to cancel a new block and crank which had been ordered for the F415 from the still enthusiastic and cooperative Maserati works.

The car lay on a trailer in a Miami garden until early in 1967 when it was bought complete with some boxes of spares (including the new parts from Maserati, unopened) by Tom Wheatcroft for what was eventually to develop into the Donington Collection.

Wheatcroft drove the car quite regularly, 'just for fun', on open test days at circuits like Silverstone and Oulton Park, and crashed it heavily into a parked ambulance on one occasion when he spun off at Silverstone.

The car was rapidly rebuilt and appeared in VSCC historic racing car events driven by Tony Merrick. It now stands in the Donington Collection – still in running order – as a memorial to the ultimate in 250F development. It might have been tops so far as basic design was concerned, but it was certainly Maserati's absolute rock-bottom in postwar achievement.

During the United States Grand Prix in which the Tec-Mec covered its seven laps in Formula 1, another 'lost cause' of motor racing was making its debut. This was the C-Type Connaught which was to have represented the British private company in the latter part of the 1957 season.

Connaught Engineering contributed nobly to the resurgence in Britain's Grand Prix fortunes post-war, and when the amateur driver C.A.S. (later famous as 'Tony') Brooks won the Syracuse Grand Prix in one of their B-Type cars in 1955 he was recording the first all-British success at this level since H. O. D. Segrave won at San Sebastian in a Sunbeam in 1924!

The company took part in their last Grand Prix at Monaco early in 1957 with Stuart Lewis-Evans driving one car into fourth place. A week later, Connaught backer Kenneth McAlpine and director Rodney Clarke announced their withdrawal from racing due to the continued lack of monetary assistance.

British enthusiasts were stunned, for Connaught had proved themselves adept at building reliable and strong cars and campaigned them sensibly despite being unable to afford the best drivers. In October that year an auction was held at Connaught's Send works beside the A3 road in Surrey, and most of the racing department's effects were sold off to private owners.

One item which did not sell was the uncompleted C-Type, which employed many basic components from the B-Type installed in a newly designed tubular spaceframe which was considerably lighter than the earlier ladder-frame. Strut-type rear suspension was adopted with tall coil-spring/damper units on either side of the tail and the rear disc brakes were mounted inboard on the final drive cheeks.

The car lay around at Send after the auction, apparently unwanted, and was eventually sold off to arch special builder Paul Emery. He put it all together into running trim and took it to Sebring where Bob Said—the man who had formerly tested the Tec-Mec—drove it in the race.

He qualified 13th quickest, faster than several private Coopers, the Tec-Mec and Rodger Ward's hilarious little Offy-powered Kurtis Midget, and jumped the start mightily to be almost on the second row as stars like Moss, Brabham, Brooks and Phil Hill stuck their elbows out to hold him back! After one exuberant lap in amongst the works cars, Said spun out mightily on the North Runway and pushed the car home to the pits with the C-Type's nose badly out of joint. It was retired, to end its Grand Prix career.

But the C-Type's American travels were not at an end, for in 1962 it was rebuilt in England by 750 Motor Club members Tony Densham and Harry Worrall, and with Pierre de Villiers in the cockpit it appeared at Indianapolis for that year's '500'! Evidently the American Speedway teams were amazed to see the old English art of back-axle warming with the spinning rear wheels up on jacks on the pit apron, and perhaps not surprisingly the Connaught failed to qualify and was regarded as rather a poor English joke . . . after all, Indianapolis was a serious business.

Connaught's original 1953 project for the C-Type or 'J3' had depicted a mid-engined car of unusual design. Rodney Clarke and engineer Mike Oliver reasoned that if they used a multi-tubular spaceframe chassis they would have to cut it about to such a degree to instal their intended $2\frac{1}{2}$-litre Coventry-Climax Godiva V8 engine that any rigidity they might have gained would be lost. They then decided to produce a geodetic fuselage which was to be welded up from a large number of steel tubes and covered with a stressed-skin bodywork. A 'hole' in the top would accommodate the driver, and the engine could be 'fed-in' from one end.

At this time Kieft were also building a Formula 1 car to carry the Climax Godiva engine in the front, and John Heath of HWM also intended to use the unit, which the Midlands company decided not to proceed with, so effectively killing off all three British Grand Prix hopes. They later made up for this move many, many times over.

When Connaught finally closed down in 1957 the rear-engined car had become the D-Type and was to have been a more conventional spaceframe-chassised vehicle with one of Connaught's own Alta-based four-cylinder engines in the rear, driving to a new five-speed transaxle which was already made and performing well on the test

bed. Like the early Porsche designs the gearbox was outboard, behind
the final drive assembly, but the D-Type was never to be completed –
and the gearbox had nowhere to go.

While the unhappy Tec-Mec was being completed and Paul Emery's
tiny amateur team were cobbling the C-Type Connaught together, a
wealthy professional set-up in America was trying hard to win their
nation's first Grand Prix race since 1921.

Road racing held a special fascination for a small but growing
faction in speedway-orientated America, and one such enthusiast
was Lance Reventlow—son of Barbara Hutton and heir to the
Woolworth millions. He raced Cooper single-seater and sports cars,
and during 1957 made a European tour to shop for a new car.

The tiny workshops occupied by Cooper and Lister in England
must have shaken him rigid. It was at this time that a new Grand
Prix driver was signed-up by Charlie Cooper, asked to see his new
car, and was handed a welding-torch and directed to a pile of tubes
lying in a corner!

In a *Road & Track* magazine feature in 1963, Reventlow was
quoted as having looked at a new sports car chassis lying in Brian
Lister's Cambridge iron works, turning to his buddy Bruce Kessler
and growling 'Hell, I could build a car better 'n *that*!'

And so it all began. In August 1957 Reventlow sealed a deal with
sports car specialist Warren Olson to produce an all American sports
car to contest the 1958 World Championship. He also wanted work
to begin on a Formula 1 design with which his team could take
America back into Grand Prix racing.

At that time there was no engine size limitation in sports car
racing. Olson had great experience of Chevrolet's light and powerful
V8 and this unit naturally became first choice to power the new
car.

Then Reventlow Automobiles Incorporated's troubles began. That
September saw the powers-that-be slap an arbitrary three-litre
capacity limit on the World Sports Car Championship. This put the
Chevy engine right out of court, but Reventlow decided to concentrate on national American sports car races with this machine and
rely on the Formula 1 project to take him international.

Olson had fabricators Dick Troutmann and Tom Barnes lined up
to build RAI's new cars, and they were joined by Chuck Daigh who
combined considerable talent as both driver and engineer. Ken Miles,

an expatriate English driver, completed the original team and he helped lay out the sports car's basic design.

Reventlow chose the name 'Scarab' for his cars, after the mystical beetle of ancient Egypt, although I doubt if he appreciated that their original was the common dung-beetle.

The first Scarab car was built in Olson's works on Robertson Boulevard, Los Angeles. It had a multi-tubular spaceframe chassis in chrome-molybdenum, with coil-and-wishbone front suspension and a De Dion rear end. A 301.6 cubic inch (4.94-litre) Chevrolet V8 engine was installed initially, later to be replaced by a 339.3 cubic inch (5.56-litre) unit, both being tuned and modified by Chuck Daigh. He added Hilborn-Travers fuel injection, and mated the engine to a suitably modified four-speed Corvette production gearbox. Huge finned drum brakes were added and the whole car was clad in a suitably 'racey' flowing sports car bodyshell, designed by Chuck Pelly and hand-formed by Emil Diedt.

Three of these Scarab sports cars were built, the later numbers incorporating detail changes, and they became the outstanding sports-racers of their day in Sports Car Club of America meetings. In 1958 the prototype became the first American car to win a major international event on foreign soil for about 40 years, when Reventlow won at Nassau during the Bahamas Speed Week.

During that year design had been progressing for the front-engined (naturally) Grand Prix car. Reventlow had gone to Leo Goossen for his engine design, and with his Offenhauser ties Goossen drew broadly on vast experience with the four-cylinder Indianapolis engines.

They were now being built and developed by Meyer-Drake, a partnership formed between Lou Meyer—three-time Indy winner and a driver we met during his Sampson Special days—and Dale Drake who had taken-over Fred Offenhauser's outfit, and also acquired Goossen's highly-valued services.

A three-litre Meyer-Drake engine had been tried briefly in the third sports Scarab, to see if it could compete internationally but results at Santa Barbara indicated otherwise. For the Formula 1 project Daigh and Reventlow suggested the basic lines along which they wanted to work, and Goossen took over from there.

Troutmann-Barnes laid out a large but light multi-tubular frame similar in basics to the sports-racers. The new engine was to be laid over virtually on its side to keep the bonnet line low and to place the propeller shaft along one side of the cockpit. This feature allowed the driver to sit very low down yet maintain a superb forward view over the wide nose of his car.

A five-speed transmission was being developed to fit inside a Chevy Corvette casing, and all-independent suspension was chosen with coil-springs and wishbones at front and rear. Braking schemes included aircraft-style expanding bladders in turbo-finned drums and a clutch-like disc brake on the back of the final drive housing. Both were abject failures, young engineer Marshall Whitfield's bladder brakes proving quite impossible to develop, while the rear disc was well-shrouded by bodywork and had a lot of work to do. It would be a devil to cool, and the RAI team decided to try water-cooling, mounting it in a shroud through which engine coolant was to be forced by a belt-driven pump.

The works were now housed in their own building on Jefferson Boulevard in Culver City, next door to the Traco engine-tuning shop of Jim Travers and Frank Coons who serviced the Chevy V8s. Reventlow decided to concentrate his efforts on Formula 1 in early 1959 as the project was dragging badly, and the two Mark II sports racers were sold for $17,500 each while he bought the Mark I from himself and had it modified as a street car!

Meanwhile the Formula 1 engine was also in trouble, partly due to its advanced specification with Mercedes-like desmodromic (mechanically closing) valve gear. It was an all light-alloy four-cylinder owing much to established Offenhauser/Meyer-Drake practice, with dimensions of 85.25 x 85.73mm to give a swept volume of 2,441cc. Twin overhead camshafts actuated the desmo valves, and Hilborn-Travers fuel injection again featured.

These compound delays kept the Scarab at home throughout 1959 and there was now only one season left to the 2½-litre Formula. A 'Now or Never' spirit pervaded the RAI works, and in a mad scramble compromises were made and two cars were completed in time for their debut in the Monaco Grand Prix, opening the World Championship on 29 May 1960.

The troublesome water-cooled rear brake idea was junked, and replaced by a standard Girling caliper-type disc brake system at both front and rear. Reventlow had wanted an all-American Grand Prix car, but the British-made brakes had to be used to put his car on the line.

At Monaco the nicely-made metallic blue and white Scarabs with their huge red beetle insignia were received with friendly interest and perhaps a few patronising smiles. During the 1959 season, which Scarab had missed, the mid-engined Cooper-Climax had proved itself the most effective Grand Prix car of the season and had won the Championship. Late in the year BRM had produced a prototype mid-engined car, and for 1960 Colin Chapman had produced his Lotus 18 mid-engined model for Formula 1 and 2 and Formula Junior production use. Scarab had been overtaken by the 'Rear-Engined Revolution'.

Reventlow and Daigh drove the cars in practice at Monaco, starting on Goodyear tyres which they quickly found far too hard and then changing to European-style Dunlops which brought their lap times tumbling down.

Due to its tight round-the-houses character Monaco had a limited Grand Prix field, and only 16 of the 24 entries would be allowed to start. Neither of the raucous 230bhp Scarabs had a chance and when Reventlow persuaded Stirling Moss to test his car the maestro returned from a brief outing with a best time of 1 minute 45 seconds. This was the same as young Jimmy Clark's Formula Junior Lotus 18. Moss felt there would be more to come once he had accustomed himself to the new car and with some chassis tuning, but clearly the Scarabs were obsolete before they had begun.

This must have come as a body blow. Two years' forced development in the crucible of Grand Prix racing had taken Europe far ahead of the West Coast sports car builders.

The Dutch Grand Prix was next on the calendar, on June 6, and there things improved and Daigh rapidly got into the swing and qualified, although the timekeepers were issuing very complimentary times which even Daigh himself could scarcely credit. Then began some kind of organisational hassle over starting money and Reventlow resolutely covered his cars and refused to run, in concert with the front-engined Aston Martins from Britain's Sports Car Champion company.

On June 19th Scarabs were at Spa-Francorchamps for the Belgian Grand Prix, and on the super-fast Ardennes circuit both cars qualified and started the race. Reventlow was the quicker in practice but left the race after only three laps when a con-rod broke. Daigh was quickly left behind by the regular Grand Prix teams but his Scarab was cheered every time it howled past the grandstand, for it had the noisiest exhaust note the enthusiastic Belgians had ever heard.

47 Tec-Mec, the unfortunate finale to the Maserati 250F's classic career.

48 'Shelsley Special' – the scruffy, badly finished, unfortunate ATS Formula 1 car, first time out at Spa, 1963.

49 Imprisoned – the prototype ATS cars were so hastily finished that chassis bracing tubes were welded into place after the engine had been installed. They had to be sawn through to remove the unit, and plumber's muff-joints were subsequently fitted for this purpose.

50 Flat-12 – Alfa Romeo's Tipo 160 engine was a 2½-litre unit intended for a four-wheel drive car in 1954.

51 Sculpture – one of Harry Miller's 1932 four-wheel drive cars in the garages at Indianapolis, with its 45-degree V8 engine dismounted.

4 wheel drive
(Front)

Then the car began to gush oil and Daigh was out on his 17th lap. They had made their Grand Prix debut, but it had been a tragic race, for two drivers (Stirling Moss and Michael Taylor) had been severely injured in practice accidents, and two more (Chris Bristow and Alan Stacey) had died in separate incidents during the race.

Two weeks later, at Reims, Scarab turned out for the French Grand Prix, but there Richie Ginther appeared on leave from Ferrari in Reventlow's car, while Daigh was in his normal number two machine. Both cars were withdrawn from the race after practice problems finished-up their stock of spares, and at this point Reventlow called a halt and the sad little group trailed back to California.

Reventlow bought Cooper drives for himself and Daigh in the British Grand Prix, but he must have been a disillusioned man as he now knew his own cars were too heavy, too fragile, and too late.

Back home RAI had moved into a brand new building in Venice, California, while Leo Goossen pencilled a 1½-litre engine for the new Grand Prix Formula starting in 1961. It was a modification on the basic four-cylinder theme but with Ferrari proving their V6, and BRM and Coventry-Climax testing their V8s, the Scarab engine was again obsolete; multi-cylinder units were now clearly the way to go. Once again, the Scarabs were one pace behind. . . .

To keep in racing Reventlow shipped one of the front-engined cars to England to run in three-litre Intercontinental events in 1961. This was a rather half-hearted attempt to keep the old Formula going. It was doomed to failure but gave British crowds a chance to see Chuck Daigh and the Scarab at Goodwood and Silverstone, where he finished seventh in one race in pouring rain. In a later event on the Northampton aerodrome circuit, Daigh lost control and crashed his car heavily and hurt himself. Once again RAI withdrew from European racing, and this time was to be the last. . . .

Things looked-up briefly when Formula 366 was announced for single-seater cars with three-litre racing or five-litre production-based engines. With their great stock of Chevrolet parts and knowledge RAI set about the new Formula with gusto, and produced a light-alloy Chevy V8 capable of 310bhp which was tested initially in one of the old Grand Prix frames.

A new mid-engined chassis was being developed as the orders poured in and RAI tooled-up for an initial five-car production batch. Then the authorities knocked the whole idea on the head once more by strictly limiting permissible stock-block modifications. This move

L

would limit the Chevy to around 230bhp which couldn't possibly compete with 2.5–2.7-litre Climax racing engines then giving some 265bhp.

Intercontinental racing-cum-Formula 366 died completely in 1962, and although the single rear-engined chassis raced once that year in Australia the end was near.

In March 1962 Lance Reventlow announced that RAI was to be wound up. The American tax system allowed an unprofitable business to be written off as a loss for up to five years, and if it hadn't begun to show a profit by that time it might as well be closed or the proprietor should bear the cost himself. This Reventlow was not prepared to do and so the Scarabs passed into history.

What happened to the cars? One, possibly used as the 366 prototype, ended up in Briggs Cunningham's museum with a V8 engine and vestigial road equipment, while another (probably an uncompleted spare chassis) is at the Donington Collection awaiting an original engine. A sectioned engine stands in the Cunningham museum, and I have heard stories that a running unit lay in a store at Venice for many years after Carroll Shelby took over the plant to build his Cobra cars.

The rear-engined chassis is also in existence and somebody was offering it for sale in Europe quite recently while its apparent owner advertised in America for information as to its whereabouts!

So the last all-American Grand Prix programme ground to a halt, but nobody who heard the cars running can forget their exciting sound. Lance Reventlow had mounted a noble private effort to bring his country back into top-class road racing, and his failure was unfortunate and in many respects unlucky. Early in 1973 he was in a light aircraft which blundered into a box canyon in California. In the ensuing disaster, all on board were killed.

16

We Aim to Beat Ferrari –
Italy, 1962-1963

With their multi-cylinder engines Ferrari wiped the Grand Prix board in 1961. Only the mastery of Moss in an obsolete Lotus 18 could hold off the red cars on the two most difficult circuits—Monaco and Nürburgring—but the year was marred for Maranello when they lost Wolfgang von Trips in the Italian Grand Prix, and shocked team-mate Phil Hill took the title in his place.

Pressures within the company had been high during this successful season, and six top executives walked out for good towards the end of the year. They included team manager Romolo Tavoni, designer Carlo Chiti, Giotto Bizzarini, Fausto Galarsi, Girolamo Gardini and Enzo Selmi.

Coincidentally, 24-year old racing enthusiast Count Giovanni Volpi di Misurata was looking for someone to build him a racing car. His father, Giuseppe Volpi, had been a politician, diplomat, financier and art connoisseur. When he died he left his vast fortune and a string of hotels to his son, and sometime in 1960 Giovanni began to spend some of it on expensive racing cars.

He bought half-a-dozen, and hired all kinds of drivers to run them in national and international events at home and abroad. His family came from Venice, which had been in the old Republic of Serenissima, so he called his team the 'Scuderia Serenissima' to celebrate the fact.

He raced his own cars on occasion but after a bad accident at Modena he promised his mother to stay out of the cockpit in future and direct his races from the pits. Racing on his scale was an expensive business, and he began to feel he could spend his money better by having a car company of his own. He approached wealthy industrialists Jaime Ortiz Patiño and Giorgio Billi in 1961, and they were chewing over ideas for building competition cars when the Ferrari rebellion occurred.

In December, Billi met the six ex-Ferrari men and suggested a scheme to them, and on January 26th this septet had a long discussion with Volpi and Patiño in the Hotel Principe e Savoia in Milan, and the new company was born.

On 11 February 1962, the Societa per Azioni Automobili Turismo Sport Serenissima was founded with over 60,000,000 lire (about £35,000) capital. Billi was created President, Volpi was Vice-President and Patiño, Chiti and Gardini formed the 'administrative council' or executive board.

Work began on a factory at Sasso Marconi between Bologna and Florence, and in a pokey office above the Banco Nazionale del' Lavoro in Bologna, Chiti began the design of a new Grand Prix car to be called the Serenissima.

He outlined a very Ferrari-like spaceframe chassis, carrying a brand new 90-degree V8 engine which he intended to produce an initial output of 180bhp at 10,000rpm. The company planned to have the first car ready by the autumn and running in the Italian Grand Prix, while future projects were to include a GT car powered by two-litre versions of the V8 engine. Production figures were decided at 100-120 cars for 1963, over 300 for 1964 and 500-600 in 1965. The rebels were ambitious and intended to go far in their new employ . . . their prime aim being to put one over Ferrari in Grand Prix racing.

Volpi doesn't seem to have got on with his new partners for late that year he walked out and took the Serenissima name with him. The company now became known as *Automobili Turismo e Sport*, or ATS for short.

Chiti's first Formula 1 car was ready before the end of the year, and Billi provided the money for Tavoni to sign on two ex-Ferrari drivers—ex-World Champion Phil Hill and Giancarlo Baghetti to campaign the cars in 1963. The veteran English driver Jack Fairman was brought over to test the cars in their initial form and then ATS were introduced to the press.

The new car was a strikingly small device, with a huge flared windscreen to protect the driver as he projected way above its slender nose-line. There was also a characteristic teardrop-shaped bulge over the carburettors behind his back.

Chiti's new engine was a quad-cam all-aluminium V8 of 1,494cc and its specially modified Colotti gearbox was situated between the engine and the differential casing in similar manner to Italy's other sanguine hope, the Cisitalia-Porsche of thirteen years before.

Front springs and rear disc brakes were tucked away inboard, giving the car a purposeful appearance, and with their fairly strong driving team and considerable financial wealth things augured well for ATS.

But they were slow in appearing during 1963, and when they did make their debut at Spa in the Belgian Grand Prix they were a laughing stock! The cars obviously hadn't worked in their neat and slim original form, and at Spa the two works cars looked more like home-built British hill-climb specials, covered in grease and oil leaks, paintwork looking as though it had been sprayed from a spud-gun and tatty badly-formed body panels hanging on haphazardly. Even the engine installations had obviously been rushed, for there were massive bracing tubes welded over the engine which imprisoned it within the chassis. The spaceframe would have to be sawn through to allow an engine change!

Neither Phil Hill nor Baghetti were very happy with this sorry state of affairs, and both retired from the rainy race with transmission failures after starting from the back rows of the grid. The Italian lasted eight laps before creeping into the pits unable to change gear and the American was splashing his way round the back of the circuit when his car suddenly just rolled to a halt with the engine revving freely.

The Dutch Grand Prix followed on June 23, and there the ATS team had tidied up their cars' bodywork a little but they still looked scruffy and very second-hand. The major modification was in the tubes across the engine bay which had been cut and fitted with plumber's muff-joints to make them removable!

Once again they qualified near the back of the grid but again retired. Phil Hill's car snapped its left-rear stub axle and careered off course in a shower of sand as the wheel bounded away. This happened on lap 16, when Baghetti was already out with something variously reported as ignition or engine failure.

Tavoni decided that further development was needed before the cars raced again and his drivers heartily agreed. Consequently the cars stayed at Sasso Marconi while the French and British Grands

Prix were run, and then came the trip to Nürburgring for the gruelling German GP. With typical ATS luck and good judgement the transporter fell off an Alp on the way to Germany, wrote itself off and damaged both cars within.

So it was not until the Italian Grand Prix at Monza on September 8 that ATS reappeared, and this time their cars looked much more professional, with neat new bodies and streamlining discs let into the wheels for the very fast Autodrome circuit.

Once again it was lack of power which saw the cars qualifying slowly and then they ran steadily during the race without fireworks of any kind and trundled into the pits from time to time—Hill for fuel and Baghetti with electrical problems—and finally came home in sorry, but still mobile, 11th and 15th places, seven laps and 23 laps respectively behind the winning Lotus of new World Champion driver, Jim Clark.

The trans-Atlantic races followed in the United States and Mexico, and both ATS cars made the trip. Phil Hill's had been altered with the whole gearbox turned about so that it now overhung the back axle while a spacer piece had been inserted on the other side to maintain the same wheelbase.

The standard ATS grid positions having been acquired, the flag fell for the US GP, and as the smoke cleared from the start Baghetti was to be seen rolling gently forward and retiring after half a lap with the oil pump gone and his engine seized. On the fifth lap Phil Hill pulled off onto the grass with his car's oil pump failed . . . which left just Mexico to come.

On the Magdalena Mixhuca circuit the ATS team arrived and waited for their rebuilt engines to be flown in from Italy. They arrived late before practice and that night a violent thunderstorm broke over Mexico City which put all the lights out. Both ATS engine installations were completed by torch and car headlights, and an unkind onlooker suggested that this was how they had originally been built!

Baghetti had all kinds of misfiring troubles in the race, for the circuit is at very high altitude and carburettor settings were always difficult to judge. After eight laps and two pit stops he drove the car disgustedly into the paddock, but it was somehow revived there and then he tried to rejoin the race. He succeeded in sneaking past the marshals, had to make another pit stop with more misfiring and was finally excluded by the organisers for leaving the scene of battle!

Meanwhile Hill had been running tenth with a very rough-sounding engine. He soldiered on until lap 41 when a lower rear wishbone mounting tore completely out of the chassis in the twisting Esses section of the circuit, and after a wild few moments he straightened the car out and abandoned it on the verge.

That was the last appearance of the original ATS team and cars in Formula 1 racing, and the close of this sorry season saw Ferrari left to uphold Italian honour on his own. A number of the pretty little ATS coupés had been built during the year and two of them ran in the 1964 Targa Florio in Sicily but retired, true to form.

The company was finished as Billi and Patiño pulled out and the works survived mainly as a light engineering and foundry concern for sub-contracted work. Tavoni moved on, and Chiti joined Alfa Romeo's Autodelta competition subsidiary to design a long string of generally unsuccessful sports-racing cars which are still with us today.

One ATS appeared in the 1964 Italian Grand Prix, having been acquired by Alf Francis and British tuning and components manufacturer Vic Derrington. They had modified the car in detail and it was given to Mario Araujo Cabral, the Portuguese driver. It was slow and retired with engine trouble and that was the end of $1\frac{1}{2}$-litre Formula 1.

Count Volpi bought the remainder of the team's bits and pieces, and in 1966 Bruce McLaren Motor Racing used a Serenissima three-litre V8 engine in their first Formula 1 chassis at Spa and in the British Grand Prix at Brands Hatch. Bruce drove the car into a steady sixth place in Kent to score his first World Championship point in a car of his own construction. Probably the last Formula 1 appearance of the ATS engine was the following year in the British GP at Silverstone, where Swiss privateer Silvio Moser used another three-litre V8 mounted in an old Cooper chassis. True to form the car qualified second slowest, and after 29 laps little Moser retired it with no oil pressure.

This was the close of an unhappy chapter in Italian motor racing, but at least one car still exists, for ATS Tipo 100, No 01, was acquired by the Donington Collection as a pile of rusty bits in 1969–70. The bits were completely restored and reassembled in 1973 and a new replica bodyshell was built to present the car in its original first prototype form. It looks far, far better than the works cars ever looked, but then the Donington Collection is a Grand Prix fairyland . . . and perhaps the old ATS drivers would agree that that's the best place for their car which never came up to scratch.

17

British Racing Failures –
1939-1967

When English Racing Automobiles came into being through the efforts of Raymond Mays and Peter Berthon in 1934 they built a 1½-litre Voiturette which was capable of making a terrific impression internationally in the mid thirties. Humphrey Cook supplied the financial backing and while Berthon developed a six-cylinder engine from Riley beginnings, Reid Railton produced a kind of 'Chinese' version of the Maserati chassis which he had improved for Whitney Straight, and Murray Jamieson evolved an efficient supercharging system.

In the years which followed, ERA became an integral part of the Voiturette scene, and of the 17 A, B, C, and D-Type cars which they built in their works beside Mays' home at Bourne in Lincolnshire, no less than 16 are still in existence. The missing car was that destroyed in SEFAC driver Marcel Lehoux's fatal accident at Deauville in 1936.

When the AIACR announced a three-litre supercharged Formula for 1938, ERA planned to build a full Grand Prix car which would equal the Continentals. Unfortunately this never came about, and with money becoming short ERA concentrated on a new type of 1½-litre supercharged Voiturette which would equal the Italian Maseratis and Alfa Romeos if not the Germans.

In this way the E-Type ERA was born and in view of the later failures experienced by its distant relatives, the V16 and H16 BRMs, its unfortunate tale is worth the telling.

The Bourne concern hoped to run the prototype car in the British Empire Trophy race at Donington Park—where the world's biggest racing car collection is now housed—on 1 April 1939, but it was far from ready, and was not to appear until the beginning of May.

Details were released, showing that the six-cylinder engine was quite similar to its predecessors, having bore and stroke dimensions of 63mm x 80mm, a capacity of 1,487cc, but with power boosted to 260bhp at 7,500rpm by the addition of a revised 28psi Zoller supercharger. A brand new four-speed synchromesh gearbox had been developed which was in unit with the differential at the rear of a new tubular ladder-frame chassis, and a geared propeller shaft ran along the car six inches beneath hub height. This feature allowed a very low seating position and consequently low-slung body lines. The bodyshell was modelled closely after the 1938 Grand Prix Mercedes cars with a peculiar divided air intake in the nose, and ERA released figures showing a maximum speed of 170mph.

Raymond Mays tested the prototype car at Donington Park in late April and found it very satisfactory, and then took it to Brooklands where a rather optimistic two-car entry had been made for himself and Arthur Dobson in the JCC International Trophy race on May 2.

The solitary new E-Type ERA arrived at Brooklands amid intense interest the day before the race, having already missed much of practice. At Brooklands a mandatory silencer system had to be fitted in deference to the local residents' tender hearing, and with this in place Mays found the E-Type not taking kindly to the increased back pressure. He covered two hopelessly slow laps and then after some vain attempts to get the car running properly it was posted as a non-starter and spent race day on show to the public.

On the Monday following this unhappy 'debut' Humphrey Cook made the long-feared announcement that ERA had so far cost him £90,000 and he could not afford to continue his support. That same day saw the E-Type running in tests at Brooklands without the silencer in place and briefly it proved very quick indeed.

After Cook's disagreement with Mays the works moved from Bourne to the barns of Coppice Farm at Donington Park, and there work continued in an attempt to get the E-Type racing. It non-started again in the Coronation Trophy there, after practice oil-pump failure ruined an engine while Arthur Dobson was driving.

Back at the start of the season Peter Berthon had promised two (if not three) E-Types to the organisers of the *Coupe de la Commission Sportive* at Reims in July, and a crash programme was put in hand to get a lone car onto the grid.

During practice for the French race Dobson forced the car round the fast triangular circuit at 101.59mph to record the fastest 1½-litre time. But after a few more laps he noticed the water temperature soaring and it was found that at 160mph along the straights there was insufficient louvring in the bonnet to let hot radiator air escape. This was pressuring the engine bay to such an extent that the radiator was failing to cool normally, and while this was going on the piston rings were damaged and oil found its way into the upper cylinders and onto the plugs. Sadly disappointed after such a promising showing, ERA Ltd *again* withdrew their new car.

Cook cancelled his Albi entry and took the car to Montlhéry to do some testing. There the car performed so well that the Albi entry was reconfirmed for the following weekend and Dobson appeared there for the car's first actual race.

He qualified on the front row of the starting grid beside Mays' fast D-Type and Johnny Wakefield's new Maserati, and from the flag he dived into an immediate lead. On his fourth lap he set fastest time of the day at 98.57mph but on the ninth lap the engine began to misfire.

Albi was another public road circuit with very fast straights and fearing more overheating problems the car was signalled to stop at its pit. Dobson saw the signal early, attempted to pull into his pit without making another complete lap and in braking heavily he got himself all crossed up and spun backwards into the barrier, bashing in his car's long streamlined tail and damaging its rear suspension.

This was an unfortunate end to a promising performance and back at Donington Park another car was being prepared for the 1939 Nuffield Trophy race, but that event had to be cancelled owing to the outbreak of war on September 3.

Both E-Types were put in storage for the duration, and post-war ERA Ltd had no intention of returning to racing so sold the cars, one to Peter Whitehead and the other—when finally completed—to Leslie Brooke.

Whitehead took his new acquisition all the way to Turin for the first big postwar race in the Valentino Park. He was running steadily in fifth place when something came adrift in the supercharger and put him out. He then took his car—GP 1—to Jersey in the Channel Islands for the International Road Race, but had all kinds of troubles which culminated in the fuel tank splitting wide open.

Meanwhile Brooke took GP 2 across the Atlantic to Indianapolis where gearbox trouble foiled any attempt to qualify and he returned disconsolately home.

Whitehead unloaded GP 1 onto Reg Parnell who had been toying with his own special 1½-litre car in 1939, which he called the 'Challenger'. It was modelled very closely on Mercedes-Benz lines but the war put a stop to the project, after he had fitted an ERA engine and gearbox to get the car running at Prescott hill-climb. His own engine was planned as a Riley-based twin overhead camshaft six-cylinder. His son Tim (now manager of the BRM Grand Prix team) tells me that this unit was completed postwar, but Challenger was fitted with a 1927 straight-eight Delage engine and was raced by David Hampshire for a short time. Tim Parnell believes that it was sold to Dick Habershon but it seems to have disappeared since then.

Meanwhile Brooke and Parnell formed a kind of unofficial two-car ERA team later in 1947, doing little except qualify for their starting money at Reims and in the Ulster Trophy. Brooke's GP 2 was drastically detuned for the British Empire Trophy race on the Isle of Man and completed 38 of the scheduled 40 laps at an average of 63.71mph. It was the first time that an E-Type ERA had seen the chequered flag!

In the French Grand Prix at Lyons which saw the CTA-Arsenal's sorry debut, Brooke technically started the race in GP 2 but did so minus one rod and piston and again did so only to qualify for starting money. Parnell was running a lowly 10th in GP 1 when he stopped to hand over to 'Wilkie' Wilkinson, who was then his chief mechanic.

Wilkinson was charging along the dual carriageway which formed part of the circuit when the E-Type's steering sheared and it charged clean across the central strip between some stout trees and miraculously came to a halt without hitting anything.

In November 1947 Leslie Johnson took over the management of ERA Ltd and he bought GP 2 back from Brooke and attempted to make it properly raceworthy. Simultaneously Mays and Berthon were working hard to get the V16 1½-litre BRM project off the ground, and their earlier E-Type at last put in reasonable performances in modified form. Johnson and Wilkinson brought the car home fifth in the Isle of Man races, and tied with Parnell's new Maserati for fastest lap of the day. Later that year Johnson broke the practice lap record for the Montlhéry short circuit, but had his car's fuel tank burst during the race.

So the tale of woe went on with the cars continually breaking and developing all kinds of odd faults. Peter Walker actually drove GP 1 into fourth place in a race heat at Silverstone, and listed four reasons why he should have retired: gears jumping out, dodgy steering, a faulty exhaust system burning his foot and the radiator spraying him with hot water!

In June, 1950, GP 1 finally snapped a half-shaft on the Isle of Man, and its flailing stumps ripped open the tank which immediately dumped its contents onto a hot exhaust. The car burst into flames and Walker baled out to watch it burn to the ground.

Its engine was eventually salvaged and fitted into a Delage chassis owned by Rob Walker, who gave it to Tony Rolt to drive. The car is still in Britain today, running regularly in VSCC events.

Meanwhile, northern enthusiast Ken Flint bought the remains of both GP 1 and GP 2, fitted a Jaguar engine in the earlier chassis, fitted the later car's body, added cycle wings and turned it into a sports car. It was the best answer to the E-Type problem.

While all this was going on, the centrifugally-supercharged V16 BRM had finally been produced by the Mays-Berthon team and with hysterically enthusiastic headlines announcing Britain's world-beating Grand Prix car it embarked on the career of malfunction and misery which is so well known. It was virtually undriveable in original form and even a youthful Stirling Moss battled with it in Ulster and was rewarded by the sight of his team-mate Juan Fangio spinning backwards down the road!

The BRM V16 story has been told many times, but eleven years after its last appearances—in 1955—another sixteen-cylinder BRM was being produced in the Bourne works . . . some thought 'Will they never learn?'

After the original sixteen-cylinder nonsense had been consigned to the back store, BRM spent five seasons developing a four-cylinder engine for the 2½-litre Formula 1 which eventually won the team their first World Championship Grand Prix at Zandvoort in 1959. At the end of that season they produced their prototype mid-engined car and late in 1961 Chief Engineer Tony Rudd's new V8 1½-litre engine made its debut. In 1962 the combination of this engine, a lightweight spaceframe BRM chassis and Graham Hill's driving won BRM the coveted World Championship in a close battle with Jim Clark's brand new monocoque Lotuses with their Coventry-Climax V8 engines.

The BRMs proved consistently competitive in the remaining years of the 1½-litre Formula and Graham Hill was again in line for the world title right into the last round of the 1964 season. Then came change, for a new Formula had been announced which was to start in 1966.

The new regulations allowed unsupercharged engines a capacity of three litres, or supercharged engines 1½ litres. Chief Engineer Rudd disregarded the blown engine as being far too dicey a proposition without the use of special alcohol fuels for their internal cooling properties, and he initiated two design researches – one for a twelve-cylinder engine, the other a sixteen cylinder.

The V12 was intended to double-up as a sports car unit, but a sixteen-cylinder was much more difficult to arrange, for another vee unit would be far too long to be compatible with modern chassis.

So a compact H-layout was proposed, in which two horizontal eight-cylinder units would lie one above the other with their individual crankshafts geared together. To minimise vehicle weight it was further intended to stress this unit as an integral part of the car's chassis structure.

Rudd was particularly drawn to the H16 idea since it could use many of the V8 components which had been proved over the years, and so BRM Project 75 was committed to paper by draughtsman Geoffrey Johnson. This type of layout had been fairly common in aero engine design, where units such as the 24-cylinder Rolls-Royce Eagle, the Napier Rapier, Dagger and Sabre had all employed it with varying degrees of success.

The original idea was to have only three camshafts appearing on either side of the engine, with the centre shaft controlling both sets of inlet valves in the upper and lower banks. This would have been a neat solution and it would have saved considerable weight. Unfortunately it was found to be unworkable, for extra space was required between the two cranks and for practical reasons Rudd and Johnson decided to narrow the angle between the valves and to use a slightly larger cylinder bore to accomodate them.

This move destroyed the idea of direct interchangeability between V8 and H16 parts, for the smaller engine had dimensions of 68.5 x 50.8mm while the new unit was to measure 69.85 x 48.89mm.

Now the added complication of using four camshafts on either side pushed the unit's weight up, and the curious decision was taken to employ single eight-cylinder head castings on either side instead of a probably lighter and certainly much simpler twin four-cylinder head arrangement. The manufacture of these one-piece heads reputedly cost six months' production delay and added over 44lbs to the engine's weight.

The H16's crankcase was a square aluminium box-like structure, divided vertically and carrying both crankshafts and their associated coupling gears. Drive for all four camshafts was taken from the nose of the lower crankshaft only, viewed by technical historian Karl Ludvigsen as '. . . one of the most questionable features of the whole design. . .'.

Drives for the Lucas transistor ignition trigger and for both distributors were taken from the front of the upper crankshaft, while two water pumps and two fuel injection metering units were driven from the camshaft gears. Oil pressure and scavenge pumps were gear-driven from the lower crankshaft.

Notwithstanding its incredible complication, this compact unit was mated to the rear of a slim sheet alloy monocoque nacelle which provided fuel tankage, front suspension and radiator mounts and what one Formula 1 designer described to me as '. . . the place where the man goes in . . .'. A giant six-speed BRM gearbox with overhung multi-disc clutch protruded from the 16's rear end, and provision was made in the design for the future possible adoption of four-wheel drive.

Sir Alfred Owen, head of the organisation of which BRM was a small part, unveiled the car at Bourne on 22 April 1966. The press and enthusiast public were shaken by its specification, but it was stressed that it was a long-term project of which not too much should be expected too soon.

Unfortunately, development had to be hurried along, for after the original production delays, promises had been made to other customers which had to be fulfilled.

When the three-litre Formula had been published, Coventry-Climax had announced that they would be pulling out of racing. The company had been supplying engines to manufacturers such as Cooper, Lotus and Brabham for years, and in 1965 their own sixteen-cylinder 'FWMW' 1½-litre engine had been an ambitious final fling which failed.

Climax had been testing four-valve per cylinder heads for their V8 engines during 1963–64 and the initial results had been so disappointing that another line of attack was considered necessary, and the 'flat sixteen' project was the result.

Designer Walter Hassan accepted that for a given rpm, a 16-

cylinder would be less stressed than a 12-cylinder, and he calculated that the former unit would offer 200bhp at 10,000rpm, 220bhp at 11,000 and 240bhp at 12,000rpm. The conventional 135-degree vee-angle was chosen but he found this pushed the centre of gravity too high into the air, and then a downwards droop layout was tried with an inverted 135-degree Vee. This produced excellent results but unfortunately left no space for the chassis tubes of a car. So a compromise was reached, and the horizontally-opposed formation was chosen. Two crankshafts were used, shrunk onto a common gear in the centre from which drive was taken for traction and all auxiliaries.

Work had begun in 1963, but the first engine was not on the test-bed until late in 1964 by which time the last year of the 1½-litre Formula was about to begin and Climax's last fling was patently too late. It could have been raced had initial tests proved trouble-free, but the power take-off shaft sheared first time on the dynamometer due to internal torsional vibrations. This was corrected by the use of a larger-diameter shaft and new drive gears, but lubrication drainage and valve spring problems delayed the programme. Frictional losses were found to be very high, and with a peak output of 209bhp at 12,000rpm the sixteen could not compete with Jim Clark's new 32-valve Climax V8 which had already virtually assured him of the world title with its 210bhp at 10,500rpm. So the flat-sixteen engine was dropped, as Coventry-Climax withdrew from racing.

This move left Cooper, Lotus and Brabham looking for motive power. Cooper went to Maserati in Italy for V12 engines, Brabham went to Repco in his native Australia for a stock-block V8, and Lotus turned to Cosworth and Ford for the V8 engine which would appear in 1967 and which would win every World Championship title from 1968 to date. In the meantime, while waiting for the Cosworth-Ford to appear, Colin Chapman did a deal with BRM to use their H16.

The previous year had seen Lotus winning at Indianapolis in their last year of exclusive Ford of America backing. Since then Chapman had concluded a deal with Andy Granatelli's STP Corporation to run his Lotus cars in their vermilion colours at Indy in 1966, and another H16 deal had been cooked-up with BRM for the development and supply of a 4.2-litre version of the new engine!

During 1965 BRM had been supplying so many V8 customers with bits and pieces and maintenance services that they had come very close to breaking even, and in a burst of over-enthusiasm they

52, 53 Reventlow's Californian workshops in 1959 with three Scarab Formula 1 chassis and the prototype body-shell being built-up. The special Scarab engine was to lie on its side within those shallow spaceframes.

54 Lance Reventlow in his Scarab at La Source, Spa, during the 1960 Belgian GP.

55 The Bugatti 251's unusual rocker-arm inboard rear suspension exposed in the garage at Rheims, 1956.

56 Leaving its lair – one of the E-Type ERAs is rolled onto its truck at Reg Parnell's Derby establishment, about 1947.

57 Leaving this World – GP No 1 burns out on the Isle of Man, 1950. Everybody seems to be enjoying the cheery blaze . . .

took on this vast amount of specialised customer work for the new year.

Unfortunately, the H16 was already in deep trouble. Initial tests in the dynamometer cells on Folkingham Aerodrome had exposed terrific vibrational problems which were tackled and minimised, and then when runs at up to 10,000rpm began, the output coupling between the two crankshafts began to fail.

The instant the crankshafts went out of synchronisation a massive breakage was inevitable and immediate. Rudd and his engineers traced this problem to complex torsional vibrations building up within the complicated new engine, and much heavier crankshaft counter-weights were adopted which proved temporarily effective.

In June 1966 a Lotus-bound H16 produced 400bhp at 10,500rpm on the test-bed and that (from engine No 7504) was the best *ever* seen, despite vague predictions of 'perhaps 600bhp by the end of its development life. . . .'

The first P83 BRM with its H16 engine appeared in practice for the Monaco Grand Prix, and then in June, Graham Hill found it really 'growling' during practice on the fast Reims circuit before the French Grand Prix. He buried his foot on the throttle out of Thillois Hairpin and came bulleting down the long undulating straight past the pits at a speed and with a noise which had everyone scrambling for cover!

Unfortunately this form could not be maintained for very long, and if the engine itself didn't fail then something in the gearbox did, for with the overhung clutch arrangement it acted as a kind of fly-wheel on the mainshaft, and the driver had to make slow deliberate changes as he waited for the gearbox internals to slow down to a speed at which they could engage cleanly. No self-respecting racing driver will count to three in between gears, and consequently gearbox dogs took a terrific hammering and failed regularly.

Whatever broke, engine or transmission, something always *did* seem to break—and then there was the weight problem. Lotus designer Maurice Phillippe once told me 'We knew we had a weight problem when the first H16 engine was delivered from BRM. We had to get six mechanics out to lift it off the lorry! I think that the engine, gearbox and rear suspension assembly together represented the Formula's minimum weight limit. . . .'

BRM's engines, in fairness, seemed to lead a far more troubled life than their customers', and the works team relied heavily upon

M

their existing 2.1-litre V8-powered Tasman Formula cars for much of the season. In the United States Grand Prix late in the year Jim Clark's Lotus 43 had a practice engine failure. To get him to the line Team Lotus borrowed BRM's spare engine (a much-patched old nail, No 7502, with about 370bhp left in it) and it was hurriedly installed overnight. Clark managed to nurse it to the finish to win the H16's one and only Grand Prix victory.

The H16 was also a difficult engine to fit into a racing chassis, for it demanded cross-over exhaust systems above and below with its original simple four-cylinder design crankshafts, in which two cylinders fired simultaneously in the upper flat-eight, and then two more fired simultaneously, ninety-degrees later, in the bottom eight.

Phillippe recalled, '. . . unless one was prepared to mount the engine an extra six inches into the air—which no self-respecting designer was prepared to do—one had to compromise with a cross-over exhaust system on top of the engine and a divided system down below . . . it was a conundrum . . .'.

Late in 1966 Rudd introduced 'eight-throw' crankshafts to provide a more permanent cure for the vibration problems, and, from this point on, the engine fired and sounded like a true sixteen cylinder.

These modified engines were known as the BRM P75 Mk 2 series, and into 1967 a perfect example of backward development found them producing only 375-380bhp at 10,500rpm. Disastrous internal breakages continued and since these almost invariably resulted in the engine becoming a total write-off BRM could only hazard guesses as to the cause.

I recall them saying that after 300 miles' running it appeared that the balance-weight retaining bolts on the crankshaft would part, and that this was the time to look over one's shoulder and take cover. In Mexico Jim Clark had a serious failure at the end of the 1966 season in which the engine exploded behind his back, pieces blew a huge hole in the top of the crankcase and he climbed out of the car with his overalls saturated in hot oil.

After much investigation a broken engine was found which gave some clues to the true cause. It was found that torsional variations in the valve gear allowed the timing to drift and adjoining valves would meet during the overlap phase and break-up. The bits would drop down into the bore and chaos would ensue.

Then there was the 4.2-litre Indianapolis engine which actually appeared in the metal in 1967. Phillippe recalls that one was delivered to Lotus, installed in a chassis and tested briefly at Snetterton before failing in spectacular style as it ripped out its coupling gears.

Evidently this engine was a petrifying sight on the test bed, for in common with all the H16s it would rattle and chatter and lurch about on its mountings and be in visible torment as it fought to produce its power. With the extra 1.2 litres it misbehaved more than the rest and its appetite for output gear trains proved quite insatiable.

During 1966 and 1967 the H16 became the inevitable also-ran in Grand Prix racing. When on form it was fast, just as the V16 and the 2½-litre four-cylinder cars had been before it, but with the advent of the Cosworth-Ford engine in mid '67 it was incapable of keeping up.

Jackie Stewart brought one car into a remarkable second place in the Belgian Grand Prix at Spa where Dan Gurney won the first European Grande Epreuve for America since 1921. Stewart was holding the car in gear for lap after lap around the dauntingly fast Ardennes circuit, in the days when he still took up its challenge.

That autumn saw BRM's second-string V12 engine make its debut in Bruce McLaren's new M5A car in the Canadian Grand Prix at Mosport, and in driving rain he came very close to winning. The writing was on the wall for the H16, and at the close of the season it was decided to concentrate on the V12 in its place.

In all, the works H16 cars finished only 11 times in Formula 1 events, and only six times did they earn championship points. One of the most consistent of the cars was 8302—entered by Tim Parnell's individual semi-works team—which Mike Spence's mechanically sympathetic style brought home into four fifth and one sixth place in championship events. This car is now preserved in the Donington Collection, and has been driven at Silverstone by Tom Wheatcroft—but gently.

Despite the decision to retire the H16s, development continued at Bourne with a view to returning to the fray at a later date.

Early in 1968 the P75 Mk 3 design was initiated which virtually resulted in a brand new engine. It was built up as a test unit for four-valve-per-cylinder heads, and two separate four-cylinder head castings appeared on either side in place of the earlier vastly complicated casting, while the internal structure was totally revised and detail changes in drive-train layouts and so on had been made.

During 1969 this unit proved that the H16 could be reliable, for it ran troublefree on the Folkingham test-beds. Unfortunately it could not run really *well*, for even with four valves per cylinder its output never bettered 385bhp, and that was nothing like enough now that Cosworth were running reliably to 440bhp and beyond.

The BRM H16 engine had been a particular pet of Tony Rudd's, and when he was dismissed during BRM's salutary shake-up in the middle of 1969, the end of the programme was assured.

It was very unfortunate that development of this daring unit should have failed so dismally in realising its theoretical potential, but today's Formula 1 regulations place a twelve-cylinder limit on eligible engines and it is doubtful if we shall ever see another BRM sixteen-cylinder. Perhaps from that unfortunate company's point of view, that might be no bad thing.

18

Air-Cooling: Minor Triumphs and Major Tragedy –
1935-1968

Britain has always been richly endowed with special builders, and many of them have produced designs which were way ahead of the major manufacturers then involved in competition.

In 1935, while the Chamberlains were campaigning their splendid special in Australia, Harry Miller was building Ford cars for Indianapolis, and Count Trossi was wrestling with his radial-engined machine in Italy, a remarkable little air-cooled, four wheel drive sprint special was being put together in England.

It was the work of an enthusiastic engineer named Robert Waddy, and he based his car on an aircraft-type fuselage very similar in principle to Auguste Monaco's multi-tubular structure then being used in the Trossi car. It was welded up from 18-gauge chrome-molybdenum tubing, and borrowed its basic layout from an Avro Avian light plane fuselage. Again, it was one of the very earliest 'spaceframe' chassis.

Waddy mounted a single-cylinder two-stroke JAP dirt-track engine at either end of this tubular frame, each having its own Rudge gearbox and chain-driving to its particular pair of wheels. Each engine had a bore and stroke of 81mm x 96.8mm, and a swept volume of 498cc.

The only linkage between these two engines was a dual throttle control, which connected to an adventurous rocking pedal device in the cockpit. By pressing the pedal straight down, Waddy could accelerate both engines simultaneously, and by rocking the pedal with his toe or heel he could open up each engine individually and so make tiny corrections to avoid unnecessary wheelspin at either end!

He used trailing link front suspension with torsion bar springing as seen on the contemporary Auto Unions, and at the rear springing was by a transverse leaf and a complex link system located the wheels.

The whole car was clad in a dumpy bodyshell, in many ways prophetic of the Gulf-Millers to come in three years' time, and unlike Auto Union the cockpit was placed further back in the frame, closer to the rear wheels.

Waddy christened this delightful car 'Fuzzi' because its chassis was like an aircraft 'fuzzilage', and during its regular sprint outings from 1936–39 it became a terrific favourite with the crowds while becoming hated by the commentators. They had the onerous task of having to fit 'Robert Waddy's "Fuzzi" ' into a hectic high-speed commentary, and it regularly reached the crowd's delighted ears as 'Frobert Wuddy's "Fizzi",' or 'Wubert Fuddy's "Wazzi" '. During its career the Rudge gearboxes were replaced by a pair as used in Morgan three-wheelers, and Fuzzi proved itself capable of streaking along a standing-start half-mile course in 25.80 seconds and nipping the 100mph mark as it went through the traps. It could also climb Shelsley Walsh's hill in 44.08 seconds, and Waddy proved both the capabilities of four-wheel drive and his own skill as driver of this complicated device.

Fuzzi was put away during the war, and reappeared in 1946 when Waddy decided to use a big American V8 engine in place of the two reliable but small JAP units. He cut the existing car in half and lengthened the chassis to accommodate a Mercury V8 housed amidships. Chains and shafts drove to front and rear wheels, and every other part of the car then had to be beefed-up to absorb the Mercury's extra horsepower. Unfortunately the basic concept of simplicity had been lost and the new 'Son of Fuzzi' was never able to reproduce its parent's great performances.

It was during this postwar period that two more air-cooled hill-climb specials appeared, both using four-wheel drive, but they were much closer in layout to Waddy's postwar failure than to his prewar success.

Irishman Archie Butterworth began to build his AJB special in 1948. He was an ex-Army man, a strong protagonist of four-wheel drive. He wanted to prove the advantages of the system for high-performance vehicles, and as a fully-qualified engineer he set about basing a sprint and hill-climb car on an ex-Army Jeep chassis.

He modified the frame, boxed it for extra rigidity and added extra location links for the axles. Power came from an ex-Wehrmacht

Steyr V8 engine, which was an air-cooled unit of 3.7 litres with separate motorcycle style finned cylinder barrels and pushrod-operated overhead valves. It had obvious potential, so Butterworth designed and made new barrels and pistons with the bore increased from 79mm to 87.5mm, providing a displacement of 4,425cc with the standard 92mm stroke. The compression ratio was raised to about 14:1, and with special camshafts, eight Amal carburettors and a lethal alcohol fuel mixture, the German engine produced about 260bhp allied to a claimed 320lbs ft torque.

This was transmitted via a Steyr three-speed gearbox to a transfer box, which offset the drive to a centre differential, from which normal Jeep propeller shafts ran to the front and rear axles. Butterworth designed a foot-change gearbox for the car later in its career, with two clutches; the driver kicked the left clutch to change up and the right clutch to change down. This second clutch automatically blipped the throttle by a varying amount compatible to the car's road speed! He patented this idea but was never to use it.

Most of this complicated mechanism was covered by a stark single-seater bodyshell, leaving the massive cylinder barrels poking nakedly into the airstream on either side of a long bonnet.

The AJB was notable for its extremely spectacular sprint and hill-climb appearances, during which it regularly cornered on two wheels with its tall, bearded creator sitting apparently oblivious in the cockpit. Once it touched down on all four wheels he would open the throttle and the car would simply rocket along the next straight section with thin plumes of blue smoke flicking from all four tyres!

Archie Butterworth tells me that he drove the car with his eyes glued on the front tyres, judging throttle opening by the amount of smoke he could see. Evidently it was a pig to handle, especially on bumpy surfaces – 'You just sat there and hoped it would all be over soon. . . .'

In 1949 the AJB made a spectacular fastest time of the day at Brighton Speed Trials, along the Madeira Drive, and in 1951 Butterworth repeated the performance, this time in pelting rain.

Autosport reported: '. . . In quite the worst of the rainstorm Archie Butterworth (AJB) and Sydney Allard (Allard) set off together – or at least Archie set off, for Syd became involved in a spectacular broadside as his rival streaked away, rather like a torpedo on its way to the target. Watching Butterworth is quite an experience. One moment he's there, the next he appears to be halfway to Rottingdean.

Anyway, his 26.77secs was an astonishing performance in such appalling weather conditions. Even more remarkable was the fact that he cut his time down to 26.33 on his second run, being half-blinded by spray from numerous deep puddles on the way!'

Archie Butterworth was a brave man.

Unfortunately, that September saw him dropping the AJB into Shelsley Walsh's ravine, and the roll-over bar which he had fitted to protect his head in just such an accident unfortunately savaged his back as the car landed on top of him.

While he was in hospital a deal was finalised with the American Four-Wheel Drive Auto Company (of original 4WD Miller frame), and the battered and mud-covered AJB was sold to them for the use of Bill Milliken—a great four-wheel drive enthusiast—of the Cornell Aeronautical Laboratory in Buffalo, Michigan. He ran the car in all kinds of research programmes, and extensively modified it with a lengthened wheelbase, new steering, suspension and rear axle. Today, 'Butterball' as the car was renamed, stands in the FWD museum at Clintonville, Wisconsin, where the original decision to back Harry Miller's effort of the Depression years had been taken.

Incidentally, the AJB had qualified as a 4½-litre unsupercharged Formula 1 car, and Butterworth raced it whenever he could in minor club events. He actually became the first constructor-driver of a four-wheel drive Grand Prix car when he ran AJB in the 1950 International Trophy race at Silverstone. Unfortunately he was using an aluminium crankcase for the Steyr there, and it flexed, allowing the main bearings to go out of line which caused an immediate engine failure almost as he left the starting grid. 'Kenneth MacAlpine had the Connaught pit [sic] next to ours. He leaned across and offered me £300 not to repair the car for Brighton, the next big speed event. . . !'

Sydney Allard was one of Butterworth's main competitors, using a similar car in many respects, although his Steyr engine retained its 3.7-litre capacity and was mounted in a chassis used for the famous Ford and Cadillac V8-powered sports cars which his small company constructed.

The Allard-Steyr was light and proved quite reliable, bringing Allard the British Hill-Climb Championship in 1949. It used two-wheel drive only for most of its career, but when a front-drive unit was added Syd Allard took some time to become acquainted with the new driving style required. These Steyr-engined specials were renowned for the sheer shattering volume of noise which they produced, and both cars proved tremendously popular with spectators.

While Butterworth was running his sprint and hill-climb car, he was also working on an ambitious project to produce an air-cooled racing engine of his own. It was intended as a proprietary unit to be sold to customers interested in unsupercharged 2-litre Formula 2 racing, and details were released in February 1951.

The new AJB engine was a horizontally-opposed four-cylinder, with bore and stroke dimensions of 87.5mm x 82.5mm giving a displacement of 1,986cc. The nearside cylinders were staggered forward by $2\frac{1}{8}$ inches to allow the use of a four-throw three-bearing crankshaft housed in a light alloy crankcase. Camshafts were housed in the top of the crankcase, operating overhead poppet valves in modified Steyr cylinder heads through short pushrods which ran through separate tubes into the cylinder barrels. Butterworth also designed a 'swing valve' as part of a development programme for this basic engine, which was intended to fold right away from the inlet port to allow an unrivalled free-flow to the incoming charge.

His engine was intended to produce something like 180bhp for a weight of only 180lbs. There was only one customer, test pilot Bill Aston, who bought two engines and mounted them in modified Cooper-Bristol front-engined type chassis frames. The flat-four engine was mounted well-forward in the frame and drove through an MG TD clutch and four-speed gearbox to an open Hardy-Spicer propeller shaft and thence to the back axle.

Bill Aston was to drive one of the cars himself, while Robin Montgomerie-Charrington took over the other. They were among the lightest cars in Formula 2, and were known as Aston-Butterworths, although the engine designer himself insisted that his products should be known as 'AJBs'.

The cars ran during the 1952 season but were uncompetitive and unreliable for all kinds of obscure reasons, not the least being the lack of adequate backing to develop their ambitious little engines. Aston and Montgomerie-Charrington had some enjoyable outings while the cars lasted, but they disappeared from the scene at the end of the season. Montgomerie-Charrington's car is in VSCC member Nigel Woollet's garage not five miles from here as I write, but its AJB engine has proved very reluctant to run properly in recent years.

It was not until 1957 that the AJB $1\frac{1}{2}$-litre swing-valve engine appeared in British club racing, installed in an Elva sports-racing chassis. The car was known affectionately as 'Sabrina' in view of its bulbous air-cooling ducts jutting proudly from its bonnet, and with the famous disabled driver Scott-Brown behind the wheel it proved immensely fast, immensely noisy, and still far from right.

Problems were experienced with outside supplies of swing-valves being improperly made, and then with replacements taking an inordinately long time to be produced. Eventually Scott-Brown won a minor event with the Elva, and Archie Butterworth already had a single-seater Cooper chassis modified to accept a 1½-litre version of the flat-four engine for Formula 2 in 1958. Archie Scott-Brown was scheduled to drive it, but tragically this wonderfully courageous driver died after crashing a Lister-Jaguar in the 1958 Spa sports-car race. This proved a body blow to the tiny Butterworth AJB operation, which was never to re-enter serious racing.

France also had its air-cooled race engine adherents during this period, with Charles Deutsch and René Bonnet being the most notable. They began building specials together in 1948 and after experimenting with all kinds of available power units they decided that the air-cooled Panhard flat-twin engine with its associated front-wheel drive transmission was the best for their requirements.

So they established a small business, building, selling and racing small sports cars under the name DB-Panhard. The cars proved very successful in their class, and when their handicapping was favourable they were capable of winning such major events as the 1954 RAC Tourist Trophy, in which Gérard Laureau and Paul Armagnac brought their streamlined DB-Panhard home ahead of Ferrari and Maserati.

Deutsch and Bonnet eventually dropped the Panhard tag, and continued as DB, but when they decided to attempt Formula 1 racing in 1955 they already had experience of some similarly ambitious projects. For example, in the autumn of 1951 the duo had been seen at Montlhéry, testing a four-wheel drive Formula 2 car.

This vehicle consisted of a pair of their '500' chassis frames, halved and welded together to produce a single car carrying a 750cc Panhard engine and drive system at either end. Each horizontally-opposed overhead valve engine had twin mechanical fuel pumps feeding a pair of 1¼-inch Solex carburettors, while ignition was provided by a single Morel magneto for each engine.

The two gearboxes were operated by a single lever, connected to the forward unit in standard fashion and with a long drag-link to the rear unit. Deutsch and Bonnet intended to build a 'proper racing car powered by a pair of highly-tuned 850cc engines' for the Formula, with a combined output of about 120bhp in a car totalling less than 1,000lbs—if their tests proved successful. Unfortunately we must presume that the tests were unsuccessful, for the uprated *Bi-Moteur* DB-Panhard failed to appear.

When the new Grand Prix Formula was introduced in 1954, it admitted unsupercharged engines of up to 2½-litres while restricting supercharged units to 750cc. This was not a very fair division, and effectively spelled the end of supercharged engines in Grand Prix racing. Only one company produced a blown 750cc GP car – and that, after a fashion, was DB.

In 1954 Bonnet had started a racing driver's school using 850cc Panhard-engined cars with very slender Deutsch-designed bodies. The cars were called 'Monomills', and they toured the country to run in specially arranged races, in a similar circus to the Cisitalia-organised troupe of the immediate postwar years. With no other competition Monomill races were misleadingly fast and impressive, and Bonnet took one of these cars and reduced its engine capacity to 750cc, then added a single Roots-type supercharger to produce his prototype Formula 1 'challenger'.

The car was displayed at the Paris Salon late in 1954, and when tests proved fairly promising Bonnet built a second vehicle and entered them both in the Pau Grand Prix the following Easter. He chose this tight round-the-houses circuit since it would level the performance of his cars with the far more powerful but less wieldy 2½-litre cars . . . or so he thought.

The 'Formula 1' DB Monomill consisted of a simple box-section twin-longeron frame, carrying all-independent suspension by wishbones and a transverse leaf-spring at the front, and by trailing arms and torsion bars at the rear. There was no rear axle beam.

Bonnet's overhead-valve flat-twin engine mounted transversely ahead of the front suspension, coupled directly to the gearbox and final-drive casing, from which universally-jointed half-shafts took power to the wheels. A tiny Roots supercharger was mounted on the front of the crankcase, being driven from the timing gears, and it drew mixture from a large downdraught double-choke Solex carburettor.

Messier, the French aviation company, produced specially cast magnesium-alloy disc wheels for the car, and also aircraft-pattern disc front brakes. Orthodox drum brakes were used on the rear, where they would have very little work to do in this decidedly nose-heavy vehicle.

Its French designers made no move to take advantage of the lack of a rearward drive line by seating their driver low down and building a low-slung car. On the contrary, the new Monomill had an enormous ground clearance and its driver was thrust well into the air in a very exposed cockpit.

Claude Storez and Paul Armagnac were to drive the cars at Pau. Both were experienced DB front-drive exponents, but although the town circuit was tight and twisty it also had some very hilly sections, and on these up-grades the DBs proved hopelessly inadequate and their drivers could make no impression at all – even against the Gordinis. Both drivers were notably fast through the corners, simply hurling their cars into them, but power was woefully lacking on the way out. Storez gave up in disgust, while Armagnac gritted his teeth and came home last by miles. Bonnet put the two cars away and forgot about Formula 1.

It was at this same Pau Grand Prix that an Italian Formula 1 car—not air-cooled but an interesting special by any standards—made a tragic debut. It was built by Gianpaolo Volpini to a design by himself and Egidio Arzani. They were Milanese enthusiasts who had cooperated in the production of various Formula 3 specials in earlier years, and their new Arzani-Volpini Formula 1 car was to be backed and driven by a wealthy young amateur driver named Mario Alborghetti.

Very little expense was spared in the car's construction, for Volpini had a special engine constructed in addition to the chassis which was put together in his own workshop. The engine was an in-line water-cooled four-cylinder with 94mm x 90mm bore and stroke, giving a displacement of 2,496cc. It had twin overhead camshafts driven by gear train from the crankshaft, with two camshaft-driven magnetos firing twin plugs per cylinder. It breathed through four single-choke Weber 48DOM sidedraught carburettors, and exhausted through a sweeping four-branch paired manifold into a long tail-pipe which looped along the left-side of the neat and attractive slipper body.

Volpini's chassis had oval-section tubing side members with a lightweight superstructure supporting the body panels. Upper and lower wishbones formed the front suspension, sprung by torsion bars mounted longitudinally and actuated on either side by a link from the lower wishbones. The rear suspension consisted of two parallel trailing arms with the lower one connected to a transverse leaf spring.

The propeller shaft ran rearwards right under the differential housing to a gearbox mounted behind the axle line. Gigantic drum brakes with delicately finned drums of great width were mounted in the wheels, having two leading shoes in each.

This was a very workmanlike approach to Formula 1 for a one-off builder with comparatively little experience, and Alborghetti was entered in it for the Turin race in Valentino Park early in the year. He tested the car extensively at Modena just before the race, but it was considered unready and so the entry was withdrawn.

Pau was the next race on the calendar, and the little Milanese *scuderia* arrived there with high hopes for their slowly developing new car. It stood no chance of becoming properly competitive, but it could give them a lot of enjoyable racing with the faint prospect of picking up some place money if it ran reliably.

Tragically, young Alborghetti seemed very much out of his depth with the supposedly 240bhp Formula 1 car. He started from the back row of the grid, with only Storez's DB qualifying slower, and after three pit stops the Arzani-Volpini came rushing into the Virage de la Gare on the 19th lap, apparently out of control. It made no attempt to take the corner and crashed heavily into the straw bales, injuring nine spectators and killing its unfortunate driver.

The sad little Arzani group returned to Milan, and the car reappeared very briefly in practice for the Italian Grand Prix in September, driven by Luigi Piotti—another wealthy amateur. Unfortunately something major went wrong with the car, and it was taken home before race-day.

While this tragedy was being enacted another—better-known—Milanese group were building a far more mysterious and ambitious Grand Prix car.

This was the Ruggeri brothers' Scuderia Milan, who had made their name in 1949 when the Maserati 4CLT/48 was reaching the end of its development. When the AC Milano offered a substantial cash prize for any new cars running in the Italian Grand Prix, the Ruggeris backed an engineer named Mario Speluzzi in modifying two old 4CLT/48s.

Speluzzi had been modifying the Maserati engine for use in racing speed boats, and much of his established marine practice was built into the 'new' Grand Prix cars with a two-stage supercharger delivering at 44psi. With the addition of newly designed brakes the Ruggeris called their cars Maserati-Milans and claimed the Milan club's prize money at Monza.

Farina and Taruffi drove the two cars, which proved very noisy and fast but unreliable, and after this financial success development continued into 1950. New chassis were built, one with wishbone and torsion bar independent front suspension, and a De Dion rear end, while another used trailing link rear suspension. Speluzzi's very much modified 1½-litre Maserati engines were used, and during 1950 the new Milans impressed only by their ear-splitting exhaust note. The Scuderia ran out of money in 1951 and faded from the scene, but in 1955 the Ruggeris were building something entirely new.

With designer Enrico Franchini they were developing an air-cooled eight-cylinder engine for the 2½-litre Formula 1, to be mounted transversely in the rear of a compact, basically twin-tube chassis, and driving Bugatti-style to the rear wheels!

This most unusual design was to have bore and stroke dimensions of 72mm x 76.5mm (curiously undersquare but so quoted in *Auto-Italiana*) which would give a quoted capacity of 2,489.884cc! Eight Dell'Orto motorcycle carburettors were to be fitted, and the unit's projected output was to exceed 305bhp at 9,000rpm. Franchini's engine lay completely flat, with its head behind the driver's seat, the eight carburettors bristling from its upper side and eight individual exhaust pipes sweeping rearwards in a decidedly aggressive manner. A combined gearbox and final-drive unit coupled up directly to the engine's crankcase, and photographs of the whole assembly show it to have been nicely made with some very complex finned castings.

The Ruggeri chassis for this remarkable engine was to have torsion bar front suspension and a transverse-leaf and link arrangement at the rear. Work on the whole project had started in 1952, but inability to find further financial support finally saw the Ruggeris regretfully abandon their plans late in 1955. The uncompleted chassis and engine are still in existence, and were being offered for sale as recently as December 1973.

An interesting parallel to the Ruggeri air-cooled car story which appeared in *Auto-Italiana* in December 1962 was a feature complete with cutaway drawing in an American magazine which purported to provide a sneak preview of the transverse, eight-cylinder air-cooled,

Dell'Orto-carburated Formula 1 Ferrari for 1963 . . . its engine layout looked exactly like that of the Ruggeri, as later illustrated in the now defunct Italian publication!

It was left to Porsche to bring air-cooling successfully into major Formula road-racing, for having taken all kinds of awards for many years in GT and sports-car events they introduced a works Formula 2 single-seater team during 1959 and entered 1½-litre Formula 1 racing in 1961.

Their original bulky flat-four cars were replaced in 1962 by flat-eight versions, and although number one driver Dan Gurney acidly compared his car's performance and handling to that of a VW saloon, he still managed to win the French Grand Prix at Rouen after the faster British-built V8 cars had run into all kinds of problems.

Porsche retired from Formula 1 racing at the close of the season, and it was not until 1968 that air-cooling returned to the scene, coming from an unusual direction – Japan.

Soichiro Honda's massive motorcycle company branched into producing light cars and vans in 1962. In the years which followed, Honda totally dominated world motorcycle racing, and as their four-wheeled production grew it was virtually second nature to enter the Grand Prix field.

At the Nürburgring in August 1964 the first Honda Formula 1 car made its debut, driven by the hitherto unknown American Ronnie Bucknum. It had a 1½-litre V12 engine mounted crosswise in the back, which prompted John Cooper to gasp wide-eyed, 'So it's *true* what they say about the Nips!'

In the last race of the 1½-litre Formula, at Mexico City late in 1965, Richie Ginther actually scored Honda's first Grand Prix victory in one of the 'cross-engine' cars.

The following September saw Ginther giving the brand new three-litre Honda V12 its debut in the Italian Grand Prix at Monza, where it was virtually destroyed in a terrific high-speed accident on the Curva Grande. Ginther was luckily not seriously injured, and he was out again in a replacement car at Watkins Glen, accompanied by his team-mate Bucknum in another car.

During 1965–66 Honda produced two one-litre Formula 2 engine designs, the later of which totally dominated the Formula in the works Brabham cars driven by Jack Brabham himself and Denny Hulme.

For 1967 ex-motorcycle World Champion John Surtees took on the Honda Formula 1 programme, basing it in Slough and operating under the name Honda Racing. Late in the year a brand new car was built around what was basically an Indianapolis Lola monocoque chassis. Surtees won the Italian Grand Prix with this car in a thrilling battle with Jim Clark and Jack Brabham, finally beating the Australian by just 0.2 of a second after 243 miles of racing.

Honda's original 1½-litre cars had been identified by the RA271 and RA272 type numbers, while the original 1966 three-litre was the RA273. The Lola-based 1967 car was known as the RA300, and its successor for 1968 with the V12 engine became the RA301. This car was lower than its predecessors but with its massive roller-bearing V12 engine was still far too heavy. Then, on Saturday June 30 the Tokyo company made a surprise announcement of their brand new RA302 air-cooled V8-engined car, and air-freighted it to London.

There had been rumours that the company had something else up their sleeve since the RA301 had first tested in December '67, but this sudden release surprised everybody. Surtees took the new car to Silverstone the following Tuesday for initial testing, and it was then loaded onto the Honda Racing transporter to be taken to Rouen for the French Grand Prix meeting the following weekend.

Honda's brand new car was remarkably small and compact when compared to its V12 'big brother'. A completely new form of monocoque chassis had been adopted, with the basic fuel tank-carrying nacelle shaping round the cockpit area and then terminating around a well-boxed engine bulkhead. From the top surface of this box a long monocoque beam extended rearwards, passing right over the top of the engine which was suspended from it. At the rear end of this beam the Honda engineers had mounted a hefty bridge-piece which provided suspension pick-ups and carried a Honda-built five-speed transaxle.

The engine was an unusual V8 with its heavily finned cylinder banks arranged at the wide included angle of 120 degrees instead of the more conventional 90 degrees. Bore and stroke were 88mm x 61.4mm to give a displacement of 2,987.5cc, and there were twin overhead camshafts per bank operating four valves per cylinder. Honda used their own low-pressure fuel injection system and quoted power output was 430bhp at 10,500rpm.

Suspension was by cantilever arms operating inboard coil-spring damper units with wide-based lower wishbones at the front, while

58, 59 Four exhaust tail pipes at the back and eight injection trumpets on either side – BRM's 3-litre H16, 1966. The overhung clutch assembly is also visible here.

60 A very obscure pile of parts – remains of the Ruggeri brothers' air-cooled transverse eight-cylinder engined 2½-litre Grand Prix project, from 1955.

61 The irrepressible Archie Butterworth beams happily from his four-wheel drive Steyr-engined AJB during practice for the International Trophy F1 race at Silverstone, 1950.

62 Just to recall the famous Indianapolis Novi V8s we publish this shot of Bobby Unser's Ferguson four-wheel drive version, 1964.

63 Jo Schlesser in the Honda RA302 air-cooled V8 during practice for the 1968 French GP at Rouen. He was tragically killed in this car on the third lap of the race . . .

64 Sneak preview – Graham Hill testing the 1969 Lotus-Ford 64 outside the factory at Hethel aerodrome. It was possible to spin all four wheels way above 100mph.

reversed lower wishbones, single top links, twin radius arms and outboard coil-spring/dampers appeared at the rear.

The whole car was very nicely constructed, with extensive use of magnesium panelling in the Engineer Sano-designed monocoque hull. A sharp-pointed nose cowl concealed a tiny oil cooler, while a heavily finned oil tank was outrigged on the right-side of the hull just below the driver's shoulder. This was intended to dissipate much of the engine's heat, and large cooling ducts were formed around the cockpit sides and fed a forced draught of cooling air through the finned engine galleries. A smaller duct to the left of the driver's head gulped cooling air down into the engine crankcase, where it was introduced into oil mist and then drawn-out through a de-aerator which retained the oil but expelled the heated air through a vent on top of the magnesium backbone. This feature was rumoured to be Mr Honda's own idea, but his sceptical engineers developed the engine to cool efficiently with or without the crankcase-feed. . . .

Chief Engineer Nakamura's men had done a very thorough job of work, but the car would obviously need some serious development driving by a pilot of Surtees' vast experience before it could be considered properly raceworthy.

Unfortunately, it was not to be given the chance. For political reasons Honda France requested that the brand new car be raced at Rouen to show the flag before their potential customers. Surtees maintained that his own appearance in their well-tried if perhaps not very competitive RA301 should be sufficient, and asked that the RA302 be retained for the moment as a spare car and nothing more.

The Honda management insisted that it should run, preferably in the hands of a French driver, and they arranged for the Madagascan-born veteran Jo Schlesser to take it out.

In this prototype trim the engine was giving no more than 380bhp at 9,000rpm, but even this was sufficient to make the untuned chassis rather twitchy and sensitive. The first practice session lasted only an hour, and Schlesser found the engine running too cool and had the intake ducts partially taped-over before continuing. He finally returned a time only 7.5 seconds slower than Jochen Rindt's pole position Repco Brabham when practice finished and he was to start the race on Sunday July 7 from the middle of the last row, flanked on either side by works Cooper-BRMs in their last Formula 1 season.

Rain poured down on the fast and tricky Rouen-les-Essarts circuit that Sunday morning. I was covering a Thruxton race meeting for

N

Motoring News on that day, and on the way home in a Triumph TR5 test car I tuned-in the radio to pick up Robin Richards' French Grand Prix report. The first words I heard were '. . . marred by the death of French driver Jo Schlesser in a new Japanese Honda . . . .'

Going into the third lap in pouring rain the popular hard-charging Madagascan had been struggling with a misfiring engine, probably suffering from rain water being sprayed into its electrics through the forced-draught cooling.

Down past the pits at Rouen the road drops steeply downhill through some very fast left and right-hand curves. Schlesser was pluming his new white and red car through these curves on a streaming road surface when his engine suddenly cut out, the Japanese car lost its balance and began to slither onto the broad grass verge, broad-siding off the road, across the run-off area and into the high sloping bank beneath the feet of a large crowd. The car flipped into the air, disintegrated on landing and burst into a hideous, flaring magnesium fire from which Schlesser could not be saved.

It was a tragic result for a commercially-induced race entry, and the air-cooled V8 did not reappear until the Italian Grand Prix meeting at Monza in September when a new and modified car was brought along by Honda Racing for David Hobbs to test purely in practice. They also had a second RA301 on hand for him to use in the race.

The new RA302 had been built in Surtees' own works at Slough, and had a more conventional monocoque panelled in L72 aluminium-alloy sheet with fewer internal stiffeners. This weighed the same as the ill-fated magnesium car, but was 1½ inches longer. Nakamura's engineering team had also dropped Mr Honda's idea of passing air into the crankcase and the V8 engine now cooled in the conventional external forced-draught manner.

Surtees actually took pole position in his V12 with Hobbs towards the back of the grid in his similar RA301, but the race was unlucky for both of them as 'Big John' became involved in a high-speed collision in the opening stages and Hobbs dropped out at two-thirds distance with a dropped valve in his car's engine.

After this brief outing, the RA302 was returned to Japan with a long job-list, and as Honda pulled out of Grand Prix racing from 1969 it never had another chance. John Surtees has one of the RA301 cars in perfect order to this day in the Edenbridge, Kent, works where he builds his own Grand Prix cars, while Honda have the rest in their Tokyo works.

On 5 October 1973, Honda's Arakawa Riverbed test track on the outskirts of the Japanese capital reverberated to the sound of multi-cylinder racing engines. It was twenty-five years since Mr Honda had initiated motorcycle production shortly after the nuclear bombing of Hiroshima and Nagasaki had annihilated the Japanese war effort.

In celebration of those twenty-five years of brilliant production success Honda were running a Brabham-Honda F2 car, an RA272 1½-litre F1 and the RA302 F1 for the last time. Works testers howled them round the track on a dismal rainy afternoon, and a reporter from the Japanese *Motor Magazine International* commented '. . . One could hardly contain a feeling of tremendous sadness, bearing witness to the running of these unique, historic racing machines with no more audience than a handful of journalists . . .' It was a brave try for the Rising Sun.

19

Indianapolis in the Sixties –
Oddballs on the Bowl

As we have seen, the Indianapolis Motor Speedway has been an irresistible attraction for some of the most unusual racing cars ever built.

After Jack Brabham introduced modern mid-engined road-racing design to the Speedway with his 1961 2.7-litre Cooper-Climax, the 'funny car' revolution began.

In 1962, inveterate hot-rodder Mickey Thompson produced some nicely-made mid-engined Indy cars powered by light-alloy stock-block Buick V8s. He was the first of the American builders to follow Cooper's lead, and once Lotus arrived with Ford backing and Ford V8 engines in 1963, and finally won there with Jimmy Clark driving in 1965, the road-racing régime had taken over completely.

All kinds of odd things followed, very much in the Pat Clancy Special mould, such as another Thompson car which had four-wheel steering—which didn't—and a beautiful little car known as the 'Hurst Floor Shifter Special' which appeared at the Speedway during practice in 1964.

This car had been built by Henry 'Smokey' Yunick who had been involved in all kinds of southern motor sports for years and who ran the self-proclaimed 'Best Damn Garage in Town' at Daytona Beach, Florida. His Indy car was one of the most unusual-looking devices ever to be run on the Speedway.

Its tube frame chassis consisted of a slender cigar structure clad in beautifully-made missile-like bodywork, just large enough to form a fared housing for a rear-mounted Offenhauser four-cylinder engine. Mid-mounted on top of this missile was a deep duct feeding air into a buried radiator which sat where one would normally expect the driver's cockpit to appear.

This heroic individual had been transplanted, with his cockpit formed in a neat sidecar-like nacelle outrigged on the nearside of the main frame. This 'driver pod' was complete with pedals and steering wheel, seat, instrument panel, and roll-over bar!

Veteran driver Duane Carter was engaged to drive the car and he reportedly liked it very much. In typical Yunick fashion it was impeccably finished and prepared, and in his colours of black and gold it looked absolutely immaculate.

Unfortunately stock car driver Bobby Johns took over the car for further testing, and he became disorientated due to the peculiarly offset driving position and creamed the whole thing into the wall. It was not to make the race, but Mr Yunick tells me that he still has the car, rebuilt and in full running order.

Ferguson Formula four-wheel drive units also appeared at the Speedway after the Formula 1 P99 research vehicle had been tested there and had displayed unusual speed through the corners. Andy Granatelli's Studebaker Corporation adopted the Ferguson system in their ex-Welch Novi cars—now approaching the end of their long and famously unsuccessful run at the Speedway.

In 1965 a sentimental favourite with the vast '500' crowd was Jim Hurtubise's STP-backed 'Tombstone Life Special', which was the last of the front-engined Novis, using a Kurtis chassis and rear-wheel drive. With the usual supercharged V8 luck of the Novis it staggered into retirement at the end of the opening lap, with the transmission 'gone home', leaving a field full of mid-engined cars.

That same year Mickey Thompson was back in the fray with a hastily constructed dragster-like Chevrolet V8-engined 'front-ender' which reintroduced pure front-wheel drive to the Speedway for the first time in ten years. Bob Mathouser drove, but he failed to qualify.

The following year saw Bill Cheesebourg failing to qualify in a delightful echo of the old Fageol Twin Coach, with Porsche engines at either end driving two wheels each.

Then in 1967 Granatelli's STP Corporation backed a sensational new four-wheel drive car powered by a helicopter-type Pratt & Whitney gas turbine engine. It was built for STP by English engineer Ken Wallis, and in Parnelli Jones's experienced hands it looked set for a certain win when a minor component failed in its transmission with less than ten miles to go.

This turbine car sparked off a terrific controversy within the speedway world, and many planned to adopt the aviation engine's fabled reliability and smooth power for new '500' cars. Wallis was taken on by Carroll Shelby to build two cars similar to his original 'STP Turbocar', intended for Bruce McLaren and Denny Hulme in 1968. These cars proved diabolically dangerous in practice and were withdrawn.

Meanwhile Granatelli had gone to Lotus for his 1968 fleet of Indy cars, and Colin Chapman and Maurice Phillippe produced the type 56 wedge-shaped monocoque cars which featured the Pratt & Whitney turbine engines mated to four-wheel drive transmissions.

Tragically, Mike Spence lost his life in one of the cars during practice when he hit the wall and the offside front wheel folded back and inflicted severe head injuries on the unfortunate Englishman.

Ex-motorcyclist Joe Leonard put his vermilion Lotus 56B on pole for the '500' and was solidly in the lead right at the end of the race when a 'fail-safe' fuel pump drive 'failed-safe' in aircraft style and brought his car coasting to a stunning halt. Almost simultaneously his well-placed team-mate, Art Pollard, went out with a similarly frustrating failure, while Graham Hill had long gone when his Lotus (the only one not using a 'fail-safe' pump drive) had thrown a wheel and cannoned into the retaining wall.

This further display of the whistling turbine car's remarkable suitability for all left-turn speedway racing was regarded with considerable distaste in the United States Auto Club's corridors of power, and the strong reactionary lobby situated there effectively limited turbine engines to such a vast extent that they would become totally uncompetitive in 1969. They further outlawed four-wheel drive, for many interested parties had vast sums of money tied up in more conventional equipment which they did not want to see rendered obsolete overnight.

USAC later retracted this cavalier ban, and moderated it to limit four-wheel drive cars' wheel rims to a maximum of ten inches, as compared to the two-wheel drive allowance of fourteen inches. Notice was given that four-wheel drive would be prohibited for Championship Trail racing from the start of 1970.

In 1969 one turbine car did arrive at the Speedway; the torpedo-like 'Jack Adams Airplane Special'—but veteran driver Al Miller was bumped off the starting grid on the final day of qualifications at the end of a brave attempt.

Meanwhile, the closing days of those practice and qualifying sessions had seen the drama of the last of our great 'might have beens'.

STP-Lotus had invested in the latest 2.65-litre turbocharged Ford four-cam V8 engines in view of the crushing turbine limitations, and they mounted these units in updated versions of the existing four-wheel drive monocoque wedge cars. With the engine's complex manifolding and pipe-work, and the '56' running gear's maze of propeller shafts and varying drive trains and transfer boxes, the resulting STP-Lotus 64s were the most complex cars yet built by the sophisticated Lotus Group and by Colin Chapman's innovative design team under the leadership of Maurice Phillippe.

Early in training Mario Andretti wound up his Lotus 64 to lap at an average of 170.197mph, but his team-mates Graham Hill and Jochen Rindt found it impossible to emulate this feat. Hill was hard-pushed to break the 160mph barrier and Rindt—who was suffering the after-effects of an enormous Formula 1 accident during the Spanish Grand Prix—was even slower and added to his own disillusionment by experiencing a comprehensive high-speed spin around the banking.

Huge duck-tail spoilers had been added to the cars to improve their handling, but as these extra aerodynamic loads were imposed upon the suspension and the drivers began to press them harder and harder so the rear hubs began to overheat. New tubes were made up with integral cooling fins, and after the first qualifying weekend was rained out Andretti set off to sample the new hubs in a practice period on the following Wednesday. He was lapping quickly in the modified Lotus 64 when its new right-rear hub broke up and the wheel went bounding away.

It hit the wall before the gyrating STP car which ploughed into the concrete at terrific speed and according to a following driver '. . . just disintegrated. There were so many bits flying around it looked like a whole lot of cars had piled up. . . .'

The wreck skated to a halt on its belly, beginning to burn fiercely as its very lucky Italo-American driver slipped off his safety harness and leapt out of the barely distorted cockpit. Andretti was shaken and had painful but minor burns on his upper lip, and he was later able to qualify Granatelli's old Hawk-Ford for the race and actually *won* it for the STP man, who had been coming to Indianapolis for year after year, suffering the most wretched luck every time.

Meanwhile, what had happened to the Lotus 64s? After this potentially disastrous hub failure—officially attributed to incorrect heat treatment but more likely caused, I hear, by machined corrections to a basic shortcoming—there was insufficient time for new components to be made, tested, fitted and run before qualifying ended on the final weekend.

So Colin Chapman—Lotus's intense, dynamic and forceful founder—regretfully had to withdraw the STP cars, and ten minutes before this decision was made public, Granatelli had agreed to buy the team cars for the rest of the USAC season at an agreed price—reputedly $95,000.

A little later there was a meeting at the Speedway Motel to finalise the deal between Lotus and STP executives, and Lotus team manager Andrew Ferguson was late as he walked into the motel's carpark.

He was almost flattened by his boss, who was reversing his hire car across the carpark with his foot hard down and the car's tyres squealing. 'The Old Man' caught sight of Ferguson, who saw he was boiling with rage, and Chapman wound down the car's window and bellowed orders that Granatelli was on no account to get hold of the cars!

With that he thundered off towards the airport and home.

Ferguson walked into the motel suite to find the STP men looking as bemused as he felt. Evidently Granatelli had agreed to buy the cars for the quoted figure, but then bucked over the price of spares which had formerly been supplied exclusively by Lotus. Chapman, still smarting from the loss of face caused by withdrawal and frustrated by another failure at Indianapolis took this as an immediate slight, told his would-be customer what to do with his spares and stormed out!

Ferguson now had a problem, and decided that to protect Lotus interests he should hide the cars and prevent any possible STP injunction being placed upon them. The Lotus' Ford engines had to be returned to Ford at Dearborn so he had to find somewhere secluded for them to be removed.

Mechanics Arthur Birchall and Dale Porteus had a single-car trailer tacked on to the back of a hire car with which to shift the remaining cars and a vast pile of spares, and they were hurriedly removed to a private house, just round the corner from the Speedway, which belonged to one of the team's lady friends.

Andrew acquired a hydraulic hoist to shift the engines, and while the mechanics set about craning out Ford's V8s he returned to the Speedway to be informed that a sheriff was looking for him! He hid, thinking it was an STP writ waiting to be served, but later found that Ford were under the impression that somebody had made off with their valuable engines and this sheriff was one with a relatively white hat.

One by one the engines filtered back to Fords by devious cross-country routes, and Ferguson then found a more remote hiding place for the now gutted team cars and their piles of spares in a private garage belonging to the secretary of Lotus's shipping agent at Indianapolis Airport.

The cars stayed there—about forty miles upstate from Indianapolis —while Ferguson was working away under orders to thrash out a deal with STP, but after a while the accommodating householder became thoroughly cheesed off at having the family garage jammed to the rafters with dismantled racing cars and stacks of wheels and crated spares.

Days turned into weeks, and eventually Birchall and Porteus brought the cars home through New York. Ferguson never succeeded in completing the deal with STP, and eventually—he recalls— Chapman passed sentence on his company's most complex racing cars by saying: 'Andrew, bring the cars back to Hethel, where I will *personally* put a hacksaw through them, I will *personally* dig a hole, and I will *personally bury them!*'

This towering figure in motor racing history didn't keep true to his word, but the Lotus 64s were never to be raced and as I write they are still lying mouldering in a storage hangar on the bleak Hethel aerodrome. Clint Brawner retained the wreck of Andretti's car, and I do not know the fate of that one—the last of the most complex cars yet built by the most successful concern in Grand Prix racing history. . . .

Index - Cars & Companies

Personalities

Miscellany